Reginald Stuart Poole

The Coins of the Sháhs of Persia, Safavis, Afgháns, Efsháris, Zands, and Kájárs

Reginald Stuart Poole

The Coins of the Sháhs of Persia, Safavis, Afgháns, Efsháris, Zands, and Kájárs

ISBN/EAN: 9783337288723

Printed in Europe, USA, Canada, Australia, Japan

Cover: Foto ©ninafisch / pixelio.de

More available books at **www.hansebooks.com**

CATALOGUE

OF

COINS OF THE SHÁHS OF PERSIA

IN THE

BRITISH MUSEUM.

LONDON:
PRINTED BY ORDER OF THE TRUSTEES.
1887.

LONDON:
PRINTED BY GILBERT & RIVINGTON (LIMITED),
ST. JOHN'S HOUSE, CLERKENWELL ROAD.

THE COINS

OF THE

SHÁHS OF PERSIA,

ṢAFAVIS, AFGHÁNS, EFSHÁRIS, ZANDS, AND ḲÁJÁRS.

BY

REGINALD STUART POOLE, LL.D.

CORRESPONDENT OF THE INSTITUTE OF FRANCE.

LONDON:

PRINTED BY ORDER OF THE TRUSTEES.

LONGMANS & CO., PATERNOSTER ROW; B. M. PICKERING, 66, HAYMARKET; B. QUARITCH, 15, PICCADILLY; A. ASHER & CO., 13, BEDFORD STREET, COVENT GARDEN, AND AT BERLIN; TRÜBNER & CO, 57 & 59 LUDGATE HILL; ALLEN & CO., 13, WATERLOO PLACE.

PARIS: MM. C. ROLLIN & FEUARDENT, 4, RUE DE LOUVOIS.

1887.

PREFACE.

The present Volume contains the description of the Coins of the Ṣafavi and subsequent dynasties of Persia, from the enthronement of Sháh Isma'íl I., A.H. 907= A.D. 1502, to the present day.

The work follows the system of previous volumes describing Oriental Coins, and is similarly illustrated. As however it is the first Catalogue of Persian coins of its class, yet issued, the number of plates is larger than usual.

The absence of any authoritative history of Persia in a European language has made research in Persian manuscripts a first necessity, while the imperfection of the few lists of Persian coins in numismatic works has rendered their decipherment a new inquiry. In both cases this labour could not have been performed without the generous aid of my colleague Dr. Charles Rieu, Keeper of Oriental Manuscripts, who has not only allowed me to refer to him throughout the composition of the work, but has also read the proof-sheets. While such merit as the work may possess is largely due to him, he has not catalogued the coins, and is therefore not responsible for any defects. I would also express my sincere acknowledgments to Professor Dr. Wold Tiesenhausen, Keeper of Coins in the Imperial Museum of the Hermitage, and to Professor Dr. Mehren, Keeper of Oriental Coins in the Royal Museum of Copenhagen, for valuable notices of coins in the collections under their charge. I owe my thanks to General Houtum Schindler for authoritative information bearing on the reckoning of time and coin-denominations of the Persians. I am also indebted to Mr. Grueber for help in the correction of the proofs.

REGINALD STUART POOLE.

CONTENTS.

	PAGE
Preface	v
Introduction	xv
§ I. CHRONOLOGY	xv
Persian mode of reckoning reigns	xv
Persian reckoning of time	xv
Night and day	xv
Muḥammadan year	xvi
Almanacs	xviii
Solar year and Tatar Cycle	xviii
Correspondence of solar and lunar years	xix
Julús	xx
Regnal years	xxi
Determination of dates	xxii
Ṣafavi Dynasty	xxii
Isma'íl I.	xxii
Relations of Isma'íl and Bábar	xxiv
Ṭahmásp I.	xxix
Isma'íl II.	xxx
Muḥammad Khudabanda	xxxi
'Abbás I.	xxxiii
Ṣafí I.	xxxiv
'Abbás II.	xxxv
Ṣafí II., Sulaimán I.	xxxvi
Ḥusain I.	xxxvi
Ṭahmásp II.	xxxvii
'Abbás III.	xxxvii
Sám	xxxviii
Ḥusain II.	xxxix
Muḥammad	xl

PAGE

Determination of dates, *continued*—
Ṣafavis, maternally . . . xl
The Family of Dá-úd . . . xli
Aḥmad . xli
Sulaimán II. . . xli
Isma'íl (III.) . . . xlii
Afgháns . . xlix
Maḥmúd xlix
Ashraf xlix
Efsháris xlix
Nádir Sháh . . . xlix
'Ádil Sháh . . . l
Ibráhím l
Sháh Rukh li
Bakhtiárí liii
'Alí Merdán Khán liii
Afghán . . . liii
Ázád Khán . liii
Zands . . liv
Kerím Khán liv
Abu-l-Fet-ḥ and Muḥammad 'Alí Kháns lvi
Muḥammad 'Alí Khán . . lvi
Abu-l-Fet-ḥ Khán, second reign . lvii
Sadiḳ Khán lvii
'Alí Murád Khán lvii
Ja'afar Khán lviii
Luṭf-'Alí Khán . . lviii
Ḳájárs lviii
Muḥammad Ḥasan Khán . . lviii
Ḥusain-ḳulí Khán . lix
Aḳa Muḥammad Khán . lix
Fet-ḥ-'Alí, Bábá Khán lix
Ḥusain 'Alí lx
'Alí lx
Muḥammad lx
Ḥasan Khán Sálár . . lx
Náṣir-ed-dín lxi

PAGE

§ 11. Coinage lxi
Denominations . . . lxi
Hanway's tables lxi
Gold coins Isma'íl I, to Khâns. lxii
Hanway's statements as to silver money compared with coins lxiii
Table of weights of silver coins, Muḥammad to Ṭahmásp II.. lxiii
Information of Chardin and Tavernier as to silver money lxiv
Evidence of table lxiv
Later silver coins lxiv
Coinage of Ḳájár Sháhs lxiv
Art of coins lxvi
Inscriptions lxvi
Obverse. Formulæ lxvi
Reverse. Royal style to Ṭahmásp II. . lxvii
'Alí-Riza coins. Their origin lxix
Style of Nádir and successors to Isma'íl (III). lxx
Mahdí coins, &c., of Kháns . . . lxxii
Coins of Ḳájár Sháhs lxxiv
Mints lxxv
Dates . . . lxxv
Distichs lxxvi
Ṣafavis lxxvi
Isma'íl II. lxxvi
'Abbás II. lxxviii
Sulaimán I. (Safi II). . . . lxxix
Sultán Ḥusain lxxx
Ṭahmásp II. lxxx
'Abbás III. . . . lxxxi
Sultán Ḥusain II. lxxxi
Sultán Muḥammad . . . lxxxi
Ṣafavis, maternally lxxxii
The family of Dá-úd lxxxii
Aḥmad lxxxii
Sulaimán II. . lxxxii
Afgháns . . . lxxxiii

PAGE
Maḥmud . . lxxxiii
Ashraf . . lxxxiv
Efsháris . lxxxv
Nádir lxxxv
'Ádil Sháh . . lxxxv
Ibráhím . . . lxxxv
Sháh Rukh . . lxxxvi
Zands lxxxvi
Luṭf-'Alí Khan . lxxxvi
'Alí-Riẓa series . . lxxxvii
Mahdí series . . lxxxvii
Ḳájárs lxxxix
Náṣir-ed-dín . . . lxxxix
Invocations . . . lxxxix
Other religious Inscriptions . . lxxxix
Autonomous Copper xc
Types and Tatar Cycle xc
Genealogical trees. . . xci
Ṣafavis . xcii
Afgháns . . xciii
Efsháris . . xciii
Zands xciv
Ḳájárs . . . xciv
Notes to the Pedigrees xcv
Errata xcvi
Chronological table . (*to follow*) xcvi
CATALOGUE 1
Ṣafavis . . . 1
Isma'íl I. 1
Ṭahmásp I. 12
Sultán Muḥammad Khudabanda . . 19
'Abbás I. 21
Ṣafí (I.) 24
'Abbás II. . . . 26
Sulaimán I. (Ṣafí II.) . . . 30
Sultán Ḥusain 39
Tahmásp II. 55
With name of Imám 'Alí-er-Riẓá . 61

	PAGE
Afgháns .	64
Maḥmúd . .	64
Ashraf .	66
Ṣafavis	69
'Abbás III.	69
With name of Imám 'Alí-er-Riẓá	71
Efsháris	72
Nádir	72
Ṣafavis	85
Sám, Pretender . . .	85
Efsháris	86
'Adil Sháh . .	86
Ibráhím	89
With name of Imám 'Alí-er-Riẓá	90
Sháh Rukh, first reign . . .	91
With name of Imám 'Alí-er-Riẓá	96
Ṣafavis (maternally) . . .	98
Sulaimán II.	98
Efsháris	100
Sháh Rukh, third reign . .	100
Ṣafavis (maternally) . .	102
Isma'íl III.	102
Under tutelage of 'Alí Merdán Khán .	102
Under tutelage of Muḥammad Ḥasan Khán	103
Zands	105
Kerím Khán . .	105
Ḳájárs	127
Muḥammad Ḥasan Khán .	127
Afghan	130
Azád Khán	130
Khán of Ganja, with name of Nádir Sháh .	131
Zands	132
Abu-l-Fet-ḥ Khán . .	132
Ṣádiḳ Khán . .	133
'Alí Murád Khán . .	136
Ja'afar Khán . . .	140
Luṭf-'Alí Khán .	142

PAGE

Ḳájárs 143
Aḳa Muḥammad Khan . . . 143
Fet-ḥ-'Alí (Bábá Khán) 148
Fet-ḥ-'Alí Sháh 150
Muḥammad Sháh 177
Rebellion of Ḥasan Khán Sálár . . 186
Náṣir-ed-dín 187
Uncertain, time of Isma'íl I. or Ṭahmásp I. . 209
Vassal king, Timúrí Bábar under Isma'íl I. . 210
Autonomous Copper . . . 212
Irán 212
Abú-Shahr 213
Bandar-Abú-Shahr 215
Ardebíl 217
Urúmí 217
Iṣfahán 219
Eriván 221
Borujird . . . 226
Baghdád 227
Bandar-'Abbás ? 227
Behbehán 228
Tabríz 229
Tiflís 234
Túï 236
Tíra ? . . . 236
Khoï 237
Demávend 238
Resht 238
Ra'násh 239
Sá-új Bulágh 240
Shemákhí . . 240
Shíráz 241
Ṭeherán 242
Ḳazvín 243
Ḳandahár 244
Kermánsháhán . . . 250
Káshán 252

PAGE

Ganja . . . 253
Mazenderán . . 257
Mesh-hed 259
Herát . . 260
Hamadán . . 261
Yazd . . . 261
Medals . . 262
Supplement 265
Isma'íl I. . . . 265
Ṭahmásp I. 268
Muḥammad Khudabanda 269
'Abbás II. 271
Sulaimán I. . . 272
Sulṭán Ḥusain 272
Maḥmúd . . . 273
Nádir . 274
INDEXES . . 275
I. Years 275
II. Mints 288
II A. Titles of Mints . . 309
III. Names . . . 311
III A. Distichs . . . 319
III B. Invocations . . 322
III C. Mottoes 322
IV. Miscellaneous 323
V. Denominations, marks and forms as of genuineness, etc. 324
VI. Types 325
TABLES 329
Comparative Table of the Years of the Hijra and of the Christian Era 329
Table of the relative weights of English grains and French grammes 334
Table for converting English inches into millimètres and into the measures of Mionnet's scale 336

INTRODUCTION.

I. Chronology.

In preparing this Catalogue it has been necessary to fix the chronology of the reigns, as to which I have found no exact information in any European work.

Persian mode of reckoning reigns.

The Persian mode of reckoning a king's reign presents two peculiarities: a reign is counted from Enthronement, and the regnal years are counted from the New-Year's Day on each vernal equinox, the Nau-rúz, whereas all other dates are given in Muhammadan lunar years and months. The adjustment of the Persian dates to our own has therefore been a matter of some difficulty, but I cannot regret the labour entailed by the endeavour to obtain historical accuracy in these dates, which, belonging as they do to modern history, demand the most precise statement possible.

Persian reckoning of time.

To explain the method of adjustment it will be necessary to state in brief the Persian mode of reckoning time. This is purely Muhammadan, except that the use of the solar year is concurrent with that of the lunar. It is, however, possible that in the Muhammadan system there may be some local peculiarities. The Persian usage is therefore here stated, without any assertion that in all particulars it represents the usage of the whole Muslim world.

Night and day.

The day begins with sunset. In Persian documents the word شب, 'night,' denotes the first moiety, روز 'day,' the second, though it is possible that 'day' is sometimes used for the civil day of twenty-four hours, instead of its division, the natural day.

There is thus a discrepancy in the beginning of any day in Muslim and European reckoning, amounting to the interval from sunset to midnight, each day of the week beginning so much earlier than with us in Muslim countries, our eve of Sunday, for instance, being their night of that day.

In the tables for converting Muslim into European reckoning, the European day given is not that on which the Muslim day began, but that with which it mainly coincided. In other words, the coincidence of natural days is given.

This is shown in Ideler's remarks on the initial day of the Hijra, reckoned by the Easterns as Thursday, July 14-15, A.D. 622; by the Europeans as the oriental Friday, 15-16 (Handbuch, ii. 482-485).

It is important to note that the European day is that of popular observation, consequently it best suits the usual Muslim custom of observation; thus, as Ideler remarks, the European date is to be taken when we have to do with popular use, the Oriental for astronomical observation (p. 485). Wüstenfeld's Tables ("Vergleichungs-Tabellen," F. Wüstenfeld, Leip., 1854), following the European reckoning, begin the calendar with Friday, July 16, which should be Thursday-Friday, 15-16. Thus, in converting dates, we can use Wüstenfeld's Tables, allowing for his neglect of the portion of the European day, and also for the possibility of the difference of a day on either side due to observation.*

Muhammadan year.

The Muhammadan year consists of twelve lunar months, alternately of thirty and twenty-nine days, the twelfth being of twenty-nine or thirty days, this month Zu-l-

* The Comparative Table of the Years of the Hijra and of the Christian Era at the close of the volume is, as in previous volumes, an abridgement of Wüstenfeld's work.

Ḥijja having thirty days eleven times in every nineteen years (see note *). In practice a difficulty may occur as to Sha'bán, the month preceding Ramaẓán, the month of fasting, and similarly with the beginning of Shawwál, the month following Ramaẓán. Properly the new moon should be seen to mark the beginning and end of the Fast. But no month can exceed thirty days, consequently there is no calendric disturbance of a serious character; the result can but be an interchange of months of twenty-nine and thirty days. In past time such variations must have often occurred: now this could only be, so far as Persia is concerned, in small and remote places, and with very strict Muslims. For in Persia, as in Egypt, the calendar is fixed by an official Almanac.*

---

* Further detail is given in the following interesting letter by General Houtum Schindler:—" The *popular* idea regarding the commencement of the months is that the first day of a month commences with the evening during which the new moon has first been seen. It sometimes happens at the end of the twenty-ninth day of a month that the moon has not been seen, on account of clouds, rain, &c., and the people then make the first of the month commence from sunset of the *next* day, counting the month as one of thirty days. This only occurs at small and out-of-the-way places, where almanacs are little known. The Persian astronomical almanac (*taqvím*) always gives the first day of the months correctly. No month can exceed thirty days, and doubt can only exist on account of the thirtieth day. After the thirtieth comes the first, even with the most fanatical part of the population, whether the moon has been seen or not. Seeing the moon is only of importance at the beginning and end of the Ramaẓân, particularly at the end. Some devout Musulmans, if they have not seen the moon continue the fast from the evening of the thirtieth till the evening of the next day, although they call this next day the first of Shevvâl. Ramaẓân always has thirty days. On the last day of Ramaẓân everybody is on the look-out for the faint crescent of the moon in the west, and every one on first seeing it rejoices, points it out to others, whom he embraces, &c. Should the sky at Teherân be overcast the courtiers are sad and gloomy. Then a telegram, sent in hot haste from the Central Telegraph Station, arrives with the announcement that the moon has been seen somewhere; for instance:

شش ساعت ربع کم ماه نو در تبریز دیده شده است

(six hours less a quarter, the new moon has been seen at Tabriz). The courtiers then 'heave' a sigh of relief—Alhamdulillah! the fast is over! but then they 'heave' another sigh, and lengthen their faces, as they think of the presents which they have to make to their people in the morning.

Almanacs.

Probably, before the use of printing, the most important days were defined by authority. It should, however, be noted that there is no certainty of agreement between Wüstenfeld's Tables and the official almanacs. In comparing these Tables with the Cairo Almanacs of A.H. 1243 to 1250 and 1259 to 1263 and 1265, it appears that in three cases the first day of the year, 1 Muḥarram, is dated one European day later by the Egyptian Almanac. In the conversion of dates we must therefore expect a degree of uncertainty as to the day of the month in both Muslim and European reckoning.

Solar year and Tatar Cycle.

Besides the Muslim year, the Persians use the native solar year, beginning at the vernal equinox, called by them the Turkí year, on account of the Tatar Cycle, which gives its name to each year. In their histories each year begins with the Nau-rúz at the vernal equinox, the year being designated according to the Tatar Cycle, and also numbered according to the Hijra year.* It consequently follows that events of the Hijra year are constantly chronicled before the heading at its Nau-rúz. The spring being the season of going to war, the difficulty does not usually arise in reference to military matters.

"The following figures regarding the Musulman reckoning may be useful; they are not always accessible. A cycle of the Muhammadan era = 10,631 days = 19 years of 354 days + 11 years of 355 days.

"The days of the week are the same after every seventh cycle; first day of the year 1 was Friday, and the first day of the year 211 was again a Friday. Divide the Muhammadan year by 30; the remainder will be the year of the cycle, and the 2nd, 5th, 7th, 10th, 13th, 16th, 18th, 21st, 24th, 26th, and 29th years of the cycle have 355 days.

"Muḥarrem, Rabi ع I, Jemádi I, Rejeb, Ramaẓán, and Zilq'adeh, always have thirty days.

Ṣafer, Rabi ع II, Jemâdi II, Sh'âbân, and Shavvâl, always have twenty-nine days.

"Zilhej has twenty-nine or thirty days."

* The formula is as in the following example:

بیان وقایع سال فرخنده فال اود ییل مطابق هزار و صد و شصت و شش هجری

Gíti-Kushái, f. 11 *a*.

The Tatar Cycle is as follows:*

سچقان	Mouse.
اود	Bull.
بارس	Tiger.
توشقان	Hare.
لوی	Crocodile.
ایلان	Serpent.
یونت	Horse.
قوی	Sheep.
بیچین	Ape.
تخاقو	Hen.
ایت	Dog.
تنگوز	Hog.

Correspondence of solar and lunar years.

In the use of the cycle there are disagreements as well as errors within a series. These are due to the confusion caused by no two years solar and lunar corresponding, and the consequent need occasionally to drop a lunar year containing no vernal equinox like A.H. 1153. Thus this year wholly disappears in the 'Histoire de Nader Chah.' We there find the heading of the year of the Sheep corresponding to A.H. 1151 (Part ii. p. 75), and the events up to 2 Zu-l-Ḥijja (p. 92), and then the heading of the year of the Ape corresponding to A.H. 1152, followed by the statement that the Nau-rúz occurred on 21 [l. 12] Zu-l-Ḥijja (p. 93). The next heading is that of the year of the Hen, corresponding to A.H. 1154, followed by the date of the Nau-rúz 3 Muḥarram (p. 119). It may be added that the date of 2 Muḥarram, 1154, occurs before the entry above cited in the record of an earlier event (p. 118). Thus a whole lunar year, A.H. 1153, had elapsed between the Nau-rúz of 1152 and that of 1154. In the case of the

* The list does not include variants, but only the ordinary names and their orthography in Persian sources, drawn up with Dr. Rieu's kind aid.

event of 2 Muḥarram, 1154, the historian has been careful to designate the Hijra year, having to deal with its second day. This is however quite exceptional, the Hijra day and month alone being usually stated where there is a long series of dates, divided by headings of the beginnings of the solar years.

In determining the reigns of the sovereigns of Persia, the Sháhs must be separated from the Kháns who arose after the first deposition of Sháh Rukh.

Julús. The beginning of a Sháh's reign is marked by the date of his جلوس *julús*, or enthronement, when he was crowned and enthroned, and acquired the right of being mentioned in the Friday prayers, خطبه *khuṭba*, and having his name on the coinage سكه *sikka*. The rights of *khuṭba* and *sikka*, which were concomitants of the *julús*, were of the first importance; and there are instances of coins in this Catalogue showing the exercise of the right of coinage prior to enthronement.

When, as usual, there was an interval between reign and reign, there must have been mention of the *sovereign de jure* in the *khuṭba*.

The *julús* usually did not immediately follow the close of a predecessor's reign, probably because few of the Sháhs enjoyed an undisturbed succession. It is necessary to ascertain the date by a collation of authorities. Some sovereigns had a first *julús* on claiming the throne, before they gained possession of the capital, when they were again enthroned.

The Zand and Ḳájár Kháns before Fet-ḥ-'Alí Sháh did not assume full rights of sovereignty. Their money shows the position they took. The founder of each line first struck money in the name of Sháh Isma'íl (III.); then Kerím Khán Zand, as vakíl (وكيل), struck in the name of the Imám Muḥammad el-Mahdí, also using an invocation allusive to his own name; Muḥammad Hasan Khán Ḳájár similarly coining in the name of the Imám 'Alí-er-Riẓa. Evidently they had no regular *julús*. The later Zand

Kháns, successors of Kerím Khán, had at least in some cases a *julús*. But on their money they assume no regal titles: there was still a Ṣafavi heir. The principle of Kerím Khán is not deviated from except in the appearance of the names without titles of his first successor Abu-l-Fetḥ and his last Luṭf-'Alí, 'Alí Murád and Jaa'far using allusive invocations, while Ṣádiḳ repeats that of Kerím Khán. Similarly the Ḳájár Aḳa Muḥammad strikes in the name of both Imáms, and is content with an allusive invocation even after he had conquered his rivals, and as sole prince had a *julús*. Probably this was because a Ṣafaví prince, Sultán Muḥammad Mírza, had been proclaimed by him at Ṭeherán, A.H. 1200, and was still living, although not in Persia.

Ázád Khán also issued Imámi coinage in the name of the Mahdí, with a mention of his own name. So far the Imámi coinage is the rule, the exceptions not bearing any sovereign titles. Fet-ḥ-'Alí Sháh made an extraordinary innovation. Before his *julús* he issued royal money, under his name Bábá Khán, with the title Sultán: this is followed by his money as Sháh.

The regnal years of each king are the Turkí years as already stated. If a king had his *julús* before the Naurúz the excess must have been reckoned to his first year. The regnal years however are usually not numbered either in books or on coins.* The sums of reigns were computed in Hijra years, months, and days. They are usually stated in the nearest number of years, or of years and months, the days rarely being given. The list of the author of the "Nukhbat-el-Akhbár" affords an extreme case of this vague method. He states the date of the death of Aḳa Muḥammad Khán and the dates of the *julús* of Fet-ḥ-'Alí Sháh and his death, and yet allows Fet-ḥ-'Alí 39 years (Or. 2837, Regnal years.

* The Persian coins, with one certain (no. 27a***, p. 270) and one possible exception (no. 17, p. 9), do not give the regnal year.

f. 194*a*-196*a*), the interval from Aḳa Muḥammad's death to his death being 38 years, 5 months, 27 days, and that from his own *julús* to his death being 38 years, 2 months, 25 days.

One coin in the series (no. 447, p. 144) struck by Aḳa Muḥammad Khán presents the date 2 Rejeb, 1209. It was issued at Káshán. This date, 22-23 January 1795, is not the date of Aḳa Muḥammad's *julús*, nor has it any significance in the calendar. It probably refers to some local event, possibly to the passage of Aḳa Muḥammad through the city on his return to Ṭeherán after the capture of Kermán, if he took this route.

Determination of dates.

The following sketch of the chronology of the Sháhs of Persia involves a sufficient historical outline for numismatic purposes, if compared with the Genealogical Trees and Chronological Table. A fuller history is alike beyond the scope of this work and the powers of the writer.

The genealogical trees give only the chief historical persons. The Persian usage of succession is in accordance with that of European nations with whom the Salic Law has prevailed; but the Sháh has the right of selecting his heir among his descendants. Under the Ḳájárs there is this peculiarity; the heir must be a Ḳájár on the side of both father and mother.

To date each reign research has been made in Persian manuscripts, in some cases checked by the statements of Europeans travelling in Persia in the times in question, and by the evidence of coins. The historians occasionally, and the coins in one case (that of Nádir Sháh), give a chronogram (تاریخ) expressing the year of enthronement, and the historians also give the month in the case of Ṭahmásp II. There are also chronograms of the deaths of Sháhs in the histories, those of Tahmásp I. and Ṣafí I. giving the month.

Ṣafaví Dynasty. Isma'íl I.

Sháh Isma'íl Ṣafaví was the descendant of a line of Sayyids who traced back to 'Alí through the seventh Imám, Músa el-Ḳáẓim. The first of the line to whom political importance can be assigned is Isma'íl's grandfather Junaid, who therefore heads the Ṣafaví pedigree in this Catalogue.* So slight, however, was the power of Isma'íl's predecessors, that he may be regarded as alike the founder of the greatness of his family and of the Ṣafaví dynasty.

The date of the accession of Sháh Isma'íl I., although it is the starting-point of modern Persian history, has not yet been satisfactorily determined in any European work. I am indebted to Dr. Rieu for its approximate determination.

"The best sources, Jáhán-árá, Lubb-ut-Tavaríkh, Táríkh-i-Elchí, 'Álam-árái, all agree that the actual *julús*, with *khuṭba* and *sikka*, took place at Tabríz, immediately after the battle of Shorúr. That battle, in which Elwend Mírza and his Turkomans were routed, took place in the early spring A.H. 907; the Jáhán-árá gives the date Saturday, 2 Ramaẓán, 907. The Habíb-us-Siyár, which is rather loose in its chronology for that period, stands alone in speaking of a *julús* in 906." †

It is significant that in the year A.H. 907, the first Muslim Saturday in Ramaẓán was our Friday-Saturday, 11-12 March, 1502, the vernal equinox falling on Friday, 11th, in the morning common to both reckonings. It is therefore highly probable that the Nau-rúz was kept on the Muslim Saturday. It should be observed that in Wüstenfeld's Tables the correspondence is Thursday, 2 Ramaẓán = Thursday-Friday, 10-11 March. The new moon occurred very late (9h. 40m.) in the evening of the 8th.‡ It is therefore quite probable that the month was not reckoned to begin before the evening of the 9th. But this is still a day too early. It may be noted that in

---

* The dynastic lists entitled Jannat-el-Firdaus begin the Ṣafavi line with Junaid (Or. 144, fol. 62*b*).

† Letter from Dr. Rieu.

‡ I am responsible for the calculations of the sun's place and of the new moon, which are sufficiently accurate for the purpose.

the MSS., Saturday شنبه may be a mistake for any other day but Friday, جمعه or آدينه, the numeral being liable to drop out.

The date 2 Ramazán being apparently the Nau-rúz, it may be doubted whether in the MS. of the Jehán-ár´a, cited by Dr. Rieu (Add. 7649, fol. 84*b*), it is not chosen as the nearest date known to that of the battle. In a second and inferior MS. of the Jehán-árá (Or. 141, fol. 201*a*), which is divided by rubrics giving the Nau-rúz of each year, the decisive battle of Shorúr is placed before Nau-rúz 2 Ramazán, which, by an error of the copyist, is dated in the rubric 908 for 907, and so with others at this period. Obviously the year 907 would alone suit.

The earlier *julús* in A.H. 906, mentioned in the Habíb-es-Siyár, would correspond with Isma'íl's proclamation of himself without regular *julús* in Shirván in that year, which Dr. Rieu has pointed out to me.

It would be interesting to trace the rise of Isma'íl I., and the subjugation to his sway of the small principalities which he gradually subjected, leaving the work of consolidation to be completed by his successors. Were there a series of coins of vassal princes, this would be necessary. There is, however, but one known which has a second royal name, a piece in the Museum Collection (p. 210, no. 652). This coin happily bears upon the events of the great war with Muḥammad Sheibání the Uzbeg, and, with other numismatic documents, throws new light upon the history of the time. There is also another gold coin (p. 12, no. 19) counterstruck by Ṭahmásp I., which may have been originally issued by a vassal of his, but I have been unable to form any conjecture as to the possible vassal's name by comparing the lists.

Relations of Isma'íl and Bábar.

The coin of Isma'íl with the second royal name demands a somewhat lengthened discussion. Its fabric resembles that of the cities of the north-east of Isma'íl's kingdom, as seen in coins of Asterábád, Herát, and Merv. It differs from these similar pieces in the Catalogue in bearing in what may be called the exergue, undoubtedly a position of second importance, the name سلطان محمد. The mint is lost. It cannot be argued that the term سلطان is merely applied to a moneyer as a prefix, which would be quite consonant with Persian custom, for moneyers' names never appear on the coinage of the Sháhs, nor indeed does any second name, save in this instance, and the possible parallel under Ṭahmásp I. It is well-known that Muḥammad Bábar,* the founder of the so-called Moghul Empire of Delhi, was from A.H. 916 to A.H. cir. 921 (Baber's 'Memoirs,' Suppl., p. 241-245, on no stated authority) in strict alliance with Sháh Isma'íl. They had a common enemy in the Uzbegs, and the geographical position of the two kings made political union possible. Bábar was supported by a Persian contingent, and conquered Transoxiana, but by adopting for himself and his troops the national dress of the Persian Shí'as, he so effectually alienated the strict Sunnis of Bukhára and Samarḳand as to be obliged, as much by general disaffection, as by defeats from the Uzbegs, to abandon Transoxiana and retire to Kábul.

Unfortunately the events of this period are wanting in Bábar's 'Memoirs,' and there is difficulty in establishing their exact dates. All that will be here attempted is to ascertain if Bábar gave Isma'íl during this time the rights of the *khuṭba* and *sikka*, the prayer for the sovereign, and the coinage; and if there is evidence that he did so, whether the coin under consideration could be due to this right. In the Supplement to Bábar's 'Memoirs,' it is stated that when he conquered Samarḳand the rights in question were exercised in his own name, according to the Indian authorities Ferishta and Kháfi Khán, whereas

* According to Dr. Rieu the right pronunciation, as shown by a couplet of this prince's own composition, was Bábur.

Iskandar Beg, the Persian authority, said that the *khuṭba* was said in the name of Sháh Isma'íl ('Memoirs,' p. 242). I have referred to these authorities and think it worth while to give a summary of their statements. Dr. Rieu has given me a trustworthy confirmation of Iskandar Beg by Khondemir, who was contemporary with Bábar. Ferishta states that in the middle of Rejeb, A.H. 917, Bábar, going from Bukhára to Samarḳand for the third time, made the *khuṭba* and *sikka* in his own name (و در نصف رجب سال مذکور (سبع عشر وتسعمائة *ante*) از انجا بسمرقند رفته بارسم (سیم MS.) خطبه و سکه ان بلده بنام خود کرد (MS. Add. 6569, i. 222, f. *b*. Kháfi Khán says that Bábar conquered Samarḳand, ordering the *khuṭba* and *sikka* 'again' in his own name (متوجه تسخیر سمرقند گشته انجارا نیز به تسخیر آورده از سر نو سکه و خطبه خود نموده (MS. Add. 6573, f. 17*a*, *b*. On the other hand Khondemir distinctly assigns *sikka* and *khuṭba* to Sháh Isma'íl. He says that Bábar, when applying to Isma'íl for help, promised that on the conquest of Transoxiana he would have the *khuṭba* and *sikka* in his name (امیدست که علی اسرع الحال سایر مملکة (ممالك B.T.) ما وراء آلنهر مفتوح گردد و درین ولایت خطبه و سکه بنام و القاب نواب کمیاب مزین گشته (MS. Add. 2677, f. 336 *b*; Bombay Text, iii., iv. p. 66), and after taking Samarḳand he fulfilled his promise, and *khuṭba* and *sikka* acquired fresh lustre by the commemoration of the glories and merits of the blameless Imáms, may God be well-pleased with (or bless) them all! and by the name and titles of the Padshah, &c. (خطبه و سکه بذکر مآثر و مفاخر ائمه معصومین رضوان (صلوات B. T.) الله علیهم اجمعین و اسم و لقب پادشاه سیادت پناه اسکندرآئین سمت زیب و زینت پذیرفت MS. f. 337*a*, Bombay Text, p. 66). Iskandar Beg writes to the same purpose, omitting the coinage: while emphatically stating the acquisition by Bábar of the sovereignty of his ancestors at Samarḳand, he says that he read the *khuṭba*

of the Twelve Imáms, in the name of His Majesty Isma'íl
دران بلده فردوس مانند خطبه اثنی عشر بنام نامی انحضرت
خواند ('Álam Árai, MS. Add. 16,684, f. 20*a*)

It is, therefore, evident that Bábar caused the *khuṭba* to be said and the coinage to be struck in the names of Sháh Isma'íl as overlord and himself as vassal. In the conditions stated by Khondemir we have the significant promise that if the 'kingdom' or 'kingdoms' (مملكة or ممالك) of Transoxiana are conquered this shall be done in "that province" (در ين ولايت). That there was no evasion is evident from the distinct statement that the Persian formula for *khuṭba* and *sikka* of the Twelve Imáms was used. Here we trace the true source of the disaffection of Samarḳand and Bukhára which ultimately forced Bábar to abandon Transoxiana. This was too much for the strict Sunnís of that country.

The accuracy of Khondemír is proved by the discovery of silver coins of Bábar of Transoxianian not Indian fabric with the Shí'a formula and the names of the Twelve Imáms. Unfortunately neither mint nor date is legible upon them. They are now described for the first time from the specimens in the British Museum acquired since the publication of vol. vii. of the *Catalogue of Oriental Coins.*

1.

Obv., within sixfoil, لا اله الا الله
محمد رسول الله
على ولى الله

Rev. area, within square, سلطان
بابر
بهادر

Margin, within four compartments,

. . . محمد علی | حسن محمد علی | موسی جعفر علی | . . . .

2.

Obv. area, within square, similar, varied.

Margin, in segments, obscure.

Rev. area, in leaf-shaped border, similar, varied.

Margin, الله ملكه وسلطانه . . . .

Æ ·95, Wt. 70·5

3.

Obv. area, within square,

لا اله الا الله
محمد رسول الله

Marg., in segments, obscure.

Rev. area, within square, سلطان
بابر
بهادر

Margin, within four compartments,

علی محمد حسین | جعفر علی موسی | محمد علی | . . . علی

Æ ·8, Wt. 79.

4.

Similar to (3).

(Restruck on coin of Sháh Rukh, the Timúrí.)

Æ ·95, Wt 76·5

The full inscription is here intended to be Sulṭán Bábar Bahádur Khán, the word Khán, as Dr. Rieu suggests, being omitted for want of space. Clearly vassalship is here implied, such as loyal Timúrís paid to the supreme Khán. The gold and silver currencies differ in the absence of the Persian sovereign's name on the silver; this is easily explained by the carelessness and unimportance of this issue, the gold coin being far more of a state document. They also differ in showing Sulṭán Bábar Bahádur (Khán) for Sulṭán Muḥammad. The only explanation that can be offered is that the coins, perhaps issued at different times, offered but a cramped space for the vassal king's style, and that thus in one case Bábar occurs in the other Muḥammad.

There can, therefore, be no reasonable doubt that the gold coin which has been discussed was issued by Bábar, as vassal of Sháh Isma'íl, a condition which is sufficiently proved by the Turki prince's silver money with the Shía' formulæ. We can now understand the omission in Bábar's 'Memoirs' of the occurrences which fell between the beginning of A.H. 914 and that of A.H. 925. Similarly an unexpected light is thrown on the conduct of Sháh Ṭahmásp I. to Humáyún during his residence as a fugitive at the Persian court. Clearly the Persian king held Bábar's engagement to be a personal one binding on his son Humáyún.

To return to the chronology of Isma'íl's reign:—His death took place in the morning of Monday, 19 Rejeb, 930 = 23 May, A.D. 1524 (Jehán-árá, Or. 141, f. 211*b*, the rubric of the year, 211*a*). The statement of this authority is repeated by the author of the Ḳiṣaṣ-el-Khaḳání, who gives the night of the same day (f. 9*b*), which would throw the event back to the evening of Sunday, 22 May.

The *julús* of Ṭahmásp I. is given as Monday, 19 Rejeb, 930 = 23 May, 1524. (Tárikh-i-Elchi, f. 32*b*, Jahán-árá, Or. 141, f. 211*b*; 'Álám-árái, Add. 17,927, f. 59*a**; the inferior MS., Add. 16,684, f. 21*b*, merely giving the year 930). The day was thus that of his father's death, a remarkable exception to Persian usage. Ṭahmásp I.

The death of the same king is dated in the better MS. of the 'Álam-árái the night of Saturday, 14 Ṣafar, 984 (f. 155*a*), the inferior giving the night of Tuesday, 14 Ṣafar,

* Dr. Rieu considers this to bear some traces of an earlier recension (Cat. Per. MSS., i. p. 287).

984 (f. 26*b*). Munajjim Yazdi has Tuesday, 19 Ṣafar, 984 (Add. 27,241, f. 8*b*). The Ḳiṣaṣ gives the night of Tuesday, 15 Ṣafar (f. 17*a*). By Wüstenfeld's tables, 14 Ṣafar 984 = Sunday-Monday, 12-13 May, 1576. The 15th Ṣafar exactly suits. That the 15th of Ṣafar was Monday-Tuesday is confirmed by the date of 22 Ṣafar, 984, mentioned shortly afterwards in discussing the dates of Isma'íl II. Ḥasan ibn Muḥammad el-Kháḱí seems to settle the date, which he further defines as "after the second watch of the night," adding "the 15th of the month Ṣafar"=984 as a chronogram:

بتاريخ شب سه شنبه پانزدهم شهر صفر سنة اربع وثمانين
وتسعمايه بعد از دو پهر شب شاه طهماسب بعالم بقا خراميد
پانزدهم شهر صفر تاريخ است (Or. 1649, f. 616*a*)

It is of course unnecessary to discuss the isolated date Saturday, Ṣafar 15, beyond suggesting سه having dropped out before شنبه. It is obvious that the night of Tuesday, 15 Ṣafar, 984 = morning of Tuesday, 14 May, 1576, is the true date. It must always have been natural to confuse events happening in the night after the close of the day with the events of the day preceding, hence the date 14 Ṣafar.

Isma'íl II. The *julús* of Isma'íl II. is dated Wednesday, 27 Jumáda I. [984] = Tuesday-Wednesday, 22 August, A.D. 1576, in the better manuscript of the 'Álam-árái (Add. 17,927, f. 251*a*, *b*). The passage runs thus:

در روز معهود كه چهار شنبه بيست وهفتم جمادى الاول
بود جلوس كرده در مكان مبارك شاه جنت مكان قرار
گرفت (fol. 251*a*, *b*)

In the corresponding passage of the MS. in Naskhi, Add. 16,684, the date is wanting (fol. 56*b*). The date of Isma'íl's death is given in the 'Álam-árái as the night of Sunday, 13 Ramaẓan [985] = Saturday-Sunday, 24 November, 1577 (Add. 17,927, f. 266*a*), quoted in the Ḳiṣaṣ-el-Kháḳáni without the day of the week (Add. 7656,

f. 18*b*). The length of the reign of this king is stated in the Ḳiṣaṣ-el-Khāḳání as a year and seven months, (f. 19*a*) مدت سلطنت پادشاه مرحوم مغفور یکسال وهفتماه بود. The note of the reigns of the Ṣafavís in the margin of the MS. of the Tárikh-i-Elchí, numbered Or. 153, confirms this sum by the vague statement that the length of the reign was "nearly two years" مدت سلطنتش قریب دو سال (f. 79*a*). The more precise reckoning of the Ḳiṣaṣ is in excess of the sum, a year and three months and a half, from the *julús* to Isma'íl's death. On the other hand, from the death of Ṭahmásp I. to that of Isma'íl II. is nearly one year and seven months, and it may be added that the death of Ḥaidar Mirza induced the pretension of Isma'íl, who left his confinement in the fortress of Ḳahḳah, Tuesday, 22 Ṣafar, 984 (= Monday-Tuesday, 27-28 May, 1576), thus only a week after his father's death (Ḳiṣaṣ, f. 18*a*). The Aḥsan et-Taváríkh of Ḥasan el-Kháki allows Isma'íl II. 'eighteen months and a fraction' (f. 618*a*) 'from the beginning of his Sulṭánate.'

In the Favaïd-i-Ṣafavia are two táríkhs, respectively for the accession and the death of Isma'íl II., in the following lines, which form the closing part of a short poem. The words untranslated, detected by Dr. Rieu, make the two dates 984 and 985:—

'Fancy sought two elegant chronograms, that she might engrave on the tablet of the world; one for his taking his place in the region of time, one for his departure to the realm of nought. شهنشاه روی زمین was fixed, شهنشاه زیر زمین was written.' *

Muḥammed Khudabanda was enthroned at Ḳazvín, towards the close of the year 985. The better copy of the Muḥammad Khudabanda.

* دو تاریخ زیبنده میخواست فکر • که بر لوح عالم نگارد رقم
یکی بهر جاهش در اقلیم دهر • یکی بهر عزمش بملك عدم
شهنشاه روی زمین گشت ثبت • شهنشاه زیر زمین شد رقم
(Add. 16,698, f. 22 *a*)

'Álam-árái reads, 'on Tuesday in the month of Zu-l-Ḥijja, which is the eleventh month of the year of the Ox, 985,' (Add, 17,927, f. 276*a*). The inferior MS. reads, 'on the second day of the month,' &c. (Add. 16,684, f. 65*a*), both specifying the eleventh for the twelfth month. At the close of the account of the *julús*, we read in the better MS. the statement omitted in the inferior one, that the author, Iskandar Beg Munshí, was present at Ḳazvín on the occasion, which was Tuesday the third of Zu-l-Ḥijja, though Ḥasan Beg stated it was Thursday, and the author admits that he has some doubt.

راقم حروف در قزوین بود و در روزی که نواب سکندرشان داخل شهر میشد باستقبال رفته بود روز سه شنبه سیم ذی الحجه بود وحسن بگ مورخ روز پنجشنبه ماه مذکور نوشته تحمل که ذره حقیررا عقلی با اشتباهی واقع شده باشد
(Add. 17,927, f. 276 *a*).

Unfortunately the Museum possesses no MS. of Ḥasan Beg's Aḥsan-el-Taváríkh, but it may be noted that in the book under that title of his namesake, Ḥasan-ibn Muḥammad el-Kháḳí, there is no precise date, but simply the *julús* given under the year 985 (Or. 1649, f. 618*b*). The Ḳiṣaṣ dates the event Thursday 5 Zu-l-Ḥijja [985] (f. 19*a*).

To correct these discrepancies we may first of all discard the eleventh month, as Zu-l-Ḥijja is so frequently mentioned here that there cannot be a mistake for Zu-l-Ḳa'da. In the next place we may reject the reading 'second' from the inferior MS. of the 'Álam-árái as the better reads 'third,' and a Naskhi copyist could easily mistake Nestálíḳ سیم for دویم (in the MS. دوم). The question between the third and the fifth is definitely settled by the calendar, for the fifth could not have been either Tuesday or Thursday. The question between the two week-days is also similarly settled. By Wüstenfeld's Tables, the third was Thursday-Friday 11-12 Feb. Thus it would appear that Iskandar Beg's memory failed him, and the true date is Thursday 3 Zu-l-Ḥijja 985 = Wednesday-Thursday 10-11 Feb. 1578.*

The reign of Muḥammad Khudabanda ended with his deposition, the date of which I do not find exactly stated, but it must have been immediately before the enthronement of 'Abbás I. as Sháh of Irán, at the end of A.H. 995, late in Nov. 1587, N.S.

It may be well to mention that Wüstenfeld is here followed in beginning the new style in 1582.

'Abbás I. was twice enthroned; first by the powerful 'Alí-ḳulí Khán as Sultán of Khurásán, under the name of Sháh 'Abbás, in his camp then before Níshapúr, in the year of the Serpent, corresponding with A.H. 989, whereupon his *sikka* and *khuṭba* spread through the whole of Khurásán. (See 'Álam-árái, Add. 17,927, f. 346*b*, 347*a*. For the year see also Ḳiṣaṣ, f. 19*b*; cf. 22*b*, 23*a*.) The year of the Serpent of course began at the vernal equinox, and as the troops were encamped at the time of the Sháh's proclamation, we may assume that it took place before the winter, therefore in the year A.D. 1581 N.S. This conclusion is confirmed by the statement of the author of the Ḳiṣaṣ, who assigns forty-nine years to the reign of 'Abbás in Khurásán and 'Irák (f. 37*a*). His death occurred 24 Jumáda 1038, which is forty-nine lunar years after the early part of 989. 'Abbás I.

The second enthronement as Sháh of Irán is the true beginning of the reign of 'Abbás, as recognised by the Persian historians. There is a general agreement that the date was A.H. 996. It appears, however, that the actual event took place at the very close of the previous year. Munajjim Yazdí dates it at the end, strictly last third, of Zu-l-Ḥijja (در اخر ذی الحجه) 995, the year being

* According to Dr. Rieu, Iskandar Beg was born about A.H. 968 (Catalogue of Persian MSS., i., p. 185 *b*). Consequently he was only about seventeen at the time of the *julús*, and his memory may well have been obscured by the festivities.

given in Persian and Arabic (45*b*); but he accepts as the táríkh 'Abbás Bahádur Khán عباس بهادر خان = 996 (46*a*). Similarly the 'Álam-árái (Add. 16,684), after noticing the *julús* (f. 135*b* seq.) with the táríkh عباس بهادر خان (f. 136*a*), yet later inserts the rubric of the events of the first year 996 (f. 136*b*). The Ḳiṣaṣ gives the same táríkh (f. 24*b*).

It is therefore evident that Sháh 'Abbás I. was enthroned near the close of the year 995, but that the fragment of this year was left out of account, as if he had been proclaimed 1 Muḥarram 996. Thus we obtain the enthronement in the last part of Zu-l-Ḥijja 995, which began 1 Nov. 1587 (Wüst.), and the official beginning of his reign 1 Muḥ. 996 = 1 Dec. 1587 (Wüst.).

The death of 'Abbás I. is dated Thursday 24 Jumáda I. [1038] in the 'Álam-árái (16,684, f. 420*b*). The Ḳiṣaṣ gives Thursday 22 Jumáda I., 1037 (f. 37*a*). If the author of the Ḳiṣaṣ used the 'Álam-árái, it is very easy to see how he might have inserted the year 1037 for 1038. In the copy of the 'Álam-árái cited the year 1038 is only made out by following the months cited of 1037. That the date is a mere slip is shown by its repetition with a correct chronogram for Ṣafi's accession. Thursday the 24th of Jumáda I. was Thursday-Friday 18-19 Jan. 1629.

Ṣafí I. The 'Álam-árái dates the *julús* of Ṣafí I. at Iṣfahán, 23 Jumáda II. [1038] = 16-17 Feb. 1629 Friday-Saturday, and also adds two chronograms ظل حق and صفی با بر اورنگ شاهی نهاد, both making the correct sum 1038, (16,684, f. 421*b*). The Ḳiṣaṣ gives the date as Monday 4 Jumáda II. 1037 (f. 37*b*), but gives the chronogram ظل حق (f. 38*a*). The date 1037 for 1038 should be explained by the mistake in the date of the death of 'Abbás I. already noticed. By Wüstenfeld's Tables, 4 Jumáda II., is Sunday-Monday, 28-29 Jan. 1629, and 23 Jumáda II. Friday-Saturday 16-17 Feb., as already stated. The date of the 'Álam-árái is probably preferable. There could easily be a confusion between شنبه and بيست in cursive Nestálík, and thus the first numeral (بيست) might have dropped out, but the difference between 23 and (2)4 would still remain. The week-day, Monday, might suit the 24th.

The death of Ṣafí I. is given in the Ḳiṣaṣ (f. 46*b*) as 12 Ṣafar 1052=Sunday-Monday 11-12 May 1642. This date is confirmed by a contemporary record of the event at Káshán, on the 12th of Ṣafar, A.H. 1052, on the first page of a general history without title Or. 1566 (Dr. Rieu, Cat. Pers. MSS. iii. p. 1064). The author of the Ḳiṣaṣ also gives a chronogram, ماه صفر کرد ز دنیا سفر=Ṣafar 1052 (f. 47*a*).

'Abbás II.

The enthronement of 'Abbás II. took place at Káshán on the night of Friday the 16th of Ṣafar 1052=Thursday evening 16th May 1642, four days after his father's death at the same place. Ṭáhir Vaḥíd in one MS. gives this statement of interval, but with the date Friday 11 Ṣafar.

جلوس حضرت . . . که بعد از وقوع رحلت نواب خاقان رضوان مکان در شب جمعه یازدهم[11] ماه صفر سنهٔ هزار و پنجاه و دو که چهار روز از ان واقعه جانگداز گذشته بود (Add. 11,632, f. 14*a*,*b*.)

In the copy which Dr. Rieu considers the next best, the reading is varied by the 15th of Ṣafar (Add. 10,594, 14*b*). The Zínat-et-taváríkh has the night of Friday 16 Ṣafar (Add. 23,515, f. 683*b*), the Mirát-el-'Álam, I am informed by Dr. Rieu, gives the 16th. The same date, the night of Friday being specified, is given in the Favaïd (Add. 16,698, f. 38*a*); and Dr. Rieu finds the same in the second copy. On the weight of authority, and the agreement of the 12th with the 16th, as at an interval of four days, we may accept the 16th شانزدهم and reject the impossible reading 11th یازدهم and the improbable 15th پنجدهم as due to errors of copyists. The Ḳiṣaṣ gives the chronogram ظل معبود=1052 (Add. 7656, f. 48*a*).

The death of 'Abbás II. is dated in the Ḳiṣaṣ at the halting-place Khusravábád [in the district] of Dámghán on the night of Tuesday the 26th of the month Rabi' I., year 1077 (= Friday-Saturday, Sept. 24-25, 1666, f. 151*b*). Clearly the day of the week is wrong, سه being superfluous before شنبه. Chardin gives 25 Sept. 1666, about 4 A.M., which no doubt is the exact date, though he makes the correspondence 26 Rabi' II. (Couronnement de Soleïmaan, ed. 1671, p. 6). The Favaïd gives the month, not the day (f. 46*b*).

Ṣafí II. Sulaimán I.

Ṣafí II., afterwards Sulaimán I., was twice enthroned. The first enthronement, at Iṣfahán, is dated in the Zinat-et-taváríkh 6 Sha'bán 1077 = Monday-Tuesday, Jan. 31-Feb. 1, 1667, f. 687*a*. In spite of the inaccuracy of the Arab copyist of this MS., it is hard to imagine a mistake in the Arabic name of the month. Yet Chardin, who was at Iṣfahán at the time, dates the event about 10 P.M. on Saturday, 3 Jumáda I. = 2 Oct. (ibid. pp. 83, 121, 122), whereas the correspondence should be 3 Rabi' II. = Saturday, 2 Oct., which, as the enthronement shortly followed the decease of the late king, must be correct.

In consequence of the young king's ill-health and the misfortunes of the kingdom, it was decided to enthrone him a second time. Accordingly a second ceremony, in which the name of Sulaimán was substituted for that of Ṣafí, took place at Iṣfahán on the Nau-rúz, Tuesday 20 March, 1669 (= 19 Shawwál, 1079), at 9 A.M. (ibid. p. 389). The death of Sulaimán I. is dated 1105 (Zínat-et-taváríkh, f. 689*a*). Brydges, in his "Dynasty of the Kajars," p. lxxiii, gives the date 29 Jan. 1694. (= 2-3 Jumáda II. 1105.)

Ḥusain I.

Dr. Rieu has discovered the exact date of the *julús* of Sulṭán Ḥusain. It took place after the lapse of two hours and a half of the night, the eve of Saturday 14 Zu-l-Ḥijja 1105. بعد از گذشتن دو ساعت و نیم از شب شنبه چهار دهم شهر ذی الحجه الحرام سنه خمس و مایه والف مطابق ایت ییل ترکی (Dastúr-i-Sháhriyárán, Or. 2941, f. 16*a*). The correspondence is Friday, 6 August, 1694; Wüstenfeld gives

Thursday, 5 August. According to Olivier, Ḥusain came to the throne in 1694 (Voyage, v. p. 351).

Sháh Ḥusain abdicated on the afternoon of 23 Oct. 1722 (Hanway, ii. p. 179, 180, and note *a*). This was the 11th of Moḥarram, 1135 (cf. Hist. de Nader Chah, i., p. xvii).*

The enthronement of Ṭahmásp II. at Ḳazvín took place in the same month as his father's abdication. This is proved by the táríkh given in the History of Nádir, MS. 7661, f. 9*b*, اخر ماه محرم, the end or strictly last third of Muḥarram. It is most remarkable that there are coins of Ṭahmásp of both Ḳazvín (no. 145, p. 55) and Tabríz (no. 149, p. 56) dated 1134, showing that he anticipated his proclamation by exercising the right of coinage. Riẓa-ḳulí Khán, author of the Rauẓet-es-ṣafá-i-náṣirí, states that Ashraf in his third year, equivalent to his last, as he allows him three years, beheaded Sháh Sulṭán Ḥusain, and that on the receipt of the news Ṭahmásp had a *julús* at Kaẓvín (Lithogr. Ṭeherán, 1274, jild viii, §§ 'Coming out of Sháh Sultán Ḥusain from Iṣfahán,' 'Account of Sháh Ṭahmásp.') According to Hanway, Ḥusain was murdered by Ashraf after the battle of Murcha-khurt, 13 Nov., 1729 (ii. p. 276), and Ṭahmásp heard of the event on reaching Iṣfahán (p. 278). If Sháh Ṭahmásp had a second *julús* it must have been at the capital on this occasion. Ṭahmá-p II.

Ṭahmásp was deposed about 14 Rabi' I., A.H. 1144= 15-16 Sept., A.D. 1731 (Wüst.), but probably=14-15 Sept., as appears from the date next following.

'Abbás III. was enthroned Monday, 17 Rabi' I., 1144 (Hist. de Nader, i. p. 153; cf. p. 151). If the day of the week be correct the correspondence would be Sunday-Monday, 16-17 Sept.; if the day of the month be correct, it would be Tuesday-Wednesday, 18-19 'Abbás III.

* By Wüstenfeld the coincidence would be 11 Moḥ.=22 Oct., or 12=23. It is quite possible that his 1st Moḥ. is one day too early, and thus we obtain 11 Moḥ.=23 Oct.

Sept. (Wüst.), but probably to be corrected one day to 17-18. The deposition of 'Abbás III. must have occurred before the proclamation of Nádir, 24 Shawwál, 1148= 8 March, 1736 (Wüst. corrected one day as before), when the throne had become vacant (id. ii. 3, 4). According to the Favaïd, as Dr. Rieu has pointed out to me, 'Abbás III. was deposed and exiled by Nádir to his father Sháh Ṭahmásp II. to Sebzewár in Khurásán, but returned, and in the year A.H. 1200 was living blind at Iṣfahán. By whom he was blinded we are not told.

انحضرت را عزل کرده نزد پدر بسبزوار فرستاد و در ایام توقف راقم حروف بایران در سنه یکهزار و دو صد هجری شاه عباس ثالث نابینا در اصفهان بود (Add. 16,698, f. 55*a*).

Sám. Sám Mírza is mentioned in the History of Nádir Sháh, in the narrative of the last year of his reign, 1160, as a pretender of obscure birth, in whose favour the people of Tabríz declared in that year (ii. p. 188, cf. 185). In the same year we find Nádir's successor 'Ádil Sháh striking money at Tabríz (no. 281, p. 87 *infra*); consequently the pretender must have held the town for less than a year. According to the History of Nádir, the pretension of Sám began after the vernal equinox of A.H. 1160 (ibid., ll.cc.), and before Nádir's death, Sunday midnight, 11 Jumáda II., 1160=18 June, 1747. According to Von Hammer (Hist., ed. 1839, vol. xv. p. 147), Sám Mirza, pretended son of Sháh Ḥusain, was enthroned at Ardebíl as soon as Nádir's death was known. This is a slight discrepancy, which is probably due to inference. His rule may be dated A.H. 1160=A.D. 1747, the Moḥammadan and Gregorian years being almost exactly coincident.

This Sám, although he calls himself son of Sultán Ḥusain Sháh, does not appear to be the same as his namesake, who revolted in Azerbíján prior to the autumn of A.H. 1156=A.D. 1743, and suffered the loss of his nose at the hands of the Persian governor, and again revolted in Shirván the same year (Hist. de Nader, ii. 157-8), and finally was captured by Tahmúras, King of Georgia, 24 Zu-l-Ḳa'da, 1157=28-29 Dec. 1744; soon after which, his eyes were torn out by order of Nádir (p. 164). It is probable that Ḥusain had a son called Sám personated by two pretenders. The Mírza Sám (l. Sám Mírza) mentioned by Von Hammer as confined by the Turks at Sinope (p. 123) very early in 1160 (cf. p. 122) may be either of the persons here mentioned.

Sultán Ḥusain (II.)* was proclaimed by 'Alí Merdán in the early part of the year A.H. 1166=A.D. 1753. According to the Zínat-et-tavárikh, Kerím Khán, after returning to Ṭeherán from his disastrous campaign against Muḥammad Ḥasan Khán, heard in the beginning of A.H. 1166=A.D. 1753, on his way to Iṣfahán, that 'Alí Merdán Khán had set up an unknown pretender calling himself Sháh Sultán Ḥusain II. Kerím Khán then marched against and defeated 'Alí Merdán, who thereupon slew the pretender, in order no doubt to make the alliance, next mentioned, with Ázád Khán (Add. 23,527, f. 173*a*,*b*). The Táríkh-i-Gítí-Kusháí has the same sequence of events, except that Ḥusain only disappears in the year 1166 (f. 14*a*-15*a*). The Favaïd-i-Ṣafavia takes a very different view of the pretention of Ḥusain, a view supported by Aḳa Muḥammad's proclamation of Ḥusain's son Sultán Muḥammad. This work allows him a reign of seven months, and states that he was blinded by 'Alí Merdán Khán (Add. 16,698, f. 57*b*; Or. 139, f. 19*a*). The marginal note on the later Ṣafavis in the Táríkh-i-Elchí gives his reign as nearly one year (Or. 153, f. 79*a*). The precise period of the Favaïd is however evidently correct, for the campaign of Ázád Khán, in which he defeated Kerím Khán, occurred in the same year, after the deposition of Ḥusain II. (Táríkh-i-Gítí-Kusháí, 17*a*,*b*, 18*a*; cf. Zínat-et-tavárikh, f. 173*b*). Ḥusain II.

* The details of the history of this period, here only alluded to, will be found in the discussion of the reign of Sháh Isma'íl (III).

This ephemeral reign may therefore be dated A.H. 1166 = A.D. 1753.

Sulṭán Muḥammad.

Abu-l-Fet-ḥ Sultán Muḥammad Mírza was proclaimed in his youth in A.H. 1200 by Aḳa Muḥammad Khán at Ṭeherán, and throughout his dominions (Favaïd, Add. 16,698, f. 59*a*, seqq.). That this proclamation actually took effect is evident from the description of the coins then issued at Ṭeherán for the Sháh and the Khán, the royal coins being sent for inspection to Sultán Muḥammad in Khurásán: they were rupis struck at Ṭeherán (id. f. 147*b*, 148*a*, see *infra*, pp. lxxxi, ii). The note in the margin of the Taríkh-i-Elchí, already referred to, states the proclamation in A.H. 1200 (Or. 153, f. 79*a*). In introducing the subject of the proclamation of Muḥammad Mírza the author of the Favaïd gives a prediction of the famous saint Ne'amet-Alláh, that a Sháh of the line of 'Alí should come, named Muḥammad (probably the Mahdí), and connects this with what happened after (بعد از) the year 1200 (f. 59*a*); but the later codex (Or. 139, f. 19*b*) gives the vaguer form (بعد), which may be rendered 'afterwards (in).' A good instance here occurs of proclamation without *julús*. Neither of these authorities assigns any length of reign to Muḥammad Mírza, and from the narrative in the Favaïd it appears that the young prince suspected a snare and declined to leave Ṭabas and go to Ṭeherán, and thus nothing came of the move of Aḳa Muḥammad (f. 148*a*). The date A.H. 1200 = A.D. 1786 may be considered exact, as 1200 began 3-4 Nov. 1785, and thus the portion corresponding to the earlier European year would have been unsuitable in the north of Persia to transactions involving the dispatch of couriers in many directions.

Ṣafavis, maternally.

In the decline of the Ṣafavis the claim to the throne on maternal descent began to be asserted. This was first done by the Sayyids of the 'Family of Dá-úd' آل داود, next by Sháh Rukh, and lastly for Sháh Isma'íl (III).

Sayyid Aḥmad was eldest son of Mírza Abu-l-Ḳásim, eldest son of Mírza Muḥammad Dá-úd, the husband of a daughter of Sulaimán I., himself maternally descended by a female succession from Sháh 'Abbás I. (Tezkira-i-Ál-i-Dá-úd, 32*a*). He was enthroned at Kermán, A.H. 1139 (ibid, f. 42*a*, *b*). The History of Nádir Sháh dates the event 14 Rabi' I, 1140, the year of the Sheep (i. p. xxx). The family history before cited is, however, very precise in specifying 1139 in its proper place (1138, f. 41*a*; 1139, f. 42*a*, again f. 42*b*; 1140, f. 45*a*, 50*b*). The course of events is the same in both narratives. According to the History of Nádir Sháh, Sayyid Aḥmad seized upon the management of the provinces of Fárs and Kermán, under the seal of Ṭahmásp II. (i. pp. xxix. xxx.). While marching on Shíráz he was defeated by an Afghán general and made captive, but afterwards, having made his escape, he raised an army, and assumed the royal title and functions in A.H. 1140. In the family history he assumes royalty at Kermán in 1139; in the same year advances on Shíráz, and is defeated by the Afgháns in a battle in which he wore the royal crown. After this he again made head against the enemy, until his capture and execution at the end of A.H. 1140 (f. 42*a*, seqq.) The family annalist is more likely to have been accurate as to the exact date of this pretender's enthronement than Nádir's historian. The brief account of Hanway seems to favour the same view (ii. p. 271). Consequently it seems preferable, though the month and day may be correct in the other history. Aḥmad was executed at Isfahán at the end of 1140=July-August, 1728 (Tezkira-i-Ál-i-Dá-úd, f. 50*b*). The probable dates are therefore 14 Rabi' I., 1139=8-9 Nov. 1726 to Zu-l-Ḥijja 1140=July-August, 1728.

The family of Dá-ud. Aḥmad.

The enthronement of Sulaimán II. is dated 8 Muḥarram, 1163 (= 17-18 Dec. 1749) in the family history (Tezkira, f. 97*b*). He is allowed a reign of 40 days by the Táríkh-i-

Sulaimán II.

f

Gítí-Kusháí (f. 6*b*) and the Favaïd (f. 57*b*, 58*a*, 108*a*, *b*), and was therefore deposed in Safar 1163=Jan. 1750.

Sháh Rukh. Sháh-Rukh. (See Efsháris).

Isma'íl (III.). According to the Táríkh-i-Gítí-Kusháí, Isma'íl (III.) was enthroned by 'Alí-Merdán Khán at Iṣfahán after the citadel capitulated, A.H. 1164 (Add. 23,524, f. 8*a*).* The Zínat-et-tavárikh begins its series of years not with 1164, as the work first mentioned, but with 1165, and shortly before relates the enthronement of Isma'íl III. at Iṣfahán after the capture of that city (Add. 23,527, f. 172*a*, *b*). These authorities would therefore seem to agree.

The earliest coin of Isma'íl (III.) in the Museum collection is dated 1163, and was struck at Iṣfahán.

To resolve this difference between the historians and the coin, it is important to examine the Táríkh-i-Gítí-Kusháí more particularly. I there find, under the section on the lineage of Kerím Khán (f. 4*a*, seqq.) the relation how he was elected head (داور) of his tribe, and after Ibráhím Sháh had made war on his brother 'Alí ('Ádil) Sháh, Kerím Khán was employed by the usurper (f. 4*b*, 5*a*). The next section relates the events which followed the assassination of Nádir Sháh as far as the forty days' reign of Sulaimán II. and the restoration of the blind Sháh Rukh (f. 5*a* to 6*b*), which we know took place in the first quarter of 1163 (*infra*, p. li). Then at once we find the rubric of the events of the year 1164, 'and how 'Alí Merdán Khán sought the aid of the sovereign of the age [Kerím Khán].' Then follows the narrative of the alliance with 'Alí Merdán and the surrender of Iṣfahán by Abu-l-Fet-ḥ, governor for Sháh Rukh (f. 6*b*-7*b*) after the Nau-rúz (f. 6*b*), and the *julús* of Isma'íl III. is next related (f. 8*a*,*b*). Consequently the rise of Kerím Khán is

* It is true that the Favaïd-i-Ṣafavia twice speaks of a previous proclamation by Muḥammad Ḥasan (Add. 16,698, f. 57*a*, 143*b*), but this is historically impossible, and the confusion is with a proclamation which must have taken place when Muḥammad Ḥasan later gained possession of Isma'íl, and struck money in his name, matters to be later noticed (p. xlvi seqq).

placed in 1161, the date of Ibráhím's rebellion, but his real acquisition of power in 1164.*

Thus a whole year is dropped, from the restoration of Sháh Rukh in the early natural spring of 1163 to Isma'íl's *julús*, here placed after the vernal equinox 1164.

'Alí Riza, who must be allowed to be a competent authority for the chronology and history of the Zand family, dates the rise of Kerím Khán in 1163, on the authority of Mírza Ṣádiḳ, the author of Táríkh-i-Gítí-Kushái, which he quotes, under the name of the Táríkh-i-Salṭanaṭ-i-Kerím Khán, in these words:

و بعد از وقع قتل نادر شاه از قراری که مرحوم میرزا صادق
منشی متخلص بنامی در تاریخ سلطنت کریم خان ایمای بآن
کرده است امر سلطنت بلاد ایران مغشوش و هر پنج روز نوبت
حکمرانی بنام یکی بلند اوازه بوده تا در سنه ١١٦٣ مهر منیر دولت
کریم خان زند از افق پریه ملایر عراق ظاهر و در سنه ١١٩٣ در شیراز
وفات یافت (Or. 2197, f. 3 *a*, *b*)

As Mírza Ṣádiḳ in the passages already referred to places the rise of Kerím Khán in 1161, it is clear that the reference here is not to his appointment as chief, but to his departure from his own territory at the call of 'Alí Merdán. Therefore the solution of the problem is probably this:—The Persian chroniclers, when they relate events under years, reckon from Nau-rúz to Nau-rúz by the old solar year. Consequently the first regnal year of a king proclaimed like Isma'íl III., after the Nau-rúz, would begin with that date in the year following. Hence a confusion between the Hijra year of proclamation and the first regnal year. Or it may be argued that the date 1163 either was found in 'Alí Rizá's copy of the Táríkh-i-Gítí-Kushái, which is an unlikely addition of a new rubric, or was here added by him on his own judgment.

* I am much indebted to Dr. Rieu for kind help in getting the tenor of these passages.

The historical circumstances of the time are in accordance with this result. The overthrow of Sháh Rukh's central government at Mesh-hed by Sulaimán II. must have been severe in its effects in the provinces. The usurper was more than master of Khurásán: he struck money in Mázenderán (no. 313, p. 98). His party was strong, for he united the partizans of the Ṣafavis and the fanatical Sayyids against the hated Efsharís. On the evidence of all authorities, Iṣfahán was not lost to Sháh Rukh, but 'Alí Merdán had little difficulty in gaining possession of it, and making it the centre of Isma'íl's government. For in truth Sháh Rukh, when restored, was a mere puppet, as a blind Sháh could only be. In the spring of 1163 everything was therefore ripe for a new sovereign. 'Alí Merdán had discovered another half-Ṣafavi puppet who would be the nominal head of his party. So soon as he could leave the Bakhtiári mountains the old Kurdish chief marched on Iṣfahán and there set up Isma'íl, while he maintained the real power himself.

The historians enable us to follow the subsequent fortunes of Sháh Isma'íl (III.). Suspicion arising between Kerím Khán and 'Alí Merdán, the Bakhtiári chief left Shíráz with the Sháh (در موکب شاهی) for his mountains. Kerím Khán, on hearing of this, left Iṣfahán early in the spring of 1165 (در اوائل سال بهار سال هزار و صد وشصت پنج)* The two armies joined battle on the bank of the river Gozán. Sháh Isma'íl, seeing that fortune was unfavourable to Alí Merdán, went over to his rival, who returned victorious to Iṣfahán (Zínat-et-taváríkh, Add. 23,527, f. 172*b*, 173*a*; cf. Táríkh-i-Gití-Kusháí, Add. 23,524, f. 10*a*—11*b*).

* This is a good instance of the habit of reckoning from the Nau-rúz, as if it were the beginning of the Hijra year, whereas Muḥarram 1165 began in November, four months before the Nau-rúz.

In the same year Kerím Khán turned his forces against the Ḳájár chief, Muḥammad Ḥasan Khán, and invaded Mázenderán. He was defeated by the Ḳájár, and fled to Ṭeherán, whence, in the beginning of the year 1166, he returned to Iṣfahán (Zínat-et-taváríkh, f. 173*a*). In the Táríkh-i-Gítí-Kusháí, Mírza Ṣádiḳ states more precisely, under the year 1165, that Kerím Khán was defeated by Muḥammad Ḥasan Khán at Asterábád, and implies that Sháh Isma'íl (III.) was captured by the Ḳájár chief, who returned to Ashraf in Mázenderán in the Sháh's cavalcade.
محمد حسن خان در موکب شاه متوجه اشرف مازندران شد
(f. 12*b*, 13*a*.)

Still more precisely the author of the Nukhbat-el-Akhbár relates that Kerím Khán took Isma'íl (III.) with him in this unfortunate expedition, and that the Sháh came to the fort of Asterábád evidently to give himself up, whereupon Kerím Khán took to flight, and Muḥammad Ḥasan carried the Sháh away with him to Ashraf.
و میرزا ابو تراب بپای حصار استراباد آمده کریم خان فرار نمود وبعضی از لشکریانش اسیر ترکمانیه یموت شده بعد از فرار کریم خان محمد حسن خان میرزا ابو ترابرا برداشته بجنب اشرف رفت (Or. 2837, f. 189*a*)

The subsequent position of Isma'íl (III.) may be inferred from numismatic evidence, which is as follows:

COINS STRUCK FROM A. H. 1163 TO 1173.

A.H.						
1163	Struck by 'Alí Merdán,	in name of Isma'il (III.),	Iṣfahán.			
1164						
1165						
1166				Struck by Muḥammad Ḥasan,	in name of Isma'il (III.),	Mázenderán.
				”	” ”	Resht.
1167	Struck by Kerím Khán,	in name of Imám Mahdí,	Iṣfahán.	”	” ”	Mázenderán.
	”		Ḳazvín.			
1168						
1169	”	”	Iṣfahán.	”	in name of Imám 'Alí-Riẓá,	Iṣfahán.
1170	”	”	Shíráz.	”	” ”	Mázenderán.
				”	” ”	Tabríz.
				”	” ”	Yazd.
1171				”	” ”	Mázenderán.
				”	” ”	Resht.
1172	”		Jelau.			
	”	”	Mázenderán.			
1173	”	”	Mázenderán.			

From this evidence it appears that (1) 'Alí Merdán Khán struck in Isma'íl's name; and (2) it may be inferred that this habit was continued by Kerím Khán, for (3) on gaining possession of the Sháh's person Muḥammad Ḥasan Khán repeated the coinage of 'Alí Merdán in 1166 and 1167; (4) 'Alí Merdán Khán requiring a puppet, then set up Sháh Husain II. in 1166, while Kerím Khán, having no pretender, may be presumed to have issued his own money in the name of the Imám Muḥammad El-Mahdí, as he certainly did in 1167, while Isma'íl's was still being issued by Muḥammad Ḥasan; (5) and on acquiring Iṣfahán 1169 = 1756 (Táríkh-i-Gítí-Kusháí, f. 23*b*), Muḥammad Ḥasan issued his own money in the name of Imám 'Alí-Riẓá, thenceforward dropping all acknowledgment of Sháh Isma'íl, whose name never afterwards appears on the coins. It may be here mentioned that this daring step probably caused the Ḳájár chief's downfall. The only point of difficulty here is when did Muḥammad Ḥasan drop his acknowledgment of Isma'íl (III.)? The right of the *khuṭba* and *sikka* was so important and distinctive as a royal prerogative, that from the cessation of Isma'íl's coins to the issue of Luṭf-'Alí's the sovereign's name does not appear except by allusion, save once (Abu-l-Fet-ḥ's) in a subsidiary place. Consequently the complete suppression of Isma'íl's name was a very strong act, and it could only be done evasively by making the 'Alí-Riẓá series the sole money authorized by Muḥammad Ḥasan Khán. Kerím Khán had already done the same, coining in the name of another Imám, the Mahdí, whose name then first appears in the place of the sovereign's, but the Zand chief had no puppet Ṣafavi in his hands. It cannot reasonably be doubted that Muḥammad Ḥasan changed the style when he became master of Iṣfahán in A.H. 1169, not long before the Nau-rúz (Ibid, l.c.). This, therefore, would be the date of the practical deposition of Sháh Isma'íl (III.)*

* Since writing this, I have had the advantage of examining Professor

I can find no further authentic information concerning him beyond the statement in the Favaïd-i-Ṣafavia that he died in the same year as Kerím Khán, A.H. 1193.

و در همین سال نخل حیات شاه اسمعیل امی صفوی از پا درافتاد

(Add. 16,698, f. 126*a*.) This statement immediately follows that of the death of Kerím Khán, 13 Ṣafar, 1193=1-2 March 1779 (f. 125*b*, 126*a*). It is thus probable that the event did not occur after the Khán's death, as it would then be referred to the period following (f. 129*b*). It is thus probable that Isma'íl (III.) died either in the same Hijra year, 1193, as Kerím Khán, between 1 Muḥarram=18-19 Jan. 1779 and 13 Ṣafar=1-2 Mar., or in the solar year beginning 21 Ṣafar, 1192=20 Mar. 1778. His death would therefore be dated A.H. 1192-3=A.D. 1778-9.

The chronology of Sháh Isma'íl (III.) would therefore be as follows:

Enthronement by 'Alí Merdán Khán, and reign under his tutelage, A.H. 1163, spring or summer=A.D. 1750.

Under tutelage of Kerím Khán, spring or summer of A.H. 1165=1752.

Under tutelage of Muḥammad Ḥasan Khán, summer or autumn of A.H. 1165=A.D. 1752.

Loses the right of coinage, and is thus practically deposed by Muḥammad Ḥasan Khán before Nau-rúz of A.H. 1169=A.D. 1756.

Sháh Isma'íl survives until A.H. 1192-3=A.D. 1778-9, but his pretentions do not appear to have been again officially raised.

Mehren's manuscript Catalogue of the Oriental Coins in the Royal Museum of Copenhagen. I there find the two coins of which I practically anticipated the existence: a coin of Kerím Khán, Iṣfahán, 1166, occurs with the style of the Mahdí, and another of Muḥammad Ḥasan (mint wanting), 1169, with the style of Sháh Isma'íl (III). We have therefore proof that Kerím Khán dropped the name of the Sháh in 1166, and Muḥammad Ḥasan in the course of 1169. I would observe that the issue of coins with the name of 'Alí-Riẓá would prove nothing in the case of Muḥammad Ḥasan had not he made this his sole coinage, and not merely an accessory issue, and, moreover, had he not struck it at the capital, Iṣfahán.

The *julús* of Maḥmud is well known to have taken place on the day of the abdication of Ḥusain I., 11 Moḥarram, 1135 = 23 Oct., 1722 (*supr.* p. xxxvii). On his coins he appears to use his *julús* year only. He was assassinated in the month of Sha'bán, 1137. Hanway dates the event on the same day as the proclamation of Ashraf, which he gives as 22 April, 1725 (= 8–9 Sha'bán, 1137; Hanway, ii. p. 225). In the Histoire de Nader the date is given as 12 Sha'bán, 1136, the year of the Serpent (i., p. xix). The *julús* year of Ashraf and the correspondence of the year of the Serpent to 1137 correct the figures in the text. We may therefore safely take Sha'bán, 1137 = April-May, 1725, as the true date. Afgháns. Maḥmud

The date of Ashraf's proclamation has been just given, Sha'bán, 1137 = April-May, 1725. He appears to have been shortly after enthroned (Hanway ii., p. 228).* It may be noted that, similarly to the case of Maḥmud, his *julús* year appears on nearly all his coins with, however, the Hijra year of striking sometimes indicated on the other side.† The *julús* year is 1137. The close of Ashraf's reign may be dated on the occasion when after his defeat in the battle of Murchah-Khurt 13 Nov. 1729 (Hanway, ii. 276) (= 20 Rabi' II, 1142, Hist. de Nader, i. p. 81) he fled the same night (21 Rabi' II.), which was followed by the occupation of the capital by Nádir's troops, 16 Nov. 1729 (= 23-24 Rabi' II.; Hanway ii., pp. 276, 277). In the Histoire de Nader the battle is dated 20 Rabi' II. (vol. i. pp. 80, 81), and the occupation of Iṣfahán the 23rd of the same month (p. 85). Ashraf.

The enthronement of Nádir Sháh took place in the plains of Mughán, on Thursday, 24 Shawwál, 1148, at 8h. 20m. Muslim time = 8 March, 1736, supposing that the Muslim time is reckoned from sunrise (Hist. de Nader, ii. pp. 7, 8). His coins have the well-known táríkh الخير فيما وقع = 1148. Efsháris. Nádir Sháh.

---

* This is apparently a case of proclamation followed by enthronement.

† In the Catalogue I have erroneously supposed that the *julús* date is always on a die of 1137.

Nádir was assassinated on Sunday, 11 Jumáda II., 1160, at midnight = 18 June, 1747; (id., p. 190, 'Alí Rizá, History of the Zand Family, 24,903, fol. 3*b*; and so in the other three MSS. of the work collated, 'night'). By Wüstenfeld the correspondence is the 19th June.

'Adil Sháh. 'Alí-Ḳuli Khán, the nephew of Nádir, was enthroned as 'Alí Sháh at Mesh-hed,* 27 Jumáda II., 1160 = 4-5 July, 1747 (Tezkira-i-Ál-i-Dáúd, f. 76*b*; Hist. de Nader, ii. p. 192; cf. Hanway, ii. p. 452). He was known as Alí or 'Ádil Sháh. He reigned about twelve months (Hanway, i. p. 347; cf. Hist. de Nader, ii. pp. 194-196). His deposition occurred not long before 23 Sept., 1748 = 30 Ramaẓán-1 Shawwál, 1161, which confirms the more precise period indicated above (Hanway, i. p. 349).

Ibráhím. In four of the best MSS. of the History of Nádir Sháh (Add. 6154, 7661, 26,196, 25,790), as Dr. Rieu kindly informs me, the enthronement of Ibráhím at Tabríz is uniformly dated 17 Zu-l-Ḥijja, 1161 = 7-8 Dec. 1748. So, too, the Durra-i-Nadira (Or. 1360, f. 264*b*). The printed Hist. de Nader gives 7 Zu-l-Ḥijja (ii. p. 196). Ibráhím had overthrown his brother 'Ádil Sháh (pp. 194, 195), but did not immediately assume the royal dignity. This was done in consequence of Sháh Rukh's accession, 8 Shawwál, 1161, under two months before (Ibid., ii. 196). By comparing the data under the previous reign, which show that 'Ádil Sháh reigned about twelve months, we find that there was an interregnum, of less than three months, between the deposition of 'Ádil and the proclamation of Ibráhím. During this interval Ibráhím and Sháh Rukh were practically but not officially rival sovereigns.

Ibráhím was deposed some months, probably about two, previously to Jan. 1750 (= Muḥarram, Ṣafar 1163; cf. Hanway, i. p. 353†).

---

* In the text Khurásán, implying of course Mesh-hed; so Durra-i-Nádira, Or. 1360, f. 260*a*, Dr. Rieu, but Tús equivalent to Mesh-hed, and 7 Jumada II.

† Hanway here states that after the overthrow of Ibráhím the British Caspian traders petitioned George II. for a letter to Sháh Rukh, which was

According to the Histoire de Nader Cháh, the first enthronement of Sháh Rukh took place at Mesh-hed, 8 Shawwál, 1161 (= 30 Sept. - 1 Oct. 1748; ii. p. 196; cf. 195). He was blinded and dethroned by Sulaimán II., enthroned, no doubt, immediately afterwards, 8 Muḥarram 1163 (= 17-18 Dec. 1749; cf. supr. p. xli). After a reign of forty days Sulaimán was deposed, and Sháh Rukh reinstated. (Hist. Nader, ii. p. 198). His second enthronement, according to the Tezkira-i-Ál-i-Daúd, took place before the 11 Rabi' II, 1163 = 19-20 March, 1750 (f. 116*a*). This date is not two months after the deposition of Sulaimán, and the second accession of Sháh Rukh is thus fixed to the first quarter of 1163 and 1750. Sháh Rukh.

Subsequently Sháh Rukh appears to have retained the semblance of sovereignty until the siege of Mesh-hed by Aḥmad Sháh Durrání. On the capture of his capital he surrendered himself to the conqueror, and was again enthroned by Aḥmad Sháh Durrání, on the 27 Rejeb, 1168 = 8-9 May, 1755, as Sháh of Irán, obviously in vassalage to or under the protection of Aḥmad Sháh (History of Aḥmad Sháh Durrání, Or. 196, f. 38*a*, *b*; cf. date in 39*a*). Both the date and the fact are contrary to the ordinary European statements, according to which Sháh Rukh was set up in 1164 by Sháh Aḥmad as Sháh of Khurásán. The date is very clearly established by the MS. In fol. 37*b* we have the rubric of the year 1160 stated to correspond to the year of the Hog in the Tatar Cycle, and to the 9th year of Aḥmad Sháh, immediately followed by the notice of the Nau-rúz, 9 Jumáda II. The correspondences give us the year 1168-9, the unit of the date being omitted in the manuscript. The dates on the coins of Aḥmad Sháh show that his ninth year corresponded to A.H. 1168-9. The year of the Hog began in A.H. 1168. The

written about January 1750. Allowing for the slowness of travelling, the information of Sháh Rukh's success must have been despatched from northern Persia at least two months earlier.

Nau-rúz determines the year to be 1168, 9 Jumáda II. of that year being 22-23 March, 1755, according to Wüstenfeld. A coin of Aḥmad Sháh, struck at Mesh-hed in his ninth year, shows the correspondence to be historically correct. Farther we learn, from the statements of the History of Aḥmad Sháh, that the *fainéant* Sháh Rukh was set up by him as Sháh of Irán, not of Khurásán. He was to be Sháh of Irán *de jure*, though *de facto* he was afterwards never more than Sháh of Khurásán. It would at first seem that Aḥmad Sháh would have preferred his dependent to have held a lower title than one which might well have eclipsed his own; but we should remember that the Afghán was ambitious of succeeding Nádir in his empire, and that thus it was of advantage to him to set up an imperial puppet, whom he could play at any time, not a local prince, whose petty kingdom he could indeed control, but who would have no influence beyond its limits.

Sháh Rukh was taken prisoner at the capture of Mesh-hed by Aḳa Muḥammad Khán in the course of A.H. 1210, after the *julús* of the Ḳájár (Táríkh-i-Moḥammadí, f. 220*a*, seqq.; cf. Brydges Dynasty of the Kajars, pp. 24, 25.) In the Táríkh-i-Ḳájáría, lithographed at Ṭeherán, (i. f. 23*b*) the sequence of events is the same, but the date of the *julús* is erroneously given as 1209, that of the expedition to Khurásán as 1210. In the highly ornate account of the *julús* in the Táríkh-i-Muḥammadí, Dr. Rieu finds that the time was spring, though Aries is not mentioned (l. c.). Probably the *julús* was hurried on before the Nau-rúz to avoid delaying the expedition to Khurásán, of which it was the necessary prologue, as an assertion of Aḳa Muḥammad's claim to the undivided rule of Irán. The natural spring of 1210 began in Ramaẓán=March, 1796, and the year closed on the 17th July. It is within this interval that the deposition of Sháh Rukh must have fallen in the spring or summer of 1796.

The dates of this complicated reign are therefore—

First enthronement, 8 Shawwál, 1161=30 Sept.-1 Oct. 1748.

Deposition, 8 Muḥarram, 1163=17-18 Dec. 1749.

Second enthronement, first quarter of 1163=1750.

Third enthronement, 27 Rejeb, 1168=8-9 May, 1755.

Deposition, spring or summer of 1210=1796.

Bakhtiárí. 'Alí Merdán Khán.

Among the Kháns who usurped regal power without assuming the royal title, 'Alí Merdán is probably the first in point of date. It may be well here to lay down a general principle as to the mode of dating the accession of these rulers. As we cannot in several cases calculate from a *julús*, we must take the time of the actual or practical assumption of independence in a leading city of Persia.

'Alí Merdán's rise may be dated from the fall of Sulaimán II., and the second proclamation of Sháh Rukh before 11 Rabí' II., 1163 = 19-20 March, 1750. He became wakíl on the submission of Iṣfahán just before the proclamation of Sháh Isma'íl (III.), A.H. 1163=A.D. 1750 (Zínat-et-Taváríkh, Add. 23,527, f. 172*a*, *b*; Tárikh-i-Gítí-Kusháí, f. 8*a*). He practically lost the regency to Kerím Khán, A.H. 1165=A.D. 1752, (supra, p. xliv). If he dropped the title of wakíl, no doubt he resumed it on setting up Sháh Ḥusain II. in 1166. He was assassinated by Muḥammad Khán Zand in the year 1167 (Tárikh-i-Gítí-Kusháí, f. 19*b*: cf., for the event, Zínat-et Taváríkh, Add. 23,527, f. 174*a*, *b*). The exact time must have been in spring or summer. The date is therefore A.D. 1754. It may be noted that this event was the political turning point in the war between Kerím Khán and Ázád Khán.

Afghán. Ázád Khán.

Chronologically the place of Ázád Khán follows those of Kerím Khán and Muḥammad Ḥasan Khán, and the discussion of his dates should follow those of their lines; but as he was their contemporary, and his line, unlike theirs, was not continued, it is well to fix his dates here instead of considering the matter after the chronology of the still ruling Ḳájár family. Following the rule laid down in the notice of 'Alí Merdán, we need not be embarrassed by the circumstance that Ázád Khán became independent as a border chieftain (von Hammer, Hist. de l'Emp. Ottoman, xv. 204), and thus detached districts of the eastern frontier. In this position 'Alí Merdán Khán claimed his aid in A.H. 1166 (A.D. 1753) against Kerím Khán (Zínat-et-Taváríkh, Add. 23,527, f. 173*b*). Thus so far he did not aspire openly to the sovereignty of Persia. The murder of 'Alí Merdán in the same year removed the barrier between Ázád and the heart of Persia. Accordingly, he then advanced and occupied Iṣfahán, where he set himself up as sovereign—

بعد از انجام مهام قلمرو سایر ولایات عراق عنان عزیمت
جانب دار السلطنه اصفهان کشوده و در اصفهان اساس دولت
و اسباب سلطنت و جلالت‌را چیده در اردوی او جمعیت منعقد
گردید (Gítí-Kusháí, 16*b*, 17*a*)

—and struck his own money (Zínat-et-Taváríkh, f. 173*b*). This was still in 1166=1753, as it must have occurred before the winter season. Ázád was finally defeated and his power overthrown by Muḥammad Ḥasan Khán in A.H. 1169=A.D. 1756, as the campaign again must have taken place before the winter. All the coins of Ázád known to me fall within these years. (See Fraehn Recensio 497, nos. 206-7; Tabríz, 1168, 1169; and infra, no. 416, p. 130, Tabríz, 1168.)

The dates are therefore, Accession at Iṣfahán, A.H. 1166 =A.D. 1753; overthrow, A.H. 1169=A.D. 1756.

Zands. Kerím Khán.

The dates of the rule of Kerím Khán, except that of its close, have been necessarily fixed in the discussion as to the dates of Sháh Isma'íl (III.), but here require some further elucidation. He first takes an important place as ally of 'Alí Merdán Khán in setting up Isma'íl, A.H. 1163 =A.D. 1750. 'Alí Merdán then was made wakíl, and Kerím Khán commander-in-chief (Zínat-et-Taváríkh, Add.

23,527, f. 172*a*, *b*). This was before the Sháh's proclamation (f. 172*b*). The Táríkh-i-Gítí-Kusháí agrees as to the circumstances (f. 8*a*). In this first period no doubt Kerím Khán played the second part. In the year A.H. 1165=A.D. 1752 the two chiefs quarrelled, and Kerím Khán secured the Sháh and the central authority as wakíl (Zínat-et-Taváríkh, f. 173*a*, and supra, p. xliv). In the same year (A.H. 1165=A.D. 1752) Sháh Isma'íl fell into the hands of Muḥammad Ḥasan Khán. From this date there was a conflict with Muḥammad Ḥasan until the overthrow and death of the Ḳájár chief. This event I do not find precisely dated anywhere, but I infer from the Táríkh-i-Gítí-Kusháí that it occurred shortly before the beginning of the solar year in A.H. 1172. The events of the solar year of A.H. 1171-1172, from spring A.D. 1758 to spring A.D. 1759, occupy more than twenty-one pages of the work, and comprise the siege of Shíráz by Muḥammad Ḥasan, his withdrawal, Kerím Khán's reoccupation of the country, and the death of his rival, in consequence of the Zand general Shaikh 'Alí Khán's invasion. This last subject is followed by an account of the immediately consequent submission of the Ḳájár territory. Then follows the rubric of the spring of A.H. 1172 (Add. 23,524, f. 27*a*-37*b*). From this it would seem probable that Shaikh 'Alí Khán did not march against the Ḳájár territory before the spring of A.D. 1759, at a time when military operations were practicable in that cold country. The date A.H. 1172 = A.D. 1759 is therefore the most probable.

The death of Kerím Khán occurred on Tuesday, 13 Ṣafar, 1193 = Monday-Tuesday, 1-2 March, 1779 ('Alí Riẓá Táríkh-i-Zandía, Or. 2197, f. 6*b*, and three other MSS.; Dynasty of the Ḳájárs, p. 9; other authorities agreeing as to the day of the month, but not stating that of the week).

For the Zands after Kerím Khán I have found 'Alí Riẓá's History of the family the most useful authority for chronology. I have collated the dates in four of the manuscripts in the British Museum, (Or. 2197, Add. 24,903, Add. 26,198, and Add. 23,525), accidentally omitting a fifth (Add. 27,243), to which I was not induced afterwards to resort by sufficient variants in the four. I quote preferably Or. 2197 as a good text, referring to any differences in the other manuscripts.

Abu-l-Fet-ḥ and Muḥammad 'Alí Kháns.

Abu-l-Fet-ḥ Khán was proclaimed with his younger brother, Muḥammad 'Alí Khán, by Zekí and 'Alí Murád Kháns shortly after the death of Kerím Khán ('Alí Riẓá's History, Or. 2197, f. 7*b*). This must have been very early in A.H. 1193 = A.D. 1779. It may be noted that this joint reign is a solitary exception to the usage of modern Persia. It had its rise in the difficulty of setting aside the elder son Abu-l-Fet-ḥ, and Zekí's desire to secure the succession for Muḥammad 'Alí, his nephew and connection by marriage. (Cf. id. f. 10*b*, cited note * below). Very shortly 'Alí Murád broke with Zekí Khán, who was then left free and with full power; and on the approach of Ṣádiḳ Khán to Shíráz, on some suspicion of Abu-l-Fet-ḥ's desire to join this other uncle, Zekí cast the young prince into confinement and confiscated his goods, then setting up Muḥammad 'Alí Khán alone.* This terminated in the course of a month or two the first reign of Abu-l-Fet-ḥ Khán, in the same year as his accession.

Muḥammad 'Alí Khán.

Muḥammad 'Alí thus proclaimed early in A.H. 1193 = A.D. 1779, had so ephemeral a reign as not to be counted by the Persian annalists in the Zand series. Three months after Kerím Khán's death Zekí Khán was assassinated, 27 Jumá-

---

* زکی خان هم ابو الفتح خان‌را که باعم خود دم موافقت میزد و طالب ورود او می بود با ولدان صادق خان که در شیراز بودند مقید سلسلهٔ گرفتاری و اموال اورا بحیطهٔ ضبط درآورده اسم سلطنت‌را اوبزه گردن محمد علی خان ولد دیگر خاقان مغفور که نسبت مصاهرت با زکی خان داشت کرده (Alí Riẓá, Hist., Or. 2197, f. 10*b*)

Mírza Ṣádiḳ thus states the circumstances, speaking of Zekí Khán:

پس نواب ابوالفتح خان‌را بجای پدر والا گهر نشانیده و بعد از چند روز محمد علی خان‌را نیز سهیم او گردانیده بهر صورت جناب ابوالفتح خان (*sic*) وهر دو برادران در امور فرماندهی و مهام حکم‌رانی بجز از نامی بی نشان واسمی بیمسما نداشتند (Tarikh-i-Gití-Kusháí, f. 90 *a*)

I have to thank Dr. Rieu for aiding me in the examination of the first passage.

da I. 1193 = 11-12 June 1779 ('Alí Riẓá, History, 2197, 12*b*, 13*a*, supply بیست before و هفتم from Add. 24,903, f. 14*b* بیست هفتم). Abu-l-Fet-ḥ immediately asserted his rights, and Muḥammad 'Alí seems to have offered no opposition.

Abu-l-Fet-ḥ was proclaimed on Friday, 3 Jumáda II. 1193 = Thursday-Friday, 17-18 June, 1779, with *sikka* and *khuṭba*, in his own name سکه و خطبه بنام او جریان یافت (id. 13*b*). He was deposed by Ṣádiḳ Khán, on Sunday, 9 Sha'bán, 1193=Saturday-Sunday, 21-22 August, 1779 (id. 14*b*, 15*a*). Abu-l-Fet-ḥ Khán, second reign.

The two reigns of Abu-l-Fet-ḥ and the two reigns of Muḥammad 'Alí should therefore be thus dated:

Abu-l Fet-ḥ Khán with Muḥammad 'Alí Khán, Muḥammad 'Alí alone,	3 months.
Abu-l-Fet-ḥ alone,	2 months.

The reign of Ṣádiḳ Khán dates from the deposition of Abu-l-Fet-ḥ (Sunday, 9 Sha'bán, 1193=Saturday-Sunday, 21-22 August, 1779), to the capture of Shíráz by 'Alí Murád Khán, in the morning of 18 Rabi' I, 1196 = 2 March, 1782. ('Alí Riẓá, History, Or. 2197, f. 22*b*.) Ṣádiḳ Khán.

The reign of 'Alí Murád is usually dated from his capture of Shíráz. This is erroneous. Dr. Rieu has thus determined the chronology. According to Mírza Ṣádiḳ, "'Alí Murád assumed independence in Iṣfahán immediately after Kerím's death, 1193 (Gítí-i-Kusháí, f. 92*a*). That fact is curiously confirmed by a poem (Shiháb's Khusrau Shírín) I have just got from Ṭeherán. It is dated 15 Rabi' I, 1194 [=20-21 March, 1780], and addressed to 'Alí Murád, who is eulogized as reigning sovereign (Or. 2817, f. 4*b*). It shows also that the Zínat-et-Taváríkh is right, when it says that Alí Murád's rule in 'Iráḳ lasted six years (Add. 23,527, f. 179*b*), namely, 1193-1198, counting the two broken years." —(Letter to R. S. Poole.) Alí Murád Khán.

'Alí Murád died 28 Ṣafar, 1199 = 9-10 January, 1785 (Or. 2197, f. 28*a*, *b*).

This reign is thus divisible into two periods:

a) Rule at Iṣfahán, A.H. 1193-1196 = A.D. 1779-1782.

b) Rule at Iṣfahán and Shíráz, A.H. 1196-1199 = A.D. 1782-1785

Ja'far Khán.

Ja'far Khán was proclaimed 6 Rabi' I, A.H. 1199 = 16-17 January, A.D. 1785 ('Alí Riẓá, History, Or. 2197, f. 29*b*). He was assassinated on the night of Thursday, 25 Rabi' II. 1203 (id. f. 58*a*). The day of the month corresponds to the 22-23 January, beginning on Thursday. According to the inferior authority of the Favaïd (f. 139*b*), the event took place in the morning of 25 Rabi' II. The date is probably Thursday, 22 January, 1789 (see also Olivier, vol. vi. p. 211), Wüstenfeld being one day wrong.

Luṭf-'Alí Khán.

Luṭf-'Alí Khán did not immediately succeed to the throne. His establishment in power is dated by 'Alí Riẓá 11 Sha'ban, 1203 = 6-7 May, 1789 (f. 61*b*, for the month see 61*a*). The end of his reign must be dated by the capture of Kermán, on the afternoon of Friday, 29 Rabi' I, 1209 = 24 October, 1794 (Or. 2197, f. 120*b*, for the year cf. Add. 24,903, f. 131*b*).

Ḳájárs. Muḥammad Ḥasan Khán.

The founder of the Ḳájár line, Muḥammad Ḥasan Khán, must have become practically independent during the troubles consequent on the usurpation of Sulaimán II., and therefore in A.H. 1163 = A.D. 1750. It is distinctly stated in the Nukhbat-el-Akhbár that he declared himself independent on that usurpation (Or. 2837, f. 189*a*); but this statement must be modified by the fact that we have a coin of Sulaimán II. issued in Mázenderán (no. 313, p. 98). The true time must be the general break-up of the state, consequent on the restoration of the blind Sháh Rukh, later in the same year. The overthrow of Muḥammad Ḥasan Khán has been already placed A.H. 1172 = A.D. 1759 as the most probable date (supra, p. lv). The Nukhbat-el-Akhbár allows him with hesitation a rule of nine years, though erroneously placing his death in A.H. 1181 (Ibid., fol. 190*a*). This is a slight confirmation of our two limits.

Ḥusain-ḳulí Khán made an insurrection in Mázenderán against Kerím Khán about A.H. 1185, and maintained himself for two years. It is stated in the Maásir-i-Sulṭáníya that his independence lasted two years (printed, Tabríz, f. 7*a*, *b*, Dynasty of the Ḳájárs, p. 7), and that during this time Fet-ḥ-'Alí Sháh (Bábá Khán) was born, on the night of Thursday, 18 Shawwál, 1185 (f. 7*b*,) or of Wednesday (Dynasty of the Ḳájárs, p. 8) = 21-23 January, 1772. The Nukhbat-el-Akhbár allows him one year (f. 190*b*). I can find no evidence of this Khán's having exercised sovereign rights. Had he been successful, it would have been a question whether he should not have been included in the series of sovereigns; as it is, he is like other Persian Kháns of this age who attempted to gain regal power but failed. Ḥusain-ḳulí Khán.

It is well known that Aḳa Muḥammad Khán rose agains the Zands immediately after Kerím Khán's death; therefore about Safar, 1193 = March, 1779. Aḳa Muḥammad Khán.

His enthronement occurred in the spring of A.H 1210 = A.D. 1796 (v. supra, p. lii).

His assassination took place, according to Brydges' authority (p. 26), in the early morning of Friday, 21 Zu-l-Ḥijja, 1211; according to the lithographed Tárikh-i-Ḳájária (f. 25*a*), on the night of Saturday of the same day of the month A.H. 1212; the Táríkh-i-Muḥammadía, in the early morning of the same day of the month, the year not stated but obviously 1211 (f. 235*a*). The date was probably Friday 16, but by Wüstenfeld, Saturday 17 June, 1797.

Fet-ḥ-'Alí was not enthroned immediately on the death of his uncle Aḳa Muḥammad. He took the direction of affairs, and struck money as Bábá Khán (nos. 456-7, pp. 148-9). He was enthroned on 24 Rabí' I, 1212 = 15-16 September 1797. (Táríkh-i Ḳájária, f. 26*b*, 27*a*; Nukhbat-el-Akhbár, Or. 2837, f. 195*a*; Brydges' Dynasty of the Ḳájárs, p. 40; a ceremony not to be confused with that of the Nau-rúz of the same year, which was intended to emphasize the previous Fet-ḥ-'Alí. Bábá Khán.

function, ibid. p. 41, *sqq.*) His death occurred on Thursday, 19 Jumáda II. 1250, in the afternoon = 22 October, 1834 (Táríkh-i-Ḳájária, f. 139*a*, Nukhbat-el-Akhbár, f. 196*a*).

Ḥusain 'Alí Sháh.

The enthronement of Ḥusain 'Alí Sháh is dated by the Nukhbat-el-Akhbár, at Shíraz, Thursday, 3 Sha'bán, 1250 (f. 196*b*) = 3-4 December, 1834, if the day of the week is right. Wüstenfeld has Sha'bán 3 = 4-5 December, Friday-Saturday. The author of the Nukhbat allows him a reign of six months, and dates his death at Ṭeherán, 26 Rabí' I, 1251 = 20-21 July, 1835 (f. 198*a*).

'Alí Sháh.

'Alí Sháh was enthroned at Ṭeherán, 14 Rejéb, 1250 = 15-16 November, 1834, and dethroned on 14 Sha'bán, 1250 = 15-16 December, 1834, having reigned one month (Ibid, f. 198*b*, Táríkh-i-Ḳájária, f. 154*b* for first date).

Muḥammad Sháh.

Muḥammad Sháh was enthroned at Tabríz, in the evening of 7 Rejéb, 1250 = 8 November, 1834 (Táríkh-i-Ḳájária, f. 157*a*), but he was a second time enthroned at Ṭeherán, on the Lesser Festival at the close of Ramaẓán, 1250, therefore 1 Shawwál (ibid. f. 162*a*, *b*) = 30-31 January, 1835. Watson gives the date 31 January, on the Festival before mentioned (History of Persia, p. 282). I adopt this as the true date of the Sháh's enthronement. Muḥammad Sháh died on the evening of Tuesday, 6 Shawwál, 1264 (Táríkh-i-Ḳájária, 243*a*, cf. 241*a*) = Monday, 4 September, 1848 (Watson, History of Persia, p. 354).

Ḥasan Khán Sálár.

Ḥasan Khán Sálár, although never enthroned, made himself independent after the death of Muḥammad Sháh, and struck money at Mesh-hed in 1265, continuing the formula of the late Sháh (no. 577, p. 186), which does not designate the sovereign, except allusively. His rebellion began on the news of Muḥammad Sháh's death (Watson, p. 363, cf. Táríkh-i-Ḳájária, f. 260*b*, where it is recorded among the troubles which occurred in the beginning of the reign of the present Sháh). The rebellion came to an end after the Nau-rúz, 6 Jumáda I, A.H. 1266 = 20 March, A.D. 1850, and before 16 Jumáda II = 9-10 May (ibid. f. 299*b*,

301*b*, 302*a*). The period of Ḥasan Khán is thus A.H. 1264-6 = A.D. 1848-50.

Náṣir-ed-dín Sháh was first enthroned at Tabríz on the evening of the 14 Shawwál, 1264 = 12 September, 1848 (ibid. 257*b*); and a second time on Monday, 24 Zu-l-Ḳa'da, 7 h. 20 m. after midnight, 23 October, at Ṭeherán, (ibid. 259*b*). Watson gives after midnight, the 20th of October, i.e. Saturday, the 21st (History of Persia, p. 364). As Náṣir-ed-dín had no competitor, I have dated his reign from the first *julús*. Náṣir-ed-dín.

II. Coinage.

For the denominations of Persian money I would refer to the careful Tables of Hanway. These are here put into clearer form. The weight is given by him in Misḳáls and Kiráts, the Misḳál being 80·9116 to the lb. Troy 5760 grs. The weight of the Misḳál is therefore 71·18 grs. I have ventured to use 72 as the equivalent on account of the greater convenience of division. The period referred to is the reign of Nádir Sháh. Denominations. Hanway's Tables.

Gold.

	grs.
Muhr-Ashrafí	162
Ashrafí	54
Ashrafí of Nádir	54
'Abbásí should be	72
Id. Ḥusain	84
Id. Sulaimán	114
Id. Ṣafí	120

Silver.

Rupí or Nádirí	180
6 Sháhí	108
'Abbásí	72
Maḥmúdi	36
Sháhí	18
Bistí (money of acct.)	7·2

Copper.

Kazbegi = $\frac{1}{10}$ of the Sháhí.

(Hanway, i., pp. 292-3).

This is quite consistent with the weights of Nádir's coins, except that early in his reign we find pieces as heavy as 82, and 41 in the silver; and his currency includes two unrecorded denominations, the double Muhr AV and the double Rupí AR.

Gold coins, Isma'íl I. to Kháns.

The evidence of the scanty gold coins confirms Hanway. The Ashrafí occurs under Ashraf, who plays on the coin's name as derived from that he bore, thus:

باشرفی اثر نام آنجناب رسید
شرف زسکهء اشرف بر آفتاب رسید

The name Ashrafí, however, no doubt came from an earlier Ashraf, probably the Memluk El-Ashraf Barsabáy or El-Ashraf Ḳáït-bey, under whom it became famous in commerce not long after its introduction into the Egyptian currency. The same coin was issued by Ṭahmásp II., Sulṭán Ḥusain, Ṭahmásp I., and Isma'íl I., who also issued its quarter.

The ''Abbásí of Ṣafí' is represented by the coin of 'Abbás I., weighing 118 grs., which is plainly a double 'Ashrafí. The 'Abbási of 72 grs. is found weighing 71 under Muḥammad Khudabanda, and its half 35·5 under 'Abbás I.

The relation of these pieces would be—

Multiples.	Standard.	Maximum weights.
2	108	118
$1\frac{1}{3}$	72	71
1	54	54
$\frac{2}{3}$	36	35
$\frac{1}{4}$	13·5	13

The only anomaly according to this scheme is the heavy weight of the coin of 'Abbás I. (118 grs.), but Hanway knew of such a coin under Ṣafí. The persistent use of the Ashrafí makes it probable that the gold standard of weight was not interfered with from Isma'íl I.'s time until Nádir introduced the heavier Indian standard, striking the Muhr, and its double, with the Ashrafí. Kerím Khán issued the Muhr, its half, and its quarter, which took the place of the Ashrafí. During the rest of the period of the Kháns the Muhr and its quarter were mainly issued. The gold coins of Fet-ḥ-'Alí Sháh and his successors will be noticed later.

Hanway's statements as to silver money compared with coins.

The statements of Hanway as to the silver coinage may now be compared with the evidence of the coins, as presented in the following table:—

Table of weight of silver coins, Muḥammad to Ṭahmásp II.

Multiples.	Standard.	Maximum Weights.					
		Ṭahmasp II.	Ḥusain.	Sulaimán.	'Abbás II.	'Abbás I.	Muḥammad.
30	855·		836				
20	570·			561	566		
15	427·5	413	401				
10	285		264	285			
7½	213·7	208					
5	142·5		134		140		
4	114		114	113	112		
3	85·5		83				
2	57		57	57	48	56	
1	28·5		28	28	27		28
½	14·2					14	

Information of Chardin and Tavernier as to silver money.

Chardin, who visited Persia under Sulaimán I., describes the silver money as having been the Sháhí, equal to 4½ sols, the Maḥmúdí equal to 9, and its double the 'Abbásí, thus equal to 18 (Voyages, ed. 1711, ii. p. 92). Tavernier, describing the money of 'Abbás II., makes the denominations the Bistí, Sháhí, Maḥmúdí, the 'Abbásí, the piece of 2½ 'Abbásís or 10 Sháhís, and its double the 5 'Abbásí piece. The weights are a little higher than Chardin's, the 'Abbásí being equal to 18 sols 6 deniers (Six Voyages, ed. 1676, ii. p. 6 and pl.). The weight of 18 sols is 126·54, and that of 18 sols 6 deniers 130·. Though these weights are not reached under 'Abbás II. and Sulaimán in the table above, it is obvious that the correspondent pieces to the Sháhí and its multiples are those of the standard of 28·5, 85·5, 114, 285, and 570 grs. The coins of 'Abbás I. and Muḥammad Khudabanda, though not sufficient for a safe inference, favour the lower standard of the table above. As to the silver money of Ṭahmásp I. and Isma'íl I., it certainly is as yet an enigma.

Evidence of table.

Hanway's figures show a remarkable reduction from the standard of the coins just noticed. They agree however with the evidence of the coins of Nádir under whom there must have been a reduction of the 'Abbásí first to 82 and then to 72 grains.

Later silver coins.

Working down from Nádir, the Efsháris and Sulaimán II. (who only strikes 'Abbásís) continue Nádir's system, Ibráhím innovating with a 3 'Abbásí or 18 Sháhí piece; but this confusion could not continue. The silver coins were first the rupí and Abbásí, exchanging at the rate of 1 to 2½; but Kerím Khán after a time issued the Sháhí of about 25·5, making a series of 51, 75·5, 151, the maximum weights being 25, 50, 71, 142. His successors before Fet-ḥ-'Alí struck rupís, and rarely the eighth.

I am able, thanks to the kindness of General Houtum Schindler, to give an account of the coinage of Fet-ḥ-'Alí Sháh and his successors to the present time.

Coinage of Ḳájár Sháhs.

Fet-ḥ-'Alí first issued in gold the Túmán. This can only be the piece which weighs about 95 grs., and of which there are several specimens of early dates in the Museum. His other denominations in gold, struck before 1232, I will not attempt to explain. His first silver coins were the Rupía, Rúpí, or Riál, the 'Abbásí, and its half, the Sanár (a corruption of Sad-dínár, or 100 dinars), or Mahmúdí. It is at present impossible to identify these denominations, but it seems that the 'Abbasí system and the Rúpí system went on side by side, gradually approaching one another, each denomination being affected by that nearest to it in the other system.

Fet-ḥ-'Ali's second issue, at the close of the 30th year of his reign, was in gold, the Tumán of 70 grs., soon reduced to 53 grs., thus identical in weight with the old Ashrafí: at the same time he issued the Ḳarán, called after the Ḳarn, or 30 years' period, weighing 142 grs., in silver, and equal to the 10th of the Tumán, or 20 Sháhís, in value. Riáls, 'Abbásís and Sanárs ceased to be coined. The Ḳarán was soon reduced to 107 grs.

Muḥammad Sháh continued his predecessor's last coinage, speedily reducing the Ḳarán to 89 grains. He is also stated to have struck the half, or Panabat (penáh bád).

Under Náṣir-ed-dín there have been successive reductions. By 1875 (A.H. 1291-2) the Tumán had fallen to 50 grs., and the Ḳarán to 78. The denominations were then as follows:

GOLD.	Tumán,	3·225	gram.	=	50 grs.	=	10 francs.
(·900 pure gold.)	½ ,,	1·6125	,,	=	25 ,,	=	5 ,,
	¼ ,,	·806	,,	=	12½ ,,	=	2·50 ,,
SILVER.	Ḳarán,	5	gram.	=	78 grs.	=	1·0 franc.
(·900 pure silver.)	½ ,,	2·5	,,	=	39 ,,	=	50 cent.
	¼ ,,	1·25	,,	=	19·5,,	=	25 ,,
COPPER.	2 Sháhí,	10	gram.	=	156 grs.	=	10 cent.
	1 ,,	5	,,	=	78 ,,	=	5 ,,
	½ ,,	2·5	,,	=	39 ,,	=	2·5 ,,

Besides the denominations mentioned above, 2, 5, and 10 Tumán pieces have been struck.

Subsequently the Ḳarán has fallen to 70 grs., and the Tumán to 47.

In A.H. 1294 (A.D. 1877) the provincial mints were suppressed, and all coinage ordered to be struck at Ṭeherán. It is from this date that the 'new coinage' described in the Catalogue takes its rise.

The present currency consists of Túmáns, in gold; the Ḳarán and 2 Ḳarán in silver (the 5 Ḳarán and ½ and ¼ Ḳarán being out of circulation); and in copper the ½ Sháhí, Sháhí, 2 Sháhí, and 4 Sháhí. At Mesh-hed the Jendeki is used at the rate of 85 to 90 = 1 Ḳarán.

For largesse, little pieces are struck in gold worth two Ḳaráns, and in silver, the so-called Dú-sháhi, or piece of two Sháhís, actually worth ⅛ Ḳarán.

General Houtum Schindler, in the letter from which I have taken the main facts of these remarks, acknowledges his obligations to a pamphlet on Persian mints, by Director Karl Ernst, of the Austrian Mint.

Art of Coins. Artistically the coins of the Sháhs of Persia rival those of the Emperors of Delhi. Less varied in types than those of Akbar and Jehángír, they are of more uniform calligraphic elegance than the Indian series. The character employed is at first Naskhí; Nesṭáliḳ is then introduced for the reverse inscription, and ultimately it is generally Inscriptions. used for both sides. In the arrangement of inscriptions, and in the occasional arabesque treatment of Nesṭáliḳ, much ingenuity is shown, particularly in bringing the Sháh's name into the centre of the reverse inscription.

At first the language is Arabic.

Obverse. Formulæ. The obverse area inscription, until the reign of Maḥmud the Afghán, is the Shía' formula لا اله الا الله محمد رسول الله علي ولي الله: rarely نبي is used for رسول. Mahmud, Ashraf, and later Ázád Khán, use the Sunní formula, of course omitting 'Alí. When, as usually, there is a margin, the Shia' formula is supplemented by the names of the Twelve Imáms. The proper order, علي حسن حسين علي محمد جعفر موسي علي محمد علي حسن محمد, is frequently varied for calligraphic reasons, the prolongation of the ى of على, thus, علے, serving for a border, and the recurrence of the initials, م four times, ح three times with ج once, and ع four times, suggesting, when the margin is in segments, a symmetrical arrangement. 'Abbas II. varies this formula by the full invocation on Muḥammad, 'Alí, Fátima, and the rest of the Imáms, all being mentioned by their titles or qualifications, Ḥasan and Ḥusain together, thus:

اللهم صل على النبى والولى والبتول والسبطين والسجاد والباقر
والصادق والكاظم والرضا والتقى والنقى والزكى والمهدى

The same formula, apparently incomplete, and with names instead of titles, except that Ja'afar has both, appears on an anonymous coin of the time of Isma'il I. or Ṭahmásp I. Maḥmud the Afghán, on the obverse margin of one of his coins, inscribes the names of the four orthodox Khalífas (no. 197*a*, p. 273). Ashraf issues their coinage as the "money of the four friends" سكهٔ چاريار, and it is probable that some of his pieces bore their names.

The reverse area is at first occupied by the royal name and style, and the mint and date. The style is afterwards abbreviated or else more or less varied in a distich: the mint and date are not changed. Reverse. Royal style to Ṭahmásp II.

The full style of Sháh Isma'íl I. is السلطان العادل الكامل الهادى الوالى ابو المظفر شاه اسمعيل بهادر خان الصفوى الحسينى شاه اسمعيل and اسمعيل شاه are written indifferently. On a coin, apparently of Isma'il I., published in the Supplement (no. 18*b*, p. 267), Dr. Rieu reads conjecturally بنـ[ـدهٔ] شا[ه] كربلا 'Servant of the Sháh of Kerbela,' that is, Ḥusain, which if accepted is the only special reference on the Persian coinage to their popular Imám.

The full style of Ṭahmásp I., rarely written at length, and on no coin to be completely read, is the same as Isma'íl's. He also calls himself غلام على بن ابى طالب عليه السلام

The only known coin of Isma'íl II. gives the style ابو المظفر اسمعيل شاه بن طهماسب الصفوى. It is observable that Isma'íl does not appear to be called the Second, as the fainéant Isma'íl (III.) is similarly unnumbered.

The scanty coinage of Sulṭán Muḥammad Khudabanda affords the following styles, which are no doubt abbreviated, سلطان محمد خدابنده پادشاه ـ سلطان محمد ابو المظفر پادشاه بن طهماسب شاه الحسینی. The word Sulṭán, as in the case of Sulṭan Ḥusain, is part of the proper name, which is Sulṭán Muḥammad Khudabanda. This Sháh styles himself غلام امام محمد مهدی علیه السلام و آبائه, and varies his father's formula to غلام علی ابی طالب الخ, in both showing a Persianizing tendency.

Under 'Abbás I., Persian appears on the reverse. The obverse is strangely varied by the use of both رسول and نبی in alternative formulæ. The Sháh's style is ابو . . . . . المظفر عباس, and he also terms himself 'Alí's servant in the phrase which is the most permanent of its class بندهٔ شاه ولایت عباس

Ṣafí repeats the formula بندهٔ شاه ولایت and he also adopts a new one, which Dr. Rieu reads شاه ازجان غلام صفی است, or شاه است الخ. A specimen in the Museum of Copenhagen leaves little doubt that the verb has the form هست not است and shows but a single *alif*, whereas in the Catalogue I have supplied a second for the verb. This formula implies devotion to his namesake, who gave his name to the family.

'Abbás II. is the first Sháh who takes a numeral, calling himself 'Abbas the Second. His designations are کلب علی in a distich for کلب آستان علی رضا, as watch-dog or guardian of the tomb of the Imám 'Alí Riẓa, and بندهٔ شاه ولایت. He appears to have introduced the title emperor, *lit.* 'master of the (auspicious) conjunction,' صاحبقران ṣáḥib-ḳirán, a title which had its origin with Timúr, also in a distich. The distichs will be treated below.

Sulaimán I. must have struck coins during the short period for which he bore the name of Ṣafi [II.], but their recall (Chardin, Couronnement, p. 393) was so effectual that no specimens are known. This Sháh styles himself بندهٔ شاه ولایت.

Sulṭán Ḥusain resumes but rarely the use of نبی in place of رسول in the chief religious formula. On one coin he gives his full style, showing the survival of the earliest titles, السلطان العادل الهادی الکامل الوالی ابو المظفر السلطان بن السلطان سلطان حسین شاه بهادر خان الصفوی, and a shorter and different style, in part novel, السلطان بن السلطان والخاقان بن الخاقان بندهٔ شاه ولایت حسین

Usually he is simply بندهٔ شاه ولایت. He also styles himself کلب آستان علی a term varied in one of his distichs.

Ṭahmásp II. uses a distich in which he is characterized as the Second and ṣáḥib-ḳirán. 'Abbás III. exactly agrees except that he is 'another ṣáḥib-ḳirán.'

The rule of the Afgháns, Maḥmúd and Ashraf, and that of Nádir Sháh practically changed the character of the coin inscriptions.

Maḥmúd styles himself Sháh, and in his distichs جهانگیر and عالمگیر, perhaps only poetically. Ashraf in two out of three distichs also appears as Sháh. He adopts Aurangzíb's formula جلوس میمنت مانوس, used by no other king of Persia.

'Alí Riẓa Coins. Their origin.

In the later years of Sháh Ṭahmásp II., when Nádir was endeavouring to expel the Afgháns, a new and very singular coinage made its appearance, which had a large influence on all subsequent issues before the reign of Fet-ḥ-'Alí Sháh, except the major part of those of the Efshárís. When Nádir undertook the difficult task of restoring the Persian power, the popularity of the Ṣafavi line must have been very low. The name of Ṭahmásp II. could raise no enthusiasm: the idea of supplanting a weak king by a mere phantom was, no doubt, already formed by the ambitious Nádir. Thus it was desirable to issue a coinage which should be popular, and thus accustom the people to some central power independent of the sovereign. The great shrine of 'Alí Riẓa at Mesh-hed, the most venerated building in Persia, suggested the issue there, and in other parts of the country, of a coinage in which the Imám takes the place of the sovereign, even with a quasi-regal style. From 1143 until 1147, thus until the year before Nádir's accession, this money was issued concurrently with the regal coinages of Ṭahmásp II. and 'Abbás III. 'It went a golden currency,' so runs the distich, 'from Khurásán, by the grace of God, by the aid and help of the Sháh of Religion, Alí Riẓa, son of Musa.'

از خراسان سکه برزر شد بتوفیق خدا
نصرت و امداد شاه دین علی موسی رضا

After this time weak sovereigns issued the Imám's money, and in the age of the rival Kháns the only currency was of 'Alí er-Riẓa and his rival in popularity, Muhammad el-Mahdí.

Style of Nádir and successors to Isma'il (III). Nádir Sháh, with his characteristic boldness, wholly changed the style of the regal inscriptions. When he uses no distich, he is simply called the Sultán Nádir. In his two distichs he styles himself 'King over the Kings of the world,' 'Sháh of Sháhs,' &c. He also uses on the coins of his first and second year the famous tárikh, or chronogram, الخیر فیما وقع = 1148, the date of his accession. Of course the Imám's coinage disappears.

'Ádil or 'Alí Sháh uses a distich, stating the circulation of the coinage of royalty in the name of 'Alí. As he was enthroned at Mesh-hed, which remained his capital, there can be no doubt that the name 'Alí implies that of the Imám, 'Ālí Riẓa, but is this or the Sháh's name the primary meaning?

Ibráhím on the money bearing his name follows the system of Nádir. He either is styled the Sultán Ibráhím, or, when he uses a distich, Ibráhím Sháh, also qualified as ṣáḥib-ḳirán. There is also an Imámí coinage here assigned to Ibráhím, issued under the name of 'Alí Riẓa at Tabríz in 1161. It has been earlier shown that Ibráhím was practically sovereign for roughly three months between his overthrow of his brother 'Adil Sháh and his own enthronement. This period would well suit the issue of these coins at Ibráhím's capital. They could have been issued by 'Ádil Sháh earlier in the year, but a second issue of Imámí coinage by him is unlikely, his first being either Imámí or quasi-Imámí, and still more so is this the case with Sháh Rukh.

We have coins of Sháh Rukh of his first reign (A.H. 1161–1163) and his third (A.H. 1168–1210). In his earlier coinage he follows the practice of Nádir Sháh, being styled Sháh Rukh the Sultán, and in one distich he is ṣáḥib-ḳirán. Like his grandfather Sulṭán Ḥusain he is watch-dog of the shrine of Mesh-hed كلب آستان رضا. Certain Imámí coins bearing the invocation يا على بن موسى الرضا, dated 1161, are assigned to this period of Sháh Rukh's rule. They are of Mesh-hed, Resht, and Ḳazvín. They cannot be of Ibráhím, as he never held Mesh-hed; consequently we have to choose between 'Ádil Sháh and Sháh Rukh. As before, it seems unlikely that 'Ádil Sháh had two sets of coins, directly or inferentially connected with 'Alí Riẓa. On the other hand, had Sháh Rukh in 1161 authority as far as Kazvín or Resht? Probably Ibráhím, though issuing his own Imámí coinage at Tabriz during the interregnum, did not interfere with this very inoffensive currency elsewhere. One of the coins (no. 312, pl. VIII.) seems markedly of Sháh Rukh's fabric. Practically it is not of much consequence by whom these coins were issued, inasmuch as they bear no evidence of regal authority.

Sulaimán II., who dethroned Sháh Rukh, in his two florid distichs is 'the rightful Sháh Sulaimán II,' and 'the Sháh, son of the sayyids, heir of the kingdom of Sulaimán,' his father-in-law, Sulaimán I.

Sháh Rukh, during his third reign, styles himself ṣáḥib-ḳirán, and Sháh of the world, [شاه] جهان, and repeats the title كلب آستان رضا, as well as using a new formula, 'watch-dog of the Sultán of Khurásán' ('Alí Riẓa).

Isma'íl (III.), in the coins struck by 'Alí Merdán, as well as by Moḥammad Ḥasan, is uniformly styled بندهٔ شاه ولایت, without any numeral, and with no further inscription.

Mahdí coins, &c., of Kháns.

When Sháh Isma'íl was carried away from Kerim Khán by Moḥammad Ḥasan, it became necessary for the Zand chief to issue a coinage which should not be confused with that of the Sháh, now the puppet of his rival the Ḳájár, and yet which should not be disloyal. What he did we learn from the Favaïd-i-Ṣafavia, as well as from Kerím Khan's coinage. The historian tells us that Isma'íl having been imprisoned in the Fort of Abáda, Kerím Khán proclaimed himself wakíl, ordering the *sikka* and *khuṭba* in the name of the Twelve Imáms, and then cites the well known distich of his money struck in the name of the Imám El-Mahdí.

و شاه اسماعیل امی صفوی‌را که در قلعه آباده که فی مابین
شیراز و اصفهان واقع است محبوس نموده خودرا وکیل الخلایق
خوانده سکه و خطبه‌را بنام امامان اثنی‌عشر قرار داد و سجع سکه
این فرد بود فرد "شد آفتاب و ماه زر و سیم در جهان" "از سکهٔ
امام بحق صاحب الزمان" (Add. 16,698, f. 125*b*.)

We know from his coinage that Kerím Khán did not wait until the titular sovereign was once more in his hands before issuing a new currency: otherwise the author of the Favaïd does not need correction. The circumstance of the *sikka* and *khuṭba* in the name the Imáms seems very strange. Was this done in the name of the Mahdí, who was expected to return, and of whom under the Fáṭimís in Egypt a coinage was issued with his name Muḥammad and his title as 'the Expected,' El-Muntaẓar? (Cf. *Cat. Or. Coins*, IV. p. ix. seqq. nos. 228–230, p. 55, 56.) However this may have been, there is no doubt that the Mahdí, as shown for instance by the coins of Muḥammad Khudabanda, was, among the Persians, next in popularity to 'Alí Riẓa. Another innovation seems to have been due to Kerím

Khán, the use of an allusive invocation. The primary intention of this kind of formula seems to have been a reference to the Khán's name. Thus Kerím Khán's constant invocation is يا كريم 'O Bountiful One,' where the divine epithet, after the manner of a patron saint's name, recalls an ordinary name. Kerím Khán also invokes the Mahdí as 'the Master of the Age,' يا صاحب الزمان, that is 'the Imám who was to arise at the end of the Age,' القائم فى آخر الزمان (*Cat. Or. Coins*, IV. p. xi.) It may be remembered that Kerím Khán's proper name Muḥammad may have been allusively referred to in the invocation of Muḥammad el-Mahdí. The subject of invocations will be later discussed. When Kerím Khán uses the Shía' formula he once varies it by the adoption of نبى for رسول (no. 326, p. 107).

Muḥammad Ḥasan Khán the Ḳájár strikes, as his distich tells us, in the name of 'Alí Riẓa.

Ázád Khán the Afghán uses the Sunní formula, which thus appears for the last time on Persian money. His distich mentions his name without any title, with the wish that while he remained on earth the coinage of the Master of the Age (the Mahdí) might last. This devotion to an Imám, though in this case consistent in a Sunní, must have been adopted to conciliate Ázád's Shía' subjects.

Kerím Khán's son Abu-l-Fet-ḥ, while continuing the Mahdí distich, introduces his own name without title in a subordinate place to the mint on the reverse.

Ṣádiḳ Khán repeats the distich, and restores the invocation used by Kerím Khán.

'Alí Murád Khán alone varies in introducing the invocation يا على; probably the Khalífa.

Ja'afar Khán abandons the distich and covers the whole of the reverse with an invocation of the sixth Imám, 'Ja'afar the Truthful,' يا امام جعفر الصادق. This probably does not indicate any special reverence for the Imám such as is shown by the coin without royal name, which I have assigned to either Isma'íl I. or Ṭahmásp I., on the reverse of which this Imám alone receives his title (no. 651, p. 209). It was probably chosen as an inscription allusive to Ja'afar Khán and his father Ṣádiḳ.

Luṭf-'Alí Khán goes a step beyond his father in the distich of his coin here catalogued, and styles himself Luṭf-'Alí son of Ja'afar (no. 445, p. 142).

Aḳa Muḥammad Khán issues money in the name of the Imám 'Alí Riẓa, repeating his father's distich, and also takes up the coinage of the Mahdí, repeating Kerím Khán's distichs and varying them with two new forms. Despite his enthronement, the only allusion to his name is the invocation 'O Muḥammad!' يا محمد, the Prophet and not the Mahdí. Fet-ḥ-'Alí, in the short period before his enthronement, issued money as the Sultán Bábá Khán, which is interesting as the only Persian coinage in which the title Khán appears without being preceded by Bahádur. As Sháh his style is السلطان ابن السلطان فتحعلى شاه قاجار or السلطان فتحعلى الخ, the Sulṭán son of the Sulṭán, or the Sulṭán, Fet-ḥ-'Alí Sháh Kajár. This instance of royal parentage is especially remarkable, as Ḥusain-Ḳuli does not seem ever to have exercised the prerogative of coinage. The insertion of the tribe-name Ḳájár is also a curious innovation. The two mottoes, 'The kingdom is God's,' الملك لله, and 'The glory is God's,' العزّة لله, are practically novel.

Coins of Ḳájár Sháhs.

Ḥusain 'Alí and 'Alí Sháh follow the style of their father Fet-ḥ-'Alí, except that 'Alí Sháh gives the title of Sulṭán to his father and grandfather, assuming two degrees of royal descent. Impressions of the coins of these sovereigns have been kindly communicated by Dr. Tiesenhausen.

Muḥammad Sháh, with the instinct of the Kháns, does not appear on his coins with any royal title or even by name, but adopts the allusive motto 'The king of the kings of the prophets (is) Muḥammad,' شاهنشه انبيا محمد. Thus he suggests his own name and usual title. The money of the rebel Ḥasan Khán Sálár, who resisted the authority of Náṣir-ed-dín Sháh, is, to judge from the solitary specimen in the Museum Collection, a continuation of the money of Muḥammad Sháh, which could be continued by any other ruler, like the Imámí coinage of the Kháns.

Náṣir-ed-dín follows his predecessor Fet-ḥ-'Alí in the style of his coins. On the ten-túmán piece, he assumes the titles السلطان الاعظم والخاقان الافخم ناصر الدين شاه قاجار On a medal he appears as السلطان ناصر الدين قاجار, and on another as شاهنشاه ناصر الدين. The same class gives us the allusive motto 'He is the aider,' هو الناصر, which does not appear on the coins.

The name of the mint is always preceded by the *maṣdar* or infinitive noun ضرب, 'striking.' In the reign of Isma'íl II. a custom begins, resumed by Ashraf, which becomes the rule under the Zands and Ḳájárs. A town takes its distinctive epithet, usually beginning with 'abode' دار : thus Shíráz is termed دار العلم, 'The Abode of Learning.' The epithet دار السلطنه, 'The Abode of Sovereignty,' is common to the successive capitals, except Shíráz: thus it is used for Tabríz, Ḳazvín, Isfahán, and Ṭehrán, and it may be noted that this use is long after Tabríz and Ḳazvín had lost their eminence. Mesh-hed takes the epithet 'holy' after its name, مشهد مقدس, (varied very rarely by ارض اقدس, 'most holy land,' no. 522, p. 170, no. 635, p. 205), the earliest instance in the Catalogue being under Ṭahmásp II. (no. 169, p. 58). Under Ṭahmásp I. we find مشهد امام رضا (no. 13, p. 15). The most singular mints are the following :—جلو 'Army Mint,' and ضربخانهء ركاب, the same, both Kerím Khán's; and ضرابخانهء دولتى, 'State Mint,' on a medal of Náṣir-ed-dín. The epithets will be found in a special index as well as in the Index of Mints. Mints.

The year is expressed in the figures of the Hijra date, almost always without the regnal year; the Persian money in this respect markedly differing from the otherwise similar coinages of the emperors of Delhi and the Durránis. Dates.

The regnal year occurs once (no. 27*a****, p. 270), and possibly twice (no. 17, p. 9). The word 'year,' in the Arabic سنه, is very rarely employed. There is one curious example of the statement of the month and day Hijra (no. 447, p. 144, supra p. xxii). It is scarcely necessary to add that the Persian names of months, frequent in the earlier imperial money of Delhi, are here wholly wanting. Ashraf always gives his *julús* year, and in later years the actual date also.

Distichs. The distich or *saj'*, according to Persian terminology, is a peculiar feature of the coinages on which the Persian language is employed. The earliest instance of which I know occurs on a coin of Muḥammad Kerím Sháh of Gujarát, A.H. 846-855 = A.D. 1443-1451, Catalogue of Indian Coins, Muḥammadan States, (no. 416, p. 134, pl. xi). It has been thus read, with Dr. Rieu's aid:

[تا ب]دار الضرب گردون قرص مهر و ماه باد
سکهٔ سلطان غیاث الدین محمد شاه باد

While in the mint of heaven there be the disk of moon and sun
May Sháh Sulṭán Ghias-ed-dín Muḥammad's coinage run.

I may on this first occasion of translating a distich explain that I have done so on account of the extreme difficulty that their style presents, making a rendering desirable. I have adopted verse instead of prose as less cumbrous. The rendering follows the originals, line for line and nearly word for word. I have allowed myself the liberty of rendering زد 'he struck' in the first line in some cases by 'came' at the end of the line, immediately followed by 'struck' at the beginning of the next, the Persian notions of coining and circulation being inseparable: otherwise there is no transposition from one line to another. Any word added is enclosed in parenthesis, and every paraphrastic rendering is confronted with the literal sense in foot-notes, which also explain obscurities.

Safavis: Isma'íl II. The second instance of a distich is on the only published coin of Isma'íl II., described and engraved by M. Soret

(Rev. Num. Belge, 1864, p. 355, no. 47, pl. xix. no. 39), who leaves the reverse, which he could not decipher, to other numismatists. By a happy accident I discovered the inscription written out as a distich in the Álam-árái-'Abbásí, thus:

زمشرق تا بمغرب گر امام است
علی و آل او مارا تمام است

If an Imám there be between the east and west,
'Alí* alone with 'Alí's house for us is best.†

The historian states that in devising a new coinage Isma'íl desired to avoid the sacred formula with the name of God falling into the hands of such as did not believe as well as the legally unclean, but fearing to be suspected of an intentional omission of 'Alí's name, devised the distich above mentioned. Gold and silver coins were accordingly issued with the distich on one side and the names of Isma'íl and the mint on the other.‡

---

* 'Alí the Khalífa.

† "Best" for "perfect," "all," تمام.

‡ The whole passage is so curious that I have transcribed it completely:

و چون تا غایت زر بنام خود نزده بود و به زر کهنه داد وستد میشد ضرابیان در تجدید زر و منافع ضرابخانه مبالغه میکردند اسمعیل میرزا در سکه لا اله الا الله و محمد رسول الله و علی ولی الله که در یکطرفش نقش میشود تأمّل داشت و میگفت که درم و دینار در سواد (سودا) و معاملات بدست یهود و ارامنه و مجوس و سایر کفار در می‌آید و عوام در حالت جنابت مس اسم الله که بمقتضای کلام قدسی انجام لا یمسّه الا المطهرون منهی و مذموم است مینمایند تردّد خاطر بود که در عوض آن عبارت نقش نماید که در نظر خلایق ناپسند نباشد روزی در میان مردم گفت که چون مارا بدنام کرده اند درین تفضیه خواهند گفت که غرض از بر طرف کردن این عبارت آن بود که لفظ علی ولی الله در سکه نباشد بعد از تأمّل بسیار در آخر قرار یافت که در یکطرف سکه این بیت نقش نمایند که بیت زمشرق تا بمغرب گر امام است ٭ علی و آل او مارا تمام است و در یکطرف دیگر اسم او و محلّ دار الضرب نقش کردد و در ساعتی که مختار او بود سکه کنده وجوه دراهم و دینار (دنانیر) بدین سکه آرایش یافت

(Add. 17,927, f. 265*a*; cf. Add. 16,684, f. 61*a*, *b*.)

The description of the coin should be as follows :—

Obv. [ابو] المظفر
[س]ـب
[ا]ن طهما شاه الصفو[ی]
اسـمـعـيـل شـاه
[د]ار العـبـاده يـزد ۹۸۴
ضر[؟]. سـ[نة]

Rev. تا بمغرب گر امام
زمـشـرقـ
[ا]سـ
[ع]ل[ی] وآله او ما[را]
[تـمـام اسـت]

Æ

On referring to M. Soret's plate it will be obvious that this reading is in part conjectural. On the obverse I do not find خان, which he places before اسمعيل : the sign ا I take for the *alif* of that name. On the reverse the order of the concluding words, bracketed, is doubtful. The metal of the coin raises a suspicion that it is an ancient forgery.

'Abbás II. Neither on coins nor in manuscripts do I find any poetic inscriptions until the reign of 'Abbás II., almost a century after that of Isma'íl II. This Sháh uses two distichs:

بگیتی سکهٔ صاحبقرانی
زد از توفیق حق عباس ثانی

Throughout the world imperial* money came,
Struck by God's grace in 'Abbás Sáni's name.

بگیتی انکه اکنون سکه زد صاحبقرانی
زتوفیق خدا کلب علی عباس ثانی

Lo! at this time throughout the world imperial money came,
Struck by God's grace in 'Alí's watch-dog† 'Abbás Sáni's name.

---

* Imperial صاحبقراني.

† Lit. 'dog,' guardian of 'Alí Riẓa's shrine at Mesh-hed.

We are informed in the Ḳiṣaṣ that the first of these distichs was adopted the day after this Sháh was proclaimed; and that, at the same time, for the motto of his seal this line was chosen بود کلب علی عباس ثانی,* where we may have the source of the second distich.

Sulaimán's coins in his first name as Ṣafí (II.) have not come down to us. Chardin states that they bore an inscription, which must have been a distich, as follows:

Zibad hestié chae Habas sanié
Safié zad Zikkeh saheb Karanié.

Sulaimán I. (Ṣafí II.)

Dr. Rieu thus restores the Persian, the first line in Chardin being obviously inaccurate, for it may be noted that there is no trace of 'chae' in Chardin's two translations. (Couronnement de Soleïmaan, 1671, pp. 149, 150.)

زبعد هستی عباس ثانی
صفی زد سکهٔ صاحبقرانی

Since 'Abbás Sáni from the world is passed away,
Ṣafí (the second's) money has imperial sway.

Examples of this coinage may possibly be found among the money of 'Abbás II. in some imperfectly classed collection, or among those of Ṣafí (I.)

The two distichs of Ṣafí (II.) of the second period of his reign as Sulaimán I. are as follows:

بهر تحصیل رضای مقتدای انس و جان
سکهٔ خیرات بر زر زد سلیمان جهان

For the sake of winning grace of him who men and genii leads,†
The age's Solomon struck golden money for the people's needs.

---

* در همانساعت که خطبهٔ صاحبقرانی بنام نامی شهریار بلند و قارخواندهٔ میشد وجوه
دراهم و دنانیرا بدین سکّهٔ مجلّی و مزیّن فرمودند سکّهٔ بگیتی سکّهٔ صاحبقرانی • زد از
توفیق حق عباس ثانی • و همچنین بجههٔ نقش نگین مبارك مقرر شد که این مصرع را نقش نمودند
مصرَع بود کلب علی عباس ثانی • و همدران روز یکی از نازل خیالان بلاد ایران تاریخ جلوس
میمنت مانوسرا ظلّ معبود یافته بود (Ḳiṣaṣ, Add. 7656, f. 18a.)

† 'Alí Riẓa; the poet plays on his title as 'favour' or 'grace.'

سکهٔ مهر علی‌را تا زدم بر نقد جان
گشت از فضل خدا محکوم فرمانم جهان

Since on my soul I struck the stamp of 'Alí's* love,
The world obeyed my rule by grace of God (above).

Sulṭán Ḥusain.

Sulṭán Ḥusain uses two distichs, the second of which does not occur on coins in the Museum:

گشت صاحب سکه از توفیق رب المشرقین
در جهان کلب امیر المومنین سلطان حسین

Money he struck by the grace of the Lord of east and west, the twain
Everywhere, dog of the Prince of the Faithful's † shrine, Sultán Ḥusain.

زد زتوفیق حق بچهرهٔ زر
سکه سلطان حسین دین پرور

By grace of God upon a golden face he made
His coin, Sultán Ḥusain, religion's aid.

(Fraehn, Rec., p. 470.)

Ṭahmásp II.

Ṭahmásp II. adopts the distich of 'Abbás II., merely substituting his own name, for his ordinary coinage, but on a single coin we find another distich of a wholly new turn. The two are—

بگیتی سکهٔ صاحبقرانی
زد از توفیق حق طهماسب ثانی

Throughout the world imperial coinage came,
Struck by God's grace in Ṭahmásp Sáni's name.

سکه زد طهماسب ثانی بر زر کامل عیار
لا فتی الا علی لا سیف الا ذوالفقار

Ṭahmásp the Second struck on purest gold assayed
No man but 'Alí and no sword but 'Alí's blade.‡

(*Num. Chron.*, 1884, p. 266.)

The second distich may be regarded as of medallic use, the only coin known which bears it being dated in

---

* The Khalífa.

† 'Alí Riẓa nominated heir by the Khalífa El-Má-mún.

‡ 'Alí the Khalífa and his famous two-bladed sword. Blade, *lit.* Zu-l-faḳár.

Ṭahmásp's first year, and the intention being obviously a defiance of the Sunní Afgháns. The distich is remarkable as being the only one which presents two languages, the first line being in Persian, the second in Arabic. A complete Arabic distich does not occur. It must also be noted that here the Khalífa 'Alí the possessor of the famous two-bladed sword is intended, not 'Alí-Riẓá. Notwithstanding, it is remarkable that in this reign the series of 'Alí-Riẓá coins begins. Their distichs will be noticed later.

The distich of 'Abbás III. is simply a variation of those of 'Abbás II. and Ṭahmásp II.: 'Abbás III.

سکه بر زر زد بتوفیق الهی در جهان
ظل حق عباس ثالث ثانی صحبقران

Throughout the universe by grace divine a golden money came,
Struck by God's shadow, a new emperor 'Abbás the third (by name.)

A marginal note in the Favaïd (Add. 16,698, f. 7*b*) gives the distich of the seal of Sulṭán Ḥusain II. as follows: Sulṭán Ḥusain II.

(و سجع مهر آنحضرت این فرد بود)

دارد زشاهمردان فرمان حکمرانی
فرزند شاه طهماسب سلطان حسین ثانی

The king of men* commanded, and the royal right has ta'en
The son of Sháh Ṭahmásp, the second Sháh Sultán Ḥusain.

Nothing is said of a coin inscription, yet if 'Alí Merdán issued any coins for Sulṭán Ḥusain it is probable that he would have used this distich. The title of 'Alí, here again instead of 'Alí-Riẓá, as 'King of heroes,' is, as Dr. Rieu agrees, very possibly a covert allusion to the name of the Bakhtiárí chief 'Alí-Merdán, ''Alí the hero,' by whose order Sulṭán Ḥusain was set up.

Sulṭán Muḥammad's rupís, struck probably as patterns only, by Áḳa Muḥammad Khán, bore the following distich according to the Favaïd: Sulṭán Muḥammad.

بزر زد سکه از الطاف سرمد
شه والا گهر سلطان محمد †

---

* 'Alí the Khalífa.

† Add. 16,698, f. 148*a*, where گوهر for گهر, which Dr. Rieu substitutes on account of the metre.

He struck his coin of gold by the Creator's grace,
Sulṭán Muḥammad ruler, of a noble race.

Ṣafavis, maternally. The family of Dá-úd. Aḥmad.

Aḥmad Sháh struck coins, none of which have come down to us, with the distich,

سکه زد بر هفت کشور چترزد چون مهر و ماه
وارث ملك سليمان گشت احمد پادشاه

He struck in climates seven, as sun and moon in might,
Aḥmad the Padisháh heir of Sulaimán's right.
(Tezkira-i-Ál-i-Daud, f. 42*b*.)

Sulaimán II.

Of the short reign of Sulaimán II. the coins, only known in the British Museum, bear two distichs:

زد از لطف حق سکهء کامرانی
شه عدل گشته سلیمان ثانی

By grace divine he struck a coin of happy fame,
The sovereign just, who second Solomon* became.

بر فروزد روی (؟) زمی چون طلوع مهر و ماه
وارث ملك شد سليمان بن سادات شاه

Shines as the rising sun and moon upon the earth
Heir of Sulaimán's right, the Sháh of saintly† birth.

The first of these I found in the Tezkira-i-Ál-i-Dá-úd, where a coin is fully described,

و نقش سکهء آنشهريار در وسط صحيفه لا اله الا الله محمد رسول الله علی ولی الله ودر محيط همان صحيفه اسما مقدس ايمه اثنی عشر و در صحيفه ديگر زد از لطف حق سکهء کامرانی شه عدل گشته سليمان ثانی (f. 99*a*.)

The reading of the other distich I owe to Dr. Rieu. At first I thought that I had discovered in the coin bearing it one of Aḥmad Sháh, but the similarity of the first line to the second of Aḥmad is evidently due to the same pretensions. Dr. Rieu's attribution of the distich to Sulaimán II. is confirmed by an ode in honour of his accession, which seems either to have originated the distich or to

---

* A double allusion, first to his maternal grandfather Sulaimán I., and secondly to the Hebrew king.

† Race of the Sayyids, descendants of Muḥammad.

have been originated by it. I have therefore thought it worth while to print the poem, the correct form of which is due to the great kindness of Dr. Rieu.*

The influence of the distichs of the Sulṭáns of Delhi is evident in these of the 'Ál-i-Dá-úd; and, as Dr. Rieu observes, the expression چترزد on Aḥmad Sháh's distich is characteristically Indian, though the name of the royal umbrella does not occur on the Indian imperial coinage, the object itself figuring there.

The origin of this Indian influence is to be traced earlier in the money of the Afghán princes. Maḥmud has two distichs, the first of which is now correctly given with Dr. Rieu's aid, while the unravelling of the second is due to his acute scholarship : **Afgháns: Maḥmud.**

سکه زد از مشرق ایران چو قرص آفتاب
شاه محمود جهانگیر سیادت انتساب

From the east of Irán he struck coin like the solar face,
Sháh Maḥmud world-conqueror of the saintly† race.

---

* شده زالطاف ربّانی فروزان نیر طالع — چه نیر مهر انور بادشاه مغرب و مشرق
در درج سیادت اختر برج شهنشاهی — خدیو کشور ایران بالطاف خدا واثق
سلیمان شاه عادل وارث ملك سلیمانی — که تاج و تخت شاهیرا نباشد غیر او لایق
بعقل و دانش و فطرت زآبای سلف افزون — زشان و شوکت و حشمت بشاهان جهان فایق
بکف چون ابر دریا دل بدل چون بحری بی ساحل — ید بیضا خصال او باعطای درم عاشق
سکندرشان شهنشاهی کز اخلاق کریم او — جهانی شاکر از عدلش بمدحش عالمی ناطق
عطارد کاتب امرش زحل طغراکش نهیش — قمر نورانی از مهرش ببزمش مشتری شایق
بود ناهید رامشگر شود مریخ سر عسکر — ببزم و رزم او هریك بشغلی راتق و فاتق
فلك دوری زدورانش مه و خورشید دربانش — ملك دایم ثنا خوانش نگهدارش بود خالق
سر شاهان بفتراکش زهی شمشیر بی باکش — برآرد عزم چالاکش دمار از دشمن آبق
شد از الطاف رب حی بساط دشمنانش طی — زلال مژدهء این می حلال شارب و ذایق
مزین گشت چون افسر زفرق فرقدان سایش — سریر سلطنت گردیده اورا قابل و لایق
بسیری با صبا همدم اشاراتش شفا توام — بشاراتش مسیحادم رسید از کشور مشرق
که شاه معدلت گستر سلیمان فریدون فر — بر اورنگ شهنشاهی چو مهر و ماه شد شارق
مبارك باد این دولت بر آن شاه فلك شوکت — جلال و حشمتش بادا مصون از عارض و طارق
من آن مور تهی دستم که در بزم سلیمانی — پر و بال ملخرا تحفهء پندارمش لایق
چو از پیر خرد آنم(؟) شدم تاریخ جو گفتا — بود سال جلوس شد طلوع شمس از مشرق

Tezkira i-Ál-i-Daud, f. 98*a* – 99*a*.

† Race of the Sayyids.

فرو رود بزمین ماه و آفتاب منیر
زرشك سکهٔ محمود شاه عالمگیر

Below the earth sank down the moon and shining sun,
Envying the coin of Sháh Maḥmud world-conquering one.

Here the Afghán prince takes the titles Jehángír and 'Álamgír, which had both become personal to Indian Sultáns. The second distich is evidently modelled on that of Aurangzíb 'Álamgír, which runs thus, on the gold,

در جهان سکه زد چو مهر منیر
شاه اورنگ زیب عالمگیر

Through all the world he struck his sun-like coin of golden ore,
Sháh Aurangzíb (throne ornament*) of earth the conqueror.

while on the silver بدر takes the place of مهر.

Ashraf. The three distichs of Ashraf are wholly exceptional:

باشرفی اثر نام آنجناب رسید
شرف زسکهٔ اشرف برآفتاب رسید

Upon the Ashrafi† was wrought the magic of his grace's name,
Nobility from Ashraf's coin upon the sun there came.

دست زد بر جلالة اشرف شاه
بود تعبیر سکه داد گناه

Ashraf laid hold on majesty with might:
Let his coin's legend read 'Requited be unright.'

زالطاف شاه اشرف حق شعار
بزر نقش شد سکهٔ چار یار

By grace of Ashraf Sháh, who keeps the right,
The gold of the four friends‡ now sees the light.

The first is the only case in which the name of the coin here, as already shown, of much older date, is connected with that of the reigning sovereign; the second, with its strange allusion to punishment of crime, stands quite alone, and I am at a loss to explain it; while the third, boldly substi-

* Translation of Aurangzíb.

† One would be inclined to suggest the English 'noble.'

‡ The four 'orthodox' Khalífas.

tuting the 'Four Companions,' Abu-Bekr, 'Omar, 'Osmán, and 'Alí, for the twelve Imáms, is the strongest instance of Sunní profession on the Persian coinage. The coins published in the body of the Catalogue (nos. 203, 204, p. 68) present no trace of the names of the Four Companions, but a coin of Maḥmúd since acquired (Suppl. no. 197*a*, p. 273) shows an obverse margin with the series of names in question as on some Sunní coins.

Efsháris: Nádir.

Nádir Sháh's two distichs seem wholly original, and mark, as already noticed, his claim to imperial power. They are—

سکه بر زر کرد نام سلطنترا در جهان
نادر ایران زمین و خسرو گیتی ستان

By gold in all the earth his kingship shall be famed
Phœnix* of Persia's land, world-conqueror, sovereign named.

هست سلطان بر سلاطین جهان
شاه شاهان نادر صاحبقران

Over Sulṭáns of earth is Sulṭán,
Nadír, Sháh of Sháhs, Ṣáḥibkerán.†

'Ádil Sháh.

'Alí or 'Ádil Sháh's distich may belong to the 'Alí Riẓá series, though in the name of 'Alí no doubt it refers to the Sháh's name as 'Alí: as already said (p. lxx.), we cannot decide whether the primary reference is to Sháh or Imám:

گشت رایج بحکم لم یزلی
سکهٔ سلطنت بنام علی

Decreed of Him who ceases not, a currency there came
The coinage of the sovereignty sent forth in 'Alí's‡ name.

Ibráhím.

Ibráhím reverts to a distich in the old Ṣafavi style:

سکهٔ صاحبقرانی زد بتوفیق اله
همچو خورشید جهان افروز ابراهیم شاه

By grace divine he struck a coinage of imperial worth,
Sháh Ibráhím, (his gold) sun-like illumining the earth.

---

* Nádir.
† Retained for the exigency of rhyme.
‡ 'Alí Sháh and 'Alí Riẓa.

Sháh Rukh.

Sháh Rukh uses three distichs:

[بزر تا؟] شاهرخ زد سكهٔ صاحبقرانی‌را
[دو] باره (؟) دولت ایران گرفت سر جوانی‌را

Whenas Sháh Rukh imperial money coined, 'twas then
A second time Irán renewed herself again.

سكه زد در جهان بحكم خدا
شاهرخ كلب آستان رضا

Throughout the world he struck his coin by grace divine,
Sháh Rukh the watchful dog of 'Alí Riẓa's shrine.

سكه زد از سَعْيِ نادر ثانی صاحبقران
كلب سلطان خراسان شاهرخ [شاه] جهان

Another emperor has coined, thanks to Nadír's efforts' worth,
Dog of the king of the east,* Sháh Rukh the king of the earth.

The first distich, expressing the hopes which were raised by the brilliant young sovereign's accession, belongs to his first reign; the last, dwelling on his relation to Nádir, is of the third reign, when his power was limited to a precarious hold of Khurásán, where alone Nádir's memory was held in respect. The second distich is common to both periods. It is to be noted that in both the second and third the devotion to 'Alí Riẓá is marked.

Zands: Luṭf-'Alí Khán.

Throughout the period of the rival Kháns there is but a solitary personal distich, that of the heroic and unfortunate Luṭf-'Alí Khán:

گشت زده سكه بر زر
لطفعلی بن جعفر

Its stamp has golden money won
From Luṭf-'Alí Ja'afar's son.

It will be best to give all the distichs of 'Alí Riẓá together, and then those of the Mahdí, with a few supplementary remarks:—

* For Khurásán, which I could not bring into the line.

از خراسان سکه بر زر شد بتوفیق خدا Ṭahmásp II. 'Alí-Riẓá series.
نصرت و امداد شاه دین علی موسی رضا Abbás III.

From out of Khurásán a golden coin by grace divine was sent,
And aid of 'Alí Musa's son the kingly saint* benevolent.

زفیض حضرت باری و سرنوشت قضا Ibráhím Sháh
رواج یافت بزر سکهٔ امام رضا

By the Creator's bounty, and by fate's decree,
Gold of saintly Riẓa has its currency.

بزر سکه از میمنت زد قضا Muḥammad Ḥasan,
بنام علی بن موسی رضا Aḳa Muḥammad

A golden coin by happy fate has run
In name of peaceful 'Alí Musa's son.

تا زر و سیم در جهان باشد Kerím Khán, Mahdí series.
سکهٔ صاحب الزمان باشد Aḳa Muḥammad

While gold and silver through the world shall flow,
Coin of the Age's Lord† (the true Imám) shall go.

شد آفتاب و ماه زر و سیم در جهان Kerím Khán,
از سکهٔ امام بحق صاحب الزمان Abu-l-Fet-ḥ, Ṣádiḳ,
'Alí Murád,
Aḳa Muḥammad

Silver and gold through all the world have now become the moon and sun,
Thanks to the true Imám's imprint the Age's Lord (the rightful one).

تا که آزاد در جهان باشد Ázád Khán
سکهٔ صاحب الزمان باشد

So long as Ázád on the earth shall stand
The Age's Master shall the coin command.

تا زر و سیم را نشان باشد Aḳa Muḥammad
سکهٔ صاحب الزمان باشد

While stamped shall be the gold and silver ore
The coinage of the Age's Master shall endure.

---

* Lit., Sháh of Religion, 'Alí Riẓa.

† The Lord or Master of the Age, the Mahdí.

بر زر و سیم تا نشان باشد Aḳa Muḥammad
سکهٔ صاحب الزمان باشد

While stamp shall be on gold and silver ore
The coinage of the Age's Master shall endure.

It will be observed that no name of any ruler appears, except Azád's throughout the series.

The idea of the comparison of gold and silver money to the sun and moon seems to begin on the coinage of Aurangzíb already cited, in which the symbolism of the sun occurs on the gold money, that of the moon (full moon) on the silver.* The idea of Kerím Khán's distich, in which sun and moon gold and silver are in apposition, on both gold and silver money, occurs first in the distichs of Jehándár Sháh, as follows,

در آفاق زد سکه بر مهر و ماه
ابو الفتح غازی جهاندار شاه

Through all the earth he struck his stamp upon the moon and sun,
Jehandár Sháh, the champion of the faith, victorious one.

This is varied by چون مهر و ماه. Farrukhsiyar substitutes 'gold and silver' for sun and moon, thus,

سکه زد از فضل حق بر سیم و زر
پادشاه بحر و بر فرخ سیر

By grace of God he struck his coin of gold and silver ore
The emperor Ferrukhsiyar the lord of sea and shore.

---

* The lines on the two-hundred mohur piece of Sháh Jehán handle the idea differently. The golden face of the coin is to illumine the world as the moon is illumined by the sun's ray:

سکه بر مهر دوصد مهری زد از لطف اله
ثانی صاحب قران شاه جهان دین پناه
روی زر بادا زنقش سکه اش عالم فروز
تا شود از پرتو خورشید روشن روی ماه

(From a cast in the Marsden Collection.)

Kájárs: Náṣir-ed-dín.

A distich on a medal of Násir-ed-dín Sháh (Med. no. 1, p. 262) may be added:

هر شیردل که دشمن شه‌را عیان گرفت
از آفتاب همت ما این نشان گرفت

Whoso with lion-heart the sovereign's foes withstands
This badge he takes at our refulgent* grace's hands.

Invocations.

The invocations, which form a marked characteristic of Persian coinage, do not appear in the earlier period. Excluding the pious exhortation to invoke the aid of 'Alí, ending with a prayer the close of which is an invocation, 'O 'Alí!' three times repeated, where indeed we may find the germ of the later invocations, the list is as follows:

یا علی بن موسی الرضا	Sháh Rukh
یا کریم	Kerím Khán, Ṣádiḳ.
یا صاحب الزمان	Kerím Khán.
یا علی	'Alí Murád.
یا امام جعفر الصادق	Ja'afar.
یا محمد	Aḳa Muḥammad.

Other religious inscriptions.

These invocations gained under Kerím Khán that allusive force which is made specially prominent in the appropriate inscription of Ja'far Khán's, in which he and his father Ṣádiḳ Khán are both alluded to.

Certain religious inscriptions have yet to be noticed. A gold coin of Kerím Khán (nos. 328, 328*a*, p. 108,) has above the reverse inscription هو; and in the midst of the obverse inscription, dividing the distich, کریم. These words probably represent the phrase یا من هو بمن رجاه کریم, given in the Favaïd as the inscription of Kerím Khán's seal.† This phrase evidently suggested the motto یا کریم.

Aḳa Muḥammad Khán on his largest gold pieces inscribes الملك لله. Fet-ḥ-'Alí Sháh as Bábá Khán uses two mottoes, that just mentioned, and العزة لله which alone is continued during his reign as Sháh.

* Lit., sun.

† (Add. 16,698, f. 125*b*) سجع مهرش این بود سجع یا من هو بمن رجاه کریم

The inscription of Muḥammad Sháh شاهنشه انبيا محمد may be regarded as an allusive motto. The coins of Náṣir-ed-dín bear no motto, but the allusive one هو الناصر occurs on the medal of his *ḳarn*, also the centenary of the Ḳájár Dynasty (Med. no. 3, p. 263).

Autonomous copper.

The copper coinage of Persia under the Sháhs is until the present reign, with insignificant exceptions, autonomous.

Types and Tatar Cycle.

It presents on the obverse a type, usually the figure of an animal, and on the reverse the name of the mint, preceded by ضرب فلوس, ضرب, or فلوس. No doubt the first inscription should be read فلوس ضرب, the inversion being due to the habit on gold and silver money of placing the word ضرب at the foot of the coin, to be read immediately before the mint written next above it.

As the types in several instances are identical with the eponymous animals of the Tatar Cycle, it might be supposed that these at least were chosen with a chronological intention.

The animals of the Cycle are as follows, with the equivalent, apparent or probable, on the coins, and the animals on the coins not in the cycle.

Tatar Cycle.	Equivalent.	Probable Equivalent.	Non-equivalent.
Mouse			
Ox	Bull		
Tiger			
Hare	Hare		
Crocodile	Dragon		
Serpent			
Horse	Horse		
Sheep	Ibex		
Ape	Ape		
Hen	Cock	Peacock	
Dog			
Hog		Elephant	
			Camel
			Goose (Duck)
			Fishes
			Lion and Sun
			Lion
			Sun
			Lion and Bull
			Lion and Stag
			Ship
			Sabre.

There can be no question that some of the coin-types are derived from the animals of the Tatar Cycle. There is however no chronological reference. This is sufficiently shown by the intervals at which types recur.

The Lion and Sun and the cognate types are of different origin. The Lion and Sun is of Seljuḳ derivation, or older. The Lion and Bull and Lion and Stag may be carried back to the Achæmenid times. The Ship is an isolated type. The famous two-bladed sword of 'Alí, Zu-l-fiḳár, properly Zu-l-faḳár, is of course a Shí'a symbol.

GENEALOGICAL TREES.

In the following genealogical trees the object is to exhibit the descent of the Sháhs and other rulers, whose names are distinguished by numerals. A few names have been added of personages who may have exercised royal functions, though I have found no proof that they did so, as Ḥamza the son of Muḥammad Khudabanda, and others of the first historical importance, as Ḥaidar, the brother of the king just mentioned. Where royal personages have apparently been personated their names are here given, as Ṣafí and Sám, the sons of Sultán Ḥusain Sháh. I have been able to place the sons in order of seniority with the exception of those of Sultán Ḥusain Sháh.

GENEALOGICAL TREE OF THE ṢAFAVIS.

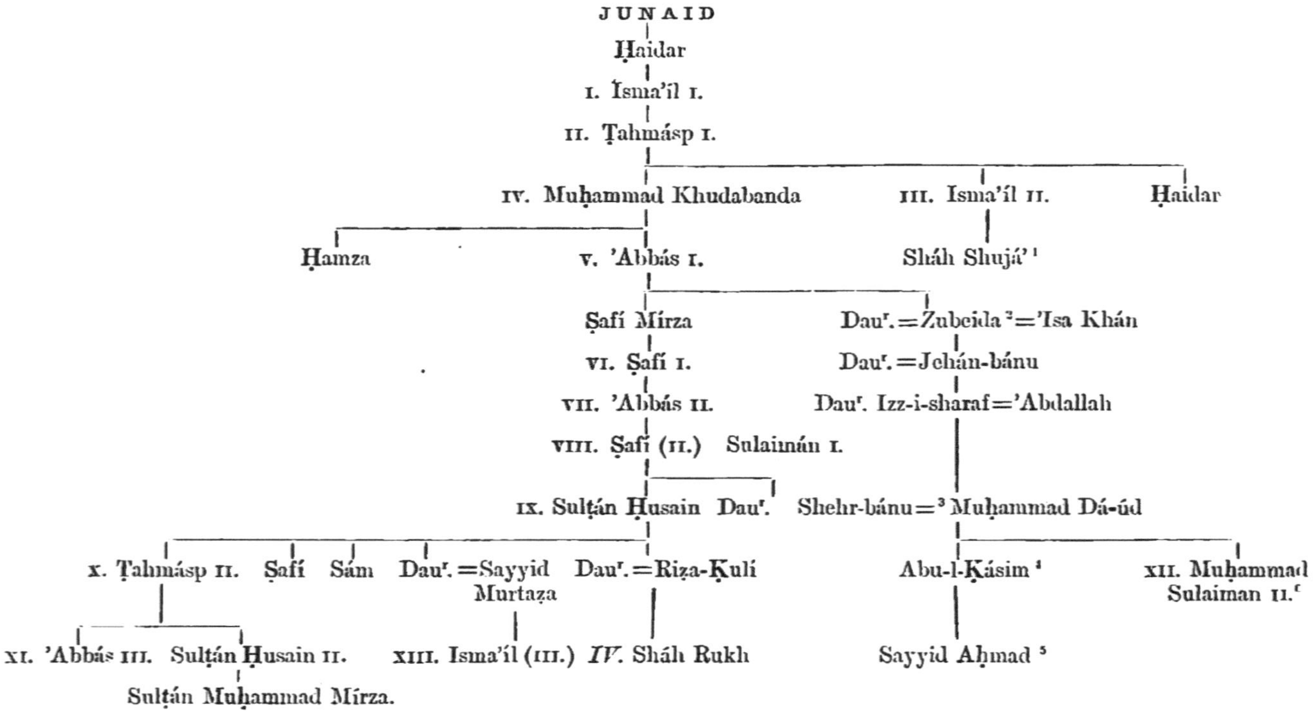

GENEALOGICAL TREE OF THE AFGHANS.

Father

- Mír Vais
  - i. Maḥmúd.
- 'Abd-el-'Azíz
  - ii. Ashraf.

GENEALOGICAL TREE OF THE EFSHÁRIS.

Imám-Ḳulí

- Ibráhím
  - *II.* 'Alí-Ḳulí, 'Ádil Sháh or 'Alí Sháh
  - *III.* Ibráhím
- *I.* Nádir
  - Riza-Ḳulí = Daughter (of Sulṭán Ḥusain Sháh)
    - *IV.* Sháh Rukh.

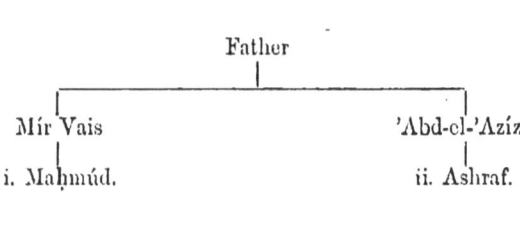

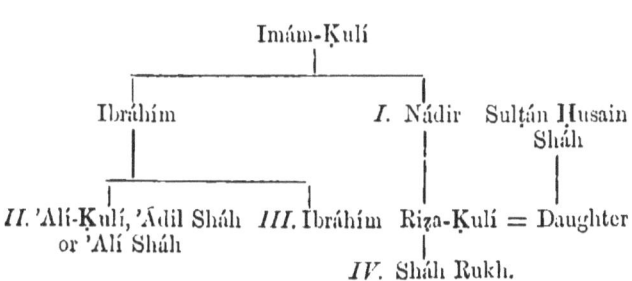

GENEALOGICAL TREE OF THE ZANDS.

- Father
  - *i.* Kerím Khán[1]
    - *ii.* Abu-l-Fet-ḥ
    - (*ii.*) Muḥammad 'Alí
  - Allah-Murád = Wife who aft. = *iii.* Ṣádiḳ[3]
    - *iv.* 'Alí-Murád[2] (son of Allah-Murád)
    - *v.* Ja'far[5] (son of Ṣádiḳ)
      - *vi.* Luṭf-'Alí
  - Zekí[4]

GENEALOGICAL TREE OF THE ḲÁJÁRS.

- Fet-ḥ-'Alí
  - A. Muḥammad Ḥasan
    - B. Aḳa Muḥammad
    - Ḥusain-Ḳulí
      - C. Bábá Khán, Fet-ḥ-'Alí Sháh
        - 'Abbás Mírza
        - D. Ḥusain 'Alí[7]
        - E. 'Alí Sháh[8]
    - Murtaẓa-Ḳ.
    - Muṣṭafa-Ḳ.
    - Ja'far-Ḳ.
    - Mahdí-Ḳ.
    - Abbás-Ḳ.
    - Riẓa-Ḳ.
    - 'Alí-Ḳ.[6]

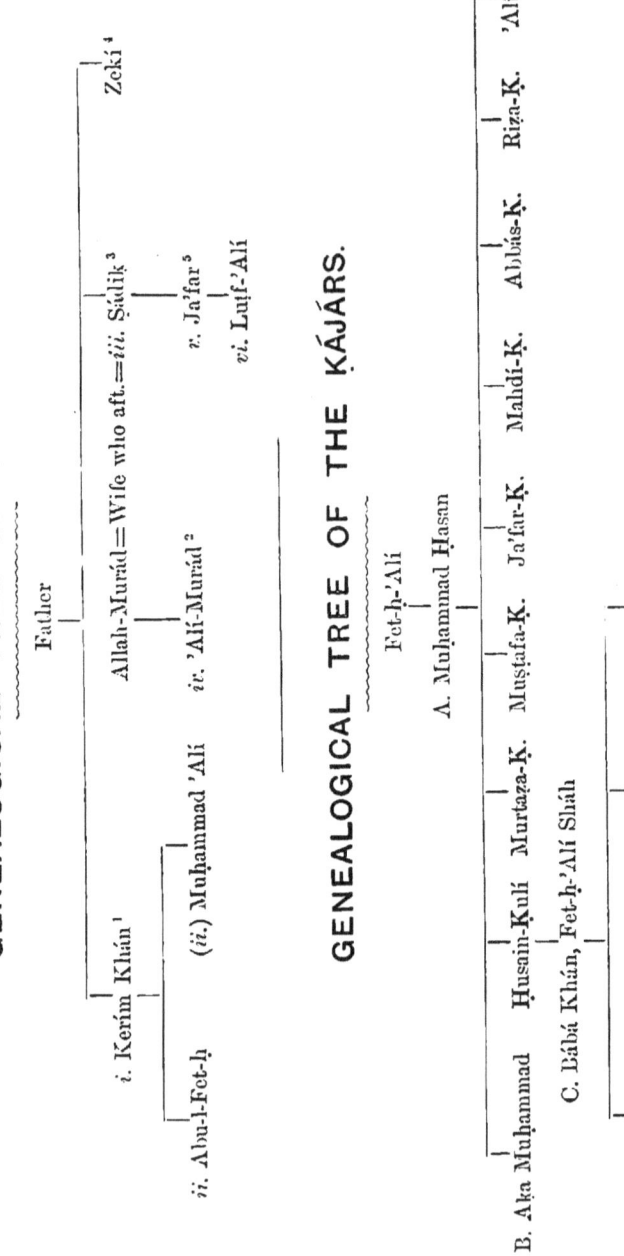

NOTES TO THE PEDIGREES.

GENEALOGICAL TREE OF THE ṢAFAVIS.

1. The infant heir of Isma'íl. *'Álam-árái*, Add. 16,684, f. 62*b*.
2. *Tezkira-i-Ál-i-Dá-úd*, f. 32 *a*, for this female descent from 'Abbás I.
3. Ib. Fol. 64 *b*—65 *b*.
4. Ib. Fol. 34 *b*.
5. Ib. Fol. 37 *a*.
6. Ib. Fol. 64 *b*.

GENEALOGICAL TREES OF THE ZANDS AND ḲÁJÁRS.

1. Muḥammad Kerím, originally called Tushmál-Kerím. *Zínat-et-Tavárikh*, Add. 23,527, f. 171 *b*.
2. 'Alí-Murád was foster-sister's son of Zekí Khán and son of 'Allah-Murád Khán. His mother, after his father's death, took refuge in Ṣádiḳ Khán's harím, and became mother of Muḥammad Ja'far Khán. *Gítí-Kushái*, f. 91 *a*. In the *Zínat*, Sayyid-Murád Khán and his fellow conspirators against Ja'far, Dín Murád and Sháh Murád, are called sons of the paternal uncle, 'Alí Murád Khán (*Ibid*. 32 *a*). 'Alí-Murád is always called a Zand, but I have been unable to ascertain his relationship to other members of the family.
3. Muḥammad Ṣádiḳ.
4. Zekí, younger brother of Kerím Khán. *Favaïd*, Add. 16,698, f. 129 *b*.
5. Muḥammad Ja'far. *Gítí-Kushái*, f. 91 *a*.
6. This list in order is taken from the Táríkh-i-Kájáría (lithogr.) 10 *a*, and given on account of the importance of the personages.
7. Fermán-Fermá.
8. Ẓill-i-Sulṭán.

ERRATA.

P. 19, l. 1, *for* Moḥammad *read* Muḥammad
" 25, ll. 8, 11, 12, *for* است *read* (?) هست
" 30, l. 2, *for* 1666 *read* 1667
" 67, " 14, 25, *dele* (die of 1137)
" 86, " 4, *for* "with name of" *read* "with allusion to"
" 91, " 4, *for* 1750 *read* 1749
" 98, " 7, transpose lines of distich
" " " 4 from foot, *for* سه *read* شه
" 108, " 15 " " با ایمن " یا من
" 122, " 9 " " الامام " الامان
" " " 13 " " م of امام " ن of امان
" 132, " 2 " " Fat-ḥ " Fet-ḥ
" 140, " 1 " " Jaa'far " Ja'far
" 153, last line, insert Pl. XIII.
" 177, l. 4, *for* انبیآ *read* انبیا
" 190, " 12, *dele* Pl. XV.
" 205, " 2, *for* Arẓ-i-ḳuds *read* Arẓ-i-aḳdas
" " " 10, " ارض قدس " ارض (ا)قدس
" 232, " 7 from foot, *for* sun *read* sun, rayed
" 266 " 13, insert Pl. I.
" 322, " 3, transfer distich to p. 319, line 15
Pl. XII., title, *for* Fat-ḥ *read* Fet-ḥ
" " " Jaa'far " Ja'far

BL

CHRONOLOGICAL TABLE OF SHAHS AND KHANS.

	AFGHANS.	SAFAVIS MATERNALLY. FAMILY OF DAÚD.	EFSHARIS.	BAKHTÍARI.	ZANDS.	
[illegible]	[illegible]	[illegible]	[illegible]	[illegible]	[illegible]	[illegible]

ṢAFAVIS.

I.—ISMA'ÍL I.

A.H. 907—930=A.D. 1502—1524.

GOLD.

1

Herát, 916.

Obverse Area, within sixfoil,

لا اله الا اللـه

مـحـمـد

رسول الله الله

على و لى

Margin, in cartouches,

محمد

حسن | حسين | [جع]فـ[ر] | موسى على | على محمد |

[على]　[على]

حسن محمد

Reverse,

السلطان العا[د]ل

الكامل الهادى الوالى ابو

[ا]لمظفر شاه اسمعيل بهادر خان خلد

اللـه تعالى ملكه و سلطانه و . . . .

| ضر ٦ هر ٨ ٩ اة

[ـبـ]

Pl. I. AV ·7, Wt. 54·3

2

Shíráz, 922.

Obv. Area, arranged in mill-sail pattern formed of على repeated, the ع making a rosette in centre,

حسين محمد على | حسن محمد على | جعفر [موسى] على | حسن محمد على

Margin, ۹۲۲ الله محمد رسول الله على ولى الله . . . .

Rev. السلطان العادل
الكامل الهادى الوا[لى]
[ا]بو المظفر اسمعيل شاه
[ش]ير ب
بهادر . . . ضر سلطانه ا . . .
. . . . ملكـ[ه]

Countermark on obv. ل
عد
شيراز

PL. I. AV ·5, Wt. 13·7

3

Mint and date obliterated.

Obv. Area within square, formed by على in margin.

لا اله الا الله
محمد رسول
الله على ولى الله

Margin, in segments,

حسين حسن على | ...... على | ...... على | محمد حسن على

Rev. Area, ...

اسمعيل شاه خلد الله . . . .

. . . المظفر بهـا[در] خان

وسـلـطـانـه

. . . ضـرب

. . . .

PL. I. AV ·45, Wt. 11·9

SILVER.

4

Mint obliterated, 908.

Obv. Area within square, formed by علي,

لا اله الا الله

محمد رسول الله

. . . .

Margin, . . . علي محمد | [علي] . . . . | علي محمد حسين | علي محمد حسن

Rev. السلطان العادل

[ا]لكامل الهادي الوالي ابو

. . . . . . شاه اسمعيل بهادر خان ٠٨ الصف[و]ي

. . . .

AR ·9, Wt. 71·5

5

Astarábád, date obliterated.

Obv. as (4), but area third line

علي ولي الله

Margin, علي محمد حسن | علي موسي جعفر | علي محمد حسين | علي محمد [حسن] |

Rev. as (4), but lines 3 foll. read

المظفر شاه اسمعيل بهادر خان الصفوي

. . . . ملكه (؟) ضرب استراباد

. سلطا[نه]

(ل of [نه]سلطا serves for ا of استراباد)

AR ·9, Wt. 69·7

6

Mint and date obliterated.

Similar, but ى instead of ے.

AR ·9, Wt. 70·3

7

Sulṭáníya, date obliterated.

Obv. Area similar to (6).

Margin, in segments,

محمد حسن علی | محمد حسن علی | مو جعفرسی علی | محمد حسین علی

Rev. Area, similar to (1) but ending

الصفوی خلد الله تعالی
. سلطانه سلطانیه . . .

AR ·95, Wt. 69·3

8

Tabríz, date obliterated.

Obv. Area in circle, لا اله الا الله محمد رسول الله
علی ولی الله

Margin, in six cartouches,

| | | علی | محمد علی | [مو]سی | | |

Rev. [السلطان العادل]
الکامل الهاد الوا[لی ابو المظفر شاه]
بهادر خان خلد الله . . . . .
اسمعیل الصفوی
سلطانه تبریز

AR ·9, Wt. 67·3

9

Merv, date obliterated.

Obv. Area, in circle, لا اله الا الله محمد ل

ل الله علي الله

رسو و

Margin, in six cartouches,

| . . . . | علي محمد | موسے . . . . | علي محمد |

| حسن علي | محمد علي

Rev. similar to (8), differently arranged, and last line

و سلطانه ضرب مرو

PL. I. AR ·9, Wt. 70·7

10

Merv, [9½]5.

Obv. Area, in square formed by علي

لا اله الا الله الله

محمد ل اولله

رسو علي ل

Margin, in segments,

| حسين حسن علي | جعفر محمد علي | موسى محمد علي | حسن محمد علي

Rev. السلطان العادل

اسمعيل شاه بهادر خان

الصفوي خلد ملكه مر[و]

سنه ٩١.

(Second line in a border.)

PL. I. AR ·8, Wt. 47·7

11

Mint and date obliterated.

Obv. Area in circle, لا اله الا الله
محمد رسول الله
على ولى الله

Margin, in six cartouches,

محمد حسن | عل محمد | [مو]سى على | | | |

Rev. السلطا[ن . . . . . .
الكامل الهاد الوا ابو ا[مظفر] . . . ل
اسمعيل خلد . . . .
[بهـا]در خان الصفو .

AR 1·1, Wt. 73·2

12

Mint obliterated, 915.

Obv., in square formed by على in margin,
لا اله الا الله
محمد رسوال لله
ولى الله
على

Margin, سى مو جعفر على | حسن محمد على | [حسن] محمد على | حسين محمد على

Rev. [الع]ا[د]ل
[ال]سلطان [ابو المظ]فر اسمعيل شاه بهاد[ر] خا[ن]
خلد [ا]لله ملكه و سلطانه
٩١٥

Pl. I. AR ·9, Wt. 134·4

13

Aberḳúh, 928.

Obv. Area, in square formed by علي in margin,

[لا اله الا الله]

محمد رسول الله

علي ولي الله

Margin, in segments,

| [علي] | . . ن محمد علي | جعفر موسى علي | علي

Rev. السلطان

الغازي في س[بيل] الل[ه]

ابو المظفر ال[له]

اسمعيل بهاد[ر خان خلد]

. . . .

In centre, within sixfoil,

ضرب

ابرقوه

٩٢٨

سنة

AR ·8, Wt. 120·6

14

Shíráz, 928.

Obv. Area, لا اله الا الله

محمد

رسول الله

. . . .

Margin, محمد علي موسى . . . .

علي حسن . . . .

Rev. سلطان

شاه اسمعيل

٩٢٨

شيراز

. . .

15

Káshán, 928.

Obv. Area, in square formed by علی repeated, within lozenge,

لا الـه الا الـلـه

محمد رسول لله (*sic*)

علی ولی الله

In angles, محمد حسین علی | محمد جعفر علی | محمد حسن علی | موسی حسن علی

Margin, in segments, the following lines:

[نـاد]علـیـا مظه[ر الـعـجائـب]

[تـجده] عو[نا]لك [فی النوائب]

[کل] هم [و] غم سینجلی

بولایـتـك یا علی یا علی یا علی

Rev. السلطان العا[دل]

الكامل ا الهادی

ابو لمظفر

شاه اسمعیل [بها]در خا[ن]

الصفوی [مل]ک[ه]

. . . .

In centre, within sixfoil, ضرب

کاشان

سنة

۹۲۸

16

Mint obliterated, 929.

Obv. Area, within square, in square Koofee,

الله
وللا
[ا]لله علي ع

Margin, in segments, وسی[م] alone legible.

Rev., within quatrefoil, شاه

اسمعي[ل]
الصفو
٩٢٩
ب

Margin obscure.

AR ·6, Wt. 30·2

17

Ámul, fifth year? (A.H. 911.)

Obv. Area, within square formed by علي in margin,

لا اله الا اللـه
محمد رسول ا[لله]
علي ولي ا[لـله]

Margin, | [علي] | [علي] | حسن محمد علي | حسين محمد علي

Rev. [السل]طا[ن] العادل
. . . . ابو المظ[فر]
ن و سلط[انه]
. . . الله ملك[ه]
. . .

In centre, within sixfoil, سنة
مال
•

AR ·7, Wt. 53·4

17*a*

Demávend, date obliterated.

Obv. Area,

لا اله الا الله
محمد ر
سول الله
و ا لى الله
على

Margin, in four cartouches,

| محمد | جعفر موسى على | محمد على حسن | |

Rev.

[ال]سلطا[ن] العا[د]ل
[ا]لكامل الهادى الوالى ابو
[الم]ظفر شاه در ن
[ا]سمعيل بهاخا
[ا]لصفوى الحسينى سنة . . .
خلد الله ملكه

In centre, within border, دماوند

AR ·95, Wt. 119·5

18.

Ḳazvín ? date obliterated.

Obv. Area, within eightfoil,

لا اله الا الله
محمد رسول الله
على ولى الله

Margin, محمد على . . . . موسى على
محمد على حسين (*sic*) محمد

Rev. [السلطـان العادل الكا[مل

(sic) الـولـى [ا]لـــهـــادى

الصفوى [ا]بو [ا]لمظفر

الله خلد

[مل]ك[ه]وسلطانه قزبنو؟

In centre, within quatrefoil,

شاه

سمعيل

بهادر خان

PL. I. Æ 1·1, Wt. 288·

18*a*

Mint and date obliterated.

Obv. Area, arranged in mill-sail pattern formed of على repeated, the ع making a rosette in centre,

محمد حسين على	محمد حسن على	محمد حسن على	مو[س]ى [جعفر] على

Margin, in four cartouches,

. . . . [ر‍س]ول | الله على و | . . . . . .

Rev. [الســ]لطــا[ن] الــعــادل

[الكـا]مـل الـهـادى الـوَلـى

سـلـطـان سمعـيـل شـاه

[خا]ن الصوى (sic) خلد الله

. . . .

Æ ·9, Wt. 120·7

II.—ṬAHMÁSP I.

A.H. 930—984=A.D. 1524—1576.

GOLD.

19

Mint and date obliterated.

Counterstruck.*

Obv. Area, within square,

[لا] اله الا الله
محمد رسول ا
لله ولى
على ا[لله]

Margin, | . . . . . | . . . . . . | . . . . | [بها]در (؟) بگ ‌. . غ . . . . ك |

Rev. . . . .
[الكا]مل الهادى الو . . .
. . . [المظ]فر . . . . . . [شا]ه
. . . . بها[د]ر
م

Counterstruck on rev., with quatrefoil enclosing

شاه
طهماسب
ضرب ل
عد

N ·7, Wt. 59·5

---

* An earlier coin of Ṭahmásp or a vassal reissued.

SILVER.

20

Hamadán, 938.

Obv. Area, within square formed by علی repeated,

لا اله الا الله
محمد رسول الله
علی ولی الله

Margin, | علی . . . . | [علی] . . . . | علی جعفر موسی | علی محمد حسین

Rev. Area, السلطان العادل الهادی
. . . خان
[المظ]فر بهادر
. . . . . . خلد الله . . . .
. . . .

Centre, within ornamental border,

شاه طهماسب
همدان
ضرب

(Letters, &c., interlaced. طهماسب written طہماسب; م united to ا, and ه to ا of همدان, which is affixed to ط.)

Pierced. Æ ·95, Wt. 92·2

21

Iṣfahán, 949.

Obv. within sixfoil,

[لا ا]له الا الـلـه

مـــحـــمـــد

[رسول] الله
[الـلـه] علی و
لی

Margin, in cartouches,

| علی | | | | محمد علی | محمد حسن

Rev. [ش]ا[ه] طهماسب

ضرب اصفهان

سـنـة

[الل]ه

٩٤٩

خلد ملکه و سلطانه

AR ·7, Wt. 80·

22

Iṣfahán, 955.

Obv. Area, in square formed by علی repeated,

لا اله الا الله
الله

محمد رسول

علی ولی الله

Margin,

حسین محمد علی | حسن [محمد] علی | حسن محمد علی |
....علی |

Rev. ....

...

[ا]لوالی ....

خان الحسینی خلد (؟) الله غلا[م]

In centre, within oblong eightfoil,

شاه طهماسب

٩٥٥

ضرب اصفهان

AR ·8, Wt. 65·3

23

Mesh-hed, 976.

Obv. within ornamented circle,

لا اله الا الله

محمد

رسول الله

ولى على

الله

Margin, in two compartments,

... ... ح ... على جعفر | موسى على م[حمد]
محمد

....

Rev., in border formed by compartments of margin,

رضا

امام

مشهد

٩٧٦

ضرب

Margin, in two compartments,

[السلطان العادل غ]لام على بن ابى طالب |

عليه السلام ابو المظ[فر] الحسينى [الصفوى]

PL. I. AR ·8, Wt. 35·1

24

Same mint and date.

Similar; but in rev. margin legible

السلطان العادل الحسينى الصفوى

[I. O. C.] AR ·95, Wt. 71·2

24a

Resht, date obliterated.

Obv. Area, within quatrefoil border,

الله

لا اله الا محمد علی

رسول الله

ولی الله

Margin, in cartouches,

. . . . . ح . . . علی | محمد حسن علی | موسی جعفر علی |
م[حمد . . . علی]

Rev. Area, [السلـ]طا[ن] العا[د]ل الکامل

[ال]هادی رشت

[ا]لوالی . . . المظفر

. . . .

In centre, within quatrefoil border, terminating in interlaced ornament on either side,

سب

طهما شاه بهادر

ب

ضر

AR ·95, Wt. 69·

25

Ḳum, date obliterated.

Obv. Area arranged in mill-sail pattern, formed of علی repeated, the ع making a rosette in centre,

محمد حسین علی | موسے جعفر علی | محمد . . . علی |
محمد حسن علی

Margin, in cartouches,

. . . . علی ولی الله | نصر من [الله] . . . .

Rev. [ا]لكامل الهـ[ـاد]ى . . . .

[ابو المظ]فر بهـادر

الله

ه [خـ]ـلـد ملكه . . . . . .

و

Centre, within quatrefoil,

سب

طهما

شا قوم (*sic*)

ضرب

AR ·75, Wt. 69·8

26

Herát, date obliterated.

Obv. Area, within lozenge formed by على repeated,

لا اله الا الله محمد

رسول الله

على

ولى الله

و

Margin, على | على | [مو]سى محمد على | محمد حسن على

Rev. [السـ]ـلطا[ن] العادل

[الـكا]مل الهادى ابو المظفر

[طهم]اسب شاه بهادر خان

. . . الله تعالى . . . . و سلطانه

. . . . مو (؟) . . .

In centre, within ornamental border,

هراة

ضرب

Pl. I. AR ·8, Wt. [illegible]1

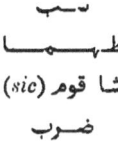

27

Mint and date obliterated.

Obv. Area, within border formed by cartouches,

لا اله الا الله
محمد رسول الله
علی ولی الله

Margin, in cartouches,

موسی
علی محمد حسین | علی جعفر | علی محمد حسن |
علی محمد حسن |

Rev. [ا]لسلطا[ن]

[ال]کا[م]ل ا لهادی

[ابو] خان

[الم]ظفر بهادر

[الص]فوی الحسینی . . .

. . . .

Centre, within ornamental border,

سب
شاه
طهما

AR ·9, Wt. 118·

IV.—SULṬÁN MOḤAMMAD KHUDABANDA.

A.H. 985—996=A.D. 1578—1587.

GOLD.

27*a*

Iṣfahán, 985.

Obv. Area, within quatrefoil border,

لا اله الا الله

محـــــمد

رسو ال لله
و علی
ی الـــله

Margin, within cartouches,

علی حسن حسین | علی محمد جعفر | [مو]سی علی محمد
| ... ...

Rev. Area, within border of many foils,

علیه و . . .

الســــــــلا[م]

غلام امام محمد مهدی

ابو ن المظفر محمد . .

سلطا * نا[د] . . . .

ضرب اصفه[ا]ن
۹۸۵

Margin, خلد الله ملکه . . . .

Pl. I. Æ 8, Wt. 71·5

---

* باد is probably the beginning of پادشاه.

27*b*

Sarí, date obliterated.

Obv., لا اله الا الله محمد رسول الله [علی ولی الله]

In centre, within fleur-de-lis border,

ی
رسا
ضرب

Rev., in centre, محمد
سلطان

Around, خدابنده با[د* غلام علی] ابی طالب علیه السلام

AR ·75, Wt. 28·

27*c*

Similar.

Obv., لا اله الا الله محمد [ر]سول الله علی ولی الله

In centre, as (27*b*),

ی
رسا
ضرب

Rev., in centre, محمد
سلطان

Around, خدابنده باد* غلام علی [ابی طالب علیه] السلام

PL. I. AR ·7, Wt. 27·3

---

* باد is probably the beginning of پادشاه, the rest being indicated by the lines surrounding the central inscription.

V.—'ABBÁS I.

A.H. 996—1038=A.D. 1587—1629.

GOLD.

28

Iṣfahán, 997.

Obv. Area, in circle,

لا اله الا الله
محمد
الله
رسول
علي
ولي الله

Margin, in cartouches,

| .... | .... | جعفر | [مو]سى علي محمد |
| .... | .... |

Rev. Area, in ornamental border,

٩٩٧
ن
اصفهـا
ضـرب

Margin,

...... | ... المظفر عباس شاه خلد .... نه و

29

Ḳazwín, date obliterated.

Obv. Area, in circle,

الله لی

علی و

Inner margin,

لا اله الا الله | محمد رسول الله

Outer margin, in cartouches,

. . . . | . . . . | [مو]سی علی محمد | علی
. . . .

Rev. Area, in border of many foils,

بنده یت

شا . لا

ضرب عباس

Centre, in border of eight foils,

قزوین

Margin,

خلد . . . . | . . . . . . من احسانه

(The inscription reads بنده شاه ولایت عباس ضرب قزوین)

Pl. II. ℛ .75, Wt. 118.6

SILVER.

30

No mint or date.

Obv. Area, within border of many foils,

لا اله الا الله

محمد

نبی الله علی و

[لی] الله

Margin, in four cartouches,

. . . . جعفر | موسی علی محمد |
علی ح[سن] . . . .

Rev. Area, as obv.,

یــــــت
بـنـده ولا
شـــــــاه
عـبـــاس
. . .

Margin,
. . [خلد] الله ملك[ه] و سلطانه و عدله و احسانه . . . . .

Pl. II. [I. O. C.] AR ·9, Wt. 14

31

No mint or date.

Obv. Area, ...

. . . . ل

علی و

Margin illegible.

Rev. Area similar to (30); beneath عباس, a letter ب? legible.

Margin illegible.

[I. O. C.] AR ·7, Wt. 56·7

32

Ḥuwaiza, 1017?

Obv. within ornamental border,

لا الـه الا الـلـه
مـــحـــمـــد
نبی الـلـه علی و
لی الـلـه

Margin, in four compartments, جعفر alone legible.

Rev. بند یت
ر
[و] ه
[شا] لاه
ضر عـبـا س

In centre, within circle, یزه
حو
ب

(The inscription reads بنده شاه ولایت عباس ضرب حویزه)

Margin, traces of inscr. with date ١٠٧١ *

AR ·85, Wt. 56·3

* From the style, this is a coin of 'Abbás I., not of 'Abbás II.

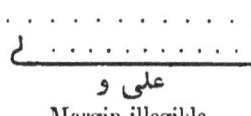

33

Ḥuwaiza, date obliterated.

Similar:

but obv. margin, | | | علی | حسین علی حسن

AR ·9, Wt. 59·1

VI.—ṢAFÍ (I.)

A.H. 1038—1052=A.D. 1629—1642.

—

SILVER.

34

Eriván, 1038.

Obv. [لله]

[لا الـــ]ـــه الا ا علی

[محـمـ]ـد رسول الله و

[ا]لله

Rev.

بـــنـــده صفی

ضـر ایـروان ۳۸

ب

34a

Iṣfahán, 1039.

Obv. لله

لا الـــه الا ا علی

محمد رسول الى لله

و

[الله]

Rev. از جان شا[ه]

[ا]ست صفی

۱۰۳۹

[غ]لام صفهان

ضر

ب

Rev. inscription reads شاه از جان غلام صفی است or

شاه است از جان غلام صفی

Pl. II. Æ ·85, Wt. 115·5

35

Iṣfahán, 103[$\frac{8}{9}$].

Obv. [لله]

لا الـه الا[ا]

مـــحـــمـــــد

[رسو]ل اعلى لله

[و]لى الله

Rev. يـت

[بنـ]ـد[ه] شاه ولا

صـفـی

[ا]صـفـهـان

۱۰۳

VII.—'ABBÁS II.

A.H. 1052—1077=A.D. 1642—1666.

DISTICHS.

بگیتی سکهٔ صاحبقرانی
زد از توفیق حق عباس ثانی

بگیتی انکه اکنون سکه زد صاحبقرانی
ز توفیق خدا کلب علی عباس ثانی

SILVER.

36

Tabríz, 1059.

Obv. Area,
لا اله الا الله
محمد
رسول الله علی و
لی الله

Margin, علی حسن حسین علی محمد جعفر موسی علی محمد
علی حسن محمد

Rev. Area,
بگیتی سکهٔ صاحبقرانی
١٠٥٩
زد از توفیق حق عباس ثانی
ضرب تبریز

Pierced. Pl. II. AR 1·, Wt. 112·6

36*a*

Tabríz, 1062.

Similar to (36), date ١٠٦٢ , and

ضرب تبريز

AR ·95, Wt. 112·7

37

Mint obliterated, 1065.

Obverse Area similar to (36): no margin.

Reverse similar to (36), but ends ٦٥ سـ . . . . . .

Pierced. AR ·65, Wt. 27·4

38

Tabríz, 1066.

Similar to (36), but rev. ends ضرب تبريز ٦٦.

AR 1·, Wt. 113·2

39

Tabríz, 1069.

Similar to (36), date ١٠٦٩

AR 1·15, Wt. 141·5

40

Tabríz, 1070.

Similar to (36), date ١٠٧٠.

AR 1·35, Wt. 141·8

41

Mint obliterated, 1071.

Similar to (36), date ١٠٧١

Pierced. AR 1·1, Wt. 135·8

42

Mint obliterated, 1072.

Similar to (36), date ١٠٧٢

Pierced. AR 1·1, Wt. 124·2

43

Mint obliterated, 1073.

Similar to (36), date ١٠٧٣.

AR 1·05, Wt. 139·4

44

Eriván, 1075.

Similar to (36), date ١٠٧٥; rev. ends ضـ[رب] ايروان.

[I. O. C.] AR 1·05, Wt. 128·4

45

Tiflís, 107*x*.

Similar to (36), date ١٠٧ ; rev. ends ضرب تفليس.

AR 1·2, Wt. 140·4

46

Tiflís, date obliterated.

Similar to (36), but order of rev. changed in details, and تفليس٧.

AR 1·2, Wt. 139·7

47

Tabríz, date obliterated.

Obv. Area,

لا اله الا الله
محمد
رسول الله علی لله
ولی ا

Margin, الـلـ[ـهـم صل على] النبى والولى والبتول والسبطين والسجاد والباقر والصادق والكاظم والرضا والتقـ[ـى و]النقـ[ـى والز]كى [و]المهدى

Rev.

بگیتی انکه اکنون سکه زد صاحبقرانی
زتوفیق خدا کلب علی عباس ثانی

ضر [تبـ]ر[یـ]ز

Pl. II. Æ 1·6, Wt. 566·9

48

Huwaiza, 1054.

Obv. Area, [ا]لله

علی و

Margin, ... رسول الله ....

Rev.

..... لا

[ض]ر عباس

In centre, [یـ]ز[ه]
حو
ب

[Rev. inscr. should read بنده شاه ولایت عباس ضرب حویزه]

Æ ·75, Wt. 41·5

49

Huwaiza, 1072?

Similar; but rev. centre, یز[ه]
حو
۱۰۷۲ (?)
ب

Æ ·75, Wt. 48·9

VIII.—SULAIMÁN I. (ṢAFÍ II.)

A.H. 1077—1105=A.D. 1666—1694.

DISTICHS.

بهر تحصیل رضای مقتدای انس وجان
سکهٔ خیرات بر زر زد سلیمان جهان

سکهٔ مهر علی‌را تا زدم بر نقد جان
گشت از فضل خدا محکوم فرمانم جهان

SILVER.

50

Iṣfahán, 1082.

Obv. Area, لا اله الا الله
محمد
رسول الله علی و
لی الله

Margin, علی حسن حسین علی محمد جعفر موسی علی محمد
علی حسن محمد

Rev. شاه ولا
یت
سلیمان بنده
ب
ضرب صفهان
۱۰۸۲

Pl. II. AR 1·85, Wt. 276·5

51

Ganja, 1086.

Similar to (50); but

١٠٨٦
گنجه

Obv. countermark of Dutch E.I.C. 

AR ·85, Wt. 111·5

52

Tabríz, 1087.

Similar to (50), but obv. no margin; rev. last line,

٨٧
تبريز

Pierced. AR ·6, Wt. 26·5

53

Iṣfahán, 1090.

Obv. Area, لا اله الا الله
محمد
رسول الله علی لله
ولی ا

Margin, traces of names of Imáms.

Rev. as (50), but ضرب
اصفهان
١٠٩٠

AR ·55, Wt. 27·9

54

Same mint, and date (?)

Similar, but obv. no margin visible.

Rev. ١٠٩
صفهان
ا

Unit of date wanting?

55

Tabríz, 1092.

Obv. Area,

لله
لا الـــه الا ا علی
محمد رسول ال لله
و الله

Margin as (50).

Rev. as (50), but سليمان and تبريز ١٠٩٢

AR ·65, Wt. 27·5

56

Iṣfahán, 1093.

Similar to (53), but date ١٠٩٣

AR ·55, Wt 27·3

57

Iṣfahán, 1096.

Obv. as (50), same die.

Rev.

رضــا ی
بهر تحصیل انس وجان مق[تدا] ی
ســکــهٔ خــیــرا بــر زر زد
ســلــیــمــان جــهــان
ضــر صــفــهــان ١٠٩٦

Pl. II. [I. O. C.] AR 1·7, Wt. 541·

58

Nakhchuván, 1096.

Similar to (50); but rev., naskhi and ١٠٩٦ بنده, and

ب
ضر
نخجون ا

PL. III. AR 1·, Wt. 113·6

59

Similar.

AR ·75, Wt. 57·1

60

Similar, but نخجون ا.

Pierced. AR ·6, Wt. 28·

61

Iṣfahán, 1097.

Similar to (50); but rev., naskhi; above first line ١٠٩٧, last lines

ب
ضر
اصفهان

AR ·6, Wt. 27·1

62

Nakhchuván, 1097.

Obv. similar to (50).

Rev.

شاه ولايت
بنده
سليمان نخجوان
١٠٩٧
ب
[ضـ]ـر

Pierced. AR 1·1, Wt. 110·7

63

Same mint and date.

Similar, but rev. ١٠٩٧ سليمان

AR ·95, Wt. 114·9

64

Same mint and date.

Similar, but rev. ١٠١٧ سليمان

Pierced. AR 1·, Wt. 111·3

65

Same mint and date.

Similar to (63), but obv. no margin.

AR ·75, Wt. 56·9

66

Hamadán, 1097.

Similar to (50); but rev., naskhi; and above first line ١٠٩٧ mint همذان

AR ·75, Wt. 57·3

67

Resht, 1098.

Similar to (62), but obv. no margin; rev. mint and date

١٠٩٨
شت
ر

AR ·6, Wt. 28·6

68

Iṣfahán, 1099.

Obv. similar to (50).

Rev. Area similar to (50), but naskhi, and above first line ١٠٩٩; inscr. ends

ب
ضر
اصفهان

Margin, nestalik, in two cartouches,

سکهٔ [مه]ر علی را تا زدم بر نقد جان
گشت از [فض]ل خدا محکوم فرمانم جهان

Pl. III. AR 1·0, Wt. 561·9

69

Iṣfahán, 1099.

Similar, but without margins.

AR ·5, Wt. 11·5

70

Tabríz, 1099.

Similar to (62), but obv. no margin; rev. mint and date

یز ۱۰۹۹

تبر

AR ·55, Wt. 29·

71

Iṣfahán, 109x.

Obv. similar to (57).

Rev. رضا

بهر [ت]حصیل مقتدا

انس و جان سکهٔ خیرا
۱۰۹

[ب]ر [زر ز]د سلیمان [جهان]

..صفهان

Pierced. AR 1·4, Wt. 252·2

72

Nakhchuván, 1101.

Similar to (62), but obv. no margin.

Rev. سلیمان ۱۱۰۱

Pierced. AR ·65, Wt. 26·1

73

Ganja, 1103.

Similar to (50); but rev., naskhi, and

۱۱۰۳
گنجه

AR 1·, Wt. 115·

74

Iṣfahán, 1104.

Obv. as (68).

Rev. Area, within border formed by two cartouches, as (68), but above,

۱۱۰۴
سنة

Margin in cartouches, as (68).

AR 1·55, Wt. 285·1

74a

Ganja, 1105.

Obv. similar to (50).

Rev. similar to (62),

۱۱۰۵
گنجه

AR ·95, Wt. 114·7

75

Ḳazvín, 10xx.

Similar to (53), but rev. ends

۱۰

.. قزوين

Twice pierced. AR ·45, Wt. 10·4

76

Mint obliterated, 10xx.

Similar to (55), date ۱۰

AR ·5, Wt. 11·6

77

Ḥuwaiza, 1084.

Obv. [محمد رسول الله] لا اله الا الله

In centre, الله لی
على و

Rev. [بنده شاه ولايت سليم]ان ضر

In centre, يـزه
حـو
۱۰۸۴
ب

Pierced. AR ·8, Wt. 48·6

78

1084 (۱۸۴).

Pierced. AR ·75, Wt. 50·6

79

1085 (۱۰۸۵).

Obv. لا اله الا الله (*sic*) الخ

PL. III. AR ·75, Wt. 53·1

80

1085 (۸۵).

Pierced. AR ·75, Wt. 49·

81

1085.

Rev. centre, يـزه
حو ۱
۰۸۵
ب

Pierced. AR ·75, Wt. 49·1

82

1086 (١٠٨٦).

Pierced. AR ·8, Wt. 53·2

83

1087 (١٠٨٧).

Date written as on (81).

Pierced. AR ·85, Wt. 52·7

84

1088 (١٠٨٨).

Date written as on (81).

AR ·7, Wt. 49·7

85

1089 (١٠٨٩).

Date written as on (81).

AR ·7, Wt. 51·4

86

Sulaimán ?

No date.

Rev. centre,

يــــزه
حـــو

Outer inscr. obscure.

Pierced. AR ·8, Wt. 54·

87

Similar to (86).

AR ·8, Wt. 53·6

IX.—SULṬÁN ḤUSAIN.

A.H. 1105—1135=A.D. 1694—1722.

DISTICH.

گشت صاحب سکه از توفیق رب المشرقین
در جهان کلب امیر المومنین سلطان حسین

GOLD.

88

Iṣfahán, 1134.

Obv. لا اله الا الله
محمد
رسول الله علی و
لی الله (*محمد)

Margin, علی حسن حسین علی محمد جعفر موسی علی محمد علی حسن محمد

Rev. شاه ولا
یت
بنده حسین
۱۱۳۴
ب
ضر
اصفهان

Pl. III. *Pierced.* AV ·85, Wt. 50·3

* Peculiar to this coin.

SILVER.

89

Tiflís, 1107.

Obv.

لله
لا الــــه الا ا
مـــحـــمـــد
رسول الله علی
ولـــی الـــلـــه

Margin similar to (88).

Rev.

گشت صاحب سکه از توفیق ر
ــــــــــ
المشرقین در جهان امیر المومنین
کلــــــــــ
ســـلـــطـــان حـــســـیـــن
۱۱۰۷
ــــــــــ
ضرب تفلیس

Æ 1·35, Wt. 134·5

90

Tabríz? 1110.

Obv.

لله
لا الــــــه الا ا علی
محمد رسول الله و لی الله

Margin similar to (88).

Rev. صاحب سکه از
گشت
توفیق المشرقین
۱۱۱۰
رب
[د]ر جهان امیر المومنین
[کل]ب
[سل]طان حسین
[ضر]ب
[تبر]یز (؟)

Æ ·95, Wt. 112·8

90*a*

Ganja, 1110.

Similar, but گنجه

Æ 1·, Wt. 111·2

91

Mint obliterated, 1110.

Similar to (90).

Pierced. Æ ·65, Wt. 26·5

92

Mint obliterated, 1112.

Similar to (90), date ۱۱۱۲.

Pierced. Æ ·9, Wt. 112·7

93

Isfahán, 1113.

Obv. لله
لا الـــــه الا ا علی
محمد رسول ولی الله
الله

Margin similar to (88).

Rev. صـــاحـــب ســـكـــه از
گشـــــــــــــــــت
تـوفـيق رب الـمشرقـين در ن
جهـــــــــــــــــا
امير المومنين سلطان حسين
١
١١٣
كلـــــــــــــــــب
ضر اصفهان
ب

Pl. III. Æ 1·25, Wt. 111·4

94

Mint obliterated, 1113.

Similar to (90).

Pierced. [I.O.C.] Æ 1·05, Wt. 112·3

95

Similar.

Pierced. Æ ·75, Wt. 51·5

96

Isfahán, 1118.

Obv. لا اله
الا الله محمد
رسـول الـله
على ولى الله

Margin within six cartouches, similar to (88).

Rev. * لله

السلطان العادل

الهادی الکامل الو ابو المظفر ل

السلطان بن بهادر خان

السلطان ضرب اصفهان

الصفو وسلطانه

خلد ا ملکه

In centre, in quatrefoil,

شاه حسین

سلطان

١١١٨

PL. III. AR 2·1, Wt. 836·6

97

Iṣfahán, 1121.

Obv. الله

لا اله الا ا

محمد

رسول الله علی و

لی الله

Rev. شاه ولا

یت

بنده حسین ن

ب

ضر اصفها

١١٢١

PL. IV. AR 3·15, Wt. 191·8

* The initial letter of خلد in خلد الله ملکه is at the base of the inscription; and "والی" is written "ولی" unless the ا of ابو has double use.

98

Iṣfahán, 1123.

Obv. similar to (88).

Rev.

شـــــاه ولا

يمـــــت

بنده ن حسين

بـــــــــ

ضـر اصـفـهـا

١١٢٣

[I.O.C.] Æ 1·7, Wt. 101·2

99

Same (same die).

Pl. IV. Æ 1·65, Wt. 264·

100

Mesh-hed, 1124.

Similar to (88), date ١١٢٤, and ضر مشهد

Æ 1·, Wt. 83·

101

Eriván, 1125.

Obv. area similar to (88); no margin.

Rev.

شـــــاه ولا

يمـــــت

١١٢٥

بنده حسين ن

بـــــــــ

ضـــر ايـــروا

102

Iṣfahán, 1127.

Obv. لا اله الا الله محمد علی
رسول الله ولی الله

Rev. ۱۱۲۷
شاه ولایت
بنده ن حسین
ضرب
اصفها

AR 1·× ·65, Wt. 129·3

103

Similar, ۱۱۲۷

PL. V. AR ·7 × ·45, Wt. 51·3

104

Same mint and date.

Obv. لله
لا اله الا ا
محمد
[ن]بی ا[لل]ه علی ولی الله

Rev. شاه ولا
یت
۱۱۲۷
بنده حسین ن
ضرب
صف[ـها]

105

Iṣfahán, date wanting.

Similar to (104).

AR ·3, Wt. 11·5

105a

Eriván, 1127.

Similar to 102; obv. varied, ۱۱۲۷ : rev. ends

بنده حسين ايروان

ضرب

AR 1·×·7, Wt. 133·5

106

Iṣfahán, 1129.

Obv. area similar to (88); no margin.

Rev. شاه ولا

يت

بنده حسين اصفهان

ضرب

۱۱۲۹

AR 1·, Wt. 82·1

107

Tabríz, 1129.

Obv. area, within ornamental oblong, similar to (102).

Margin similar to (88).

Rev. حسين

شاه يت

بنده

ضرب ولا

In centre, within ornamental oblong,

و تبريز

۱۱۲

Margin, السلطان بن السلطان و الخاقان بن الخاقان خلد الله ملكه و سلطانه

AR 1·1×·7, Wt. 131·5

108

Similar, but

Rev. centre, ١١٢٩
تبريز

PL. V. Æ 1·05 × ·75, Wt. 134·2

109

Iṣfahán, 1130.

Similar to (106), ب
ضر ١١٣٠

Pierced. Æ 1·05, Wt. 67·7

110

Similar; but rev.,

شــــاه ولا
يـــــت
١١٣٠
بنده ن حسين
ضـرب
صفها
ا

Pierced. Æ 1·05, Wt. 76·1

110*a*

Similar; but rev., ن
ـب
ضر اصفها

Æ 1·05, Wt. 83·2

111

Tabríz, 1130.

Similar to (106), but تبريز and ١١٣٠

Pierced. Æ 1·, Wt. 78·9

111*a*

Similar to (111): rev. same die.

AR 1·, Wt. 83·5

112

Tiflís, 1130.

Similar to (106), but تفليس and ضرب ۱۱۳۰

Pierced. AR ·95, Wt. 71·8

112*a*

Similar.

AR ·9, Wt. 82·8

113

Ḳazvín, 1130.

Similar, but قزوين.

Pierced. AR 1·, Wt. 82·8

114

Káshán, 1130.

Obv. similar to (106).

Rev. شـــــاه ولا
يـــــت
بنده ن حسين
ضـرب
كاشا

AR 1·05, Wt. 82·3

114*a*

Similar.

Twice pierced. AR 1·, Wt. 75·7

115

Mesh-hed, 1130 (?)

Obv. similar to (106), order of letters varied.

Rev. علی
۱۱۳
استان حسین
کلب
ضر مشهد
ب

(The order is حسین کلب استان علی)

Twice pierced. PL. V. Æ ·95, Wt. 80·8

116

Nakhchuván, 1130.

Obv. similar to (106).

Rev. شاه ولا
یت
بنده حسین ن
ب
ضر نخجوا ۱۱۳۰

Æ 1·, Wt. 82·7

116*a*

Similar.

Pierced. Æ ·9, Wt. 77·8

117

Iṣfahán, 1131.

Obv. similar to (88).

Rev. شاه ولا
یت
بنده حسین ضر اصفهان
ب
۱۱۳۱

117*a*

Obv. similar to (117); but rev. similar to (110), حسین ۱۱۳۱

Twice pierced. AR 1·05, Wt. 66·

117*b*

Eriván, 1131.

Similar to (101); but last line of rev. ends ۱۱۳۱

AR ·95, Wt. 83 2

118

Tabríz, 1131.

Similar to (111), ۱۱۳۱

AR ·95, Wt. 83·1

119

Tiflís, 1131.

Similar to (112), ۱۱۳۱

AR ·9, Wt. 83·

120, 120*a*

Tiflís, 1131.

Similar; varied.

(Rev. of 120 same die as 110.) [I. O. C.] AR ·9, Wt. 82·6
Pierced. AR ·9, Wt. 81·

121

Similar.

Pierced. AR ·55, Wt. 20·1

122

Ḳazvín, 1131.

Obv. Area, within ornamental octagonal border, similar to (88).

Margin similar to (88).

Rev., within ornamental border, similar to (113): ۱۱۳۱.

Pierced. AR 1·15, Wt. 79·4

123

Iṣfahán, 1132.

Obv. as (88).

Rev. similar to (106); but صفهان ا : ۱۱۳۲

Æ 1·05, Wt. 80·3

124

Obv. similar to (88).

Rev. similar to (106) : ۱۱۳۲

Twice pierced. Æ ·1, Wt. 62·5

125

Similar; but rev. similar to (110) : ۱۱۳۲

Æ 1·, Wt. 82·6

126

Eriván, 1132.

Similar to (101) : ۱۱۳۲

Pierced. Æ ·95, Wt. 79·2

127

Similar.

Æ ·9, Wt. 83·1

127*a*

Resht, 1132.

Obv. similar to (88).

Rev. شـــــاه ولا
يـــــــت
بنده حسين رشت
ب
ضر ۱۱۳۲

Æ ·95, Wt. 82·3

128

Ḳazvín, 1132.

Obv. as (88).

Rev, within ornamental octagonal border, similar to (113) : ١١٣٢

[I.O.C.] Æ 1·, Wt. 83·9

129

Iṣfahán, 1133.

Obv. as (88).

Rev.

شــــاه ولا
يــــتـــــب
١١٣٣
بنده ن حسين
ــــــــب
ضــر
اصـــفـــهـــا

Pierced. Æ 1·05, Wt. 67·1

130

Similar, but ١١٣٣ حسين

Æ 1·, Wt. 60·8

131

Tabríz, 1133.

Similar to (88); but ١١٣٣ and

ــــــــب
ضر تبريز

Pl. V. Æ 1·, Wt. 83·2

131*a*

Similar to (111) : ١١٣٣

Pierced. Æ ·9, Wt. 77·8

132

Tiflís, 1133.

Obv. similar to (88).

Rev., within ornamental border,

شـــــاه ولا
يـــــت
[بنـ]ـد[ه] حسين
١١٣٣
ب
[ضـر تـفـ]ـليس

With two rings, and pierced. AR ·85, Wt. 68·6

133

Nakhchuván, 1133.

Obv. similar to (88).

Rev.

شـــاه ولا
يـــت
بنده حسين
١١٣٣
ب
ضر نخجوان

Pierced. AR ·95, Wt. 82·6

134

Tabríz, 1134.

Similar; but rev., within ornamental border,

١١٣٤ and تبريز

PL. V. AR 1·1, Wt. 83·1

135—138.

Similar; varied in ornaments.

AR ·95, Wt. 83·

AR 1·, Wt. 83·3

Pierced. AR ·95, Wt. 81·2

H.O.C.! *Pierced.* AR ·95, Wt. 63·4

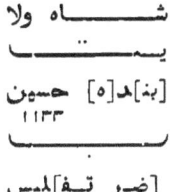

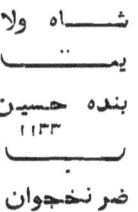

139

Similar to (135), but Tenth Imám علي omitted.

[I.O.C.] *Pierced.* AR 1·, Wt. 81·3

140

Similar to (134), but rev. border not ornamental.

Twice pierced. AR ·7, Wt. 40·9

141

Tiflís, 1134.

Similar to (134), but

تفليس
ضرب

AR 1·, Wt. 82·4

142

Tabríz, 1135.

Similar to (134) : ۱۱۳۵

Twice pierced. AR 1·1, Wt. 78·

143

Tiflís, date wanting.

Similar to (112).

Pierced and ringed. AR ·6, Wt. 23·2

144

Mint and date wanting.

Obv. similar to (90).

Rev. [صا]حب سكه [از] تو[ف]يق [رب]
[گش]ـــــــــــــــ
[الم]شر[قي]ن [د]ر جهان امير المومنين
[كلـ]ــــــــــــــ
[سلـطان] حسين
. . . .

AR ·65, Wt. 28·3

X.—ṬAHMÁSP II.

A.H. 1135—1144 = A.D. 1722—1731.

DISTICH.

بگیتی سکهٔ صاحبقرانی
زد از توفیق حق طهماسب ثانی

GOLD.

145

Ḳazvín, 1134.*

Obv. لا اله الا الله
محمد
رسول الله علی و
لی الله

Rev. بگیتی سکه صاحبقرانی
زد از توفیق حق طهماسب ثانی
ضرب قزوین ۱۱۳۴

Pierced. AV ·85, Wt. 49·1

146

Tabríz, 1136.

Obv. area similar to (145).

Margin, علی حسن حسین علی محمد جعفر موسی علی محمد
علی حسن محمد

Rev. similar to (145):

ضرب تبریز ۱۱۳۶

Pl. V. AV ·8, Wt. 53·4

---

* See Introduction, § Chronology.

147

Iṣfáhan, 1142.

Similar to (145), but mint and date

۱۱۴۲
ضرب صفهان

$\mathcal{N}$ ·9, Wt. 53·6

148

Similar:

Rev. ۱۱۴ ۲
ضرب صفهان

$\mathcal{N}$ ·95, Wt. 52·7

SILVER.

149

Tabríz, 1134.*

Similar to (147), تبريز ۱۱۳۴

Pl. V. Æ 1, Wt. 82·4

150

Tabríz, 1135.

Similar to (146), تبريز ۱۱۳

Pierced. Æ 1·05, Wt. 80·5

151—155

Similar, varied in points.

(Rev. same die as 150.) Æ 1·, Wt. 79·1

Æ 1·, Wt. 82·8

(Rev. same die as 152.) *Pierced.* Æ 1·05, Wt. 82·6

Pierced. [I.O.C.] Æ 1·15, Wt. 82·7

Æ ·85, Wt. 62·1

---

* See Introduction, § Chronology.

156

Similar to (150), ١١٣٥

AR 1·05, Wt. 83·

157

Similar to (150).

Twice pierced. [I.O.C.] AR ·8, Wt. 37·5

158

Similar.

Pierced. AR ·7, Wt. 19·6

159

Ḳazvín, 1135.

Similar to (150), قزوين ١١٣٥

Pierced and ringed. AR 1·, Wt. 88·2

160

Tabríz, 1136.

Similar, تبريز ١١٣٦

AR 1·, Wt. 82·9

161, 162

Similar; varied in points.

Pierced. AR 1·05, Wt. 82·8

Ringed. AR 1·1, Wt. 86·5

163, 164

Similar; تبريز ١١٣٦; varied in points.

AR 1·, Wt. 82·9

Ringed. AR 1·05, Wt. 86·

165

Tabríz, 1137.

Similar to (160), but obv. marg. مو for موسى; rev. ٣٧

AR ·9, Wt. 52·1

166

Mázenderán, 1138.

Obv. similar to (150).

Rev. similar to (150) ; but ١١٣ بگیتی ٨ and مازندران

Æ 1·15, Wt. 83·

167

Resht, 1139.

Similar to (150), ١١٣٩ رشت

Æ 1·, Wt. 68·5

168

Láhíján, 1139.

Similar to (150) ; but ١١ ٣ حق ٩ توفيق and لاهيجان

Æ ·85, Wt. 42·9

168*a*

Mázenderán, 1139.

Similar to (166) ; but obv. in ornamented border, forming four cartouches in margin.

Rev. سب ١١ ٣ طهماسب ثا ٩

Pierced. Æ 1·2, Wt. 82·5

169

Mesh-hed, 1139.

Similar to (150).

Rev. ١١٣٩ ضرب مشهد مقدس : rev. countermark رايج

Pierced. Æ 1·, Wt. 61·6

170, 171

Similar ; varied in points.

Twice pierced. Æ 1·, Wt. 62·4

Ringed. Æ 1·, Wt. 81·

172

Mesh-hed, 1140.

Obv. similar to (150) : but marg. ..... يا حسن م[حمد]

Rev. similar to (169) مشهد مقدس ۱۱۴

Twice pierced. Æ 1·1, Wt. 69·7

173

Similar; points varied.

Pierced. Æ 1·05, Wt. 79·1

174

Mázendarán, 1141.

Similar to (150) : but obv. area within ornamented border, dividing fourfold the marg. inscr.

Rev. مازندران ۱۱۴۱

Æ 1·15, Wt. 82·2

175

Mesh-hed, 1141.

Similar to (169), ۱۱۴۱

Twice pierced. Æ 1·05, Wt. 78·8

176

Iṣfahán, 1142.

Similar to (150); but reverse,

بگیتی سکه صاحبقرانی

زد از توفیق حق طهماسب ثانی ۱۱۴۲

ضرب صفهان

Æ 1·95, Wt. 113·8

177

Similar to (176); but صفهان ١١٤٢

Æ 1·65, Wt. 208·8

178

Similar to (176); but ضرب صفهان ١١٤٢

Pierced. Æ 1·1, Wt. 81·

179

Obv. لا اله الا الله علی

محمد رسول الله ولی

الله

Rev. as (176); but صفهان ١١٤٢

Æ 1·1, Wt. 79·0

180

Similar; but صفهان ١١٤٢

Æ 1·05, Wt. 83·5

181

Mázandarán, 1142.

Similar to (150); but rev.

مازندران ١١٤٢

Æ ·95, Wt. 82·9

182

Tabríz, 1143.

Similar to (150); but obv. within ornamented looped square; no margin; and rev.

تبریز ١١٤٣

Æ ·9, Wt. 26·5

183

Tabríz, 1144.

Obv. similar to (150); rev. similar to (182), ١١٤٤

AR ·8, Wt. 27·5

With name of Imám 'Alee er-Riẓá.

DISTICH.

از خراسان سکه بر زر شد بتوفیق خدا
نصرت و امداد شاه دین علی موسی رضا

SILVER.

184

Mázendarán, 1143.

Obv. Area,
لا اله الا الله
محمد
رسول الله علی و
ای الله

Margin, علی حسن حسین علی محمد جعفر موسی علی
محمد علی حسن محمد

Rev.
از خراسان سکه بر زر
شد
بتوفیق خدا نصر و امداد
شاه دین علی موسی رضا
۴
[ضر | مازندر۳ان

Ringed. Pl. V. AR 1·1, Wt. 83·4

185

Similar to (184); but obv. area enclosed in scroll dividing margin.

Ringed. Æ 1·1, Wt. 82·1

186

Mesh-hed, 1143.

Obv. similar to (184).

Rev. Area,

مــقـــدس

١١٤٣

ضر مشهد

Margin, in two scrolls enclosing area,

از خر[ا]سان سكه بر زر شد بتوفيق | خدا

نـصرت و امداد شاه دين على مـوسى رضا

Pierced. Æ 1·1, Wt. 78·4

187

Similar to (184); but rev.

ضر مشهد مقدس ١١٤٣

Pierced. Æ 1·15, Wt. 78·7

188

Obv.

لا الـه الا الله على

محمد رسول الله ولى

الله

Rev. similar to (187); but enclosed in border of many foils.

Pl. V. [I.O.C.] Æ 1·05, Wt. 82·5

189

Similar to (188); inscr. of obv. varied.

Twice pierced. AR 1·1, Wt. 79·6

190

Similar to (188); but rev. margin within ordinary border.

Twice pierced. AR ·8, Wt. 19·8

191*

Mázendarán, 1144.

Similar to (184); but rev.

١١۴۴
رضا

Pierced. AR 1·05, Wt. 75·5

192*

Mesh-hed, 114x.

Obv. similar to (184); but no margin.

Rev. similar to (187).

مشهد مقدس ١١۴

Pierced. AR 1·, Wt. 79·8

---

* Possibly of 'Abbás III.

AFGHÁNS.

I.—MAḤMÚD.

A.H. 1135—1137=A.D. 1722—1725.

DISTICHS.

سکه زد از مشرق ایران چو قرص آفتاب
شاه محمود جهانگیر سیادت انتساب

فرو رود بزمین ماه و آفتاب منیر
زرشك سکهٔ محمود شاه عالمگیر

SILVER.

193

Iṣfahán, 1135.

Obv. لا اله الا الله
محمد
رسول الله
۱۱۳ ۵

Rev. سکه زد
ب
از مشرق ایران چو قرص افتا
ب
۱۱۳۵
شاه محمود جهانگیر سیاد انتسا
ب
ضر اصفهان
[ب]

PL. VI. Æ ·9, Wt. 71·

194

Similar to (193), but obv. ١١٣٥ ; rev. no date; countermark, sun.

Pierced. Æ ·95, Wt. 69·5

195

Similar; rev. same die; countermark, sun.

Æ ·95, Wt. 70·

196

Similar; rev. same die; no countermark.

Pierced. Æ ·95, Wt. 69·

197

Mint effaced, 1135.

Obv. similar.

Rev. فرو رود

منير

بزمين ماه وافتاب ز

[ر]شك

سكه محمود شاه عالمگير

. . . .

Pierced. Pl. VI. Æ 1·, Wt. 69·2

II.—ASHRAF.

A.H. 1137—1142=A.D. 1725—1729.

DISTICHS.

باشرفی اثر نام آنجناب رسید
شرف زسکهٔ اشرف بر آفتاب رسید

دست زد بر جلالة اشرف شاه
بود تعبیر سکه داد گناه

زالطاف شاه اشرف حق شعار
بزر نقش شد سکهٔ چاریار

GOLD.

198

Iṣfahán, 1137.

Obv. لا اله الا الله
محمد
رسول الله
١١٣٧
(*محمد علا)

Rev. باشرفی اثر نام
انجنا رسید شرف
زسکه اشر بر افتاب رسید
ضرب صفهان
١

Pl. VI. 𝒩 ·8, Wt. 53·2

* Peculiar to this coin.

199

Iṣfahán, 1140.

Similar to (198), but ۱۱۴

N ·8, Wt. 53·5

S I L V E R.

200

Iṣfahán, 1140.

Obv.

زد بر جلالة

دست

بود تعبير سكه

گناه داد

ف

۱۱ ۴۰

اشر شاه

Rev. (die of 1137)

جلوس

ميمنت

مانوس در دار

السلطنة

۱۱۳ ۷

اصفهان

Pierced. AR (base) ·95, Wt. 58·7

201

Iṣfahán, 1141.

Similar, but obv.

ف

اشر شاه

۱ ۱۴۱

Rev. (die of 1137)

اصفهان

۱۱ ۳۷

202

Isfahán, 114x.

Similar, but obv.

فـــــــ

اشـر شـاه
۱۱۴

Rev. (die of 1137) similar to (200), but اصفهان

Twice pierced. AR ·95, Wt. 65·5

203

Isfahán, date obliterated.

Obv. لا الـه الا الله

محـــــــمد

ر[س]ول الل[ه]

Rev. [حـــــق شـــعـــار]

فـــــــ

ز[ا]لـــطـــا شـــاه اشـــر

فـــــــ

[ب]زر [نق]ش شد سكه چاريار

ضـر صـــفـهـــان . . . .

[بـــ]

Pierced. Pl. VI. AR 1·, Wt. 67·5

204

Mint and date obliterated.

Obv. similar.

Rev. زالـطـا

فـــــــ

شـــاه اشـــر حـــق شـعـــار

فـــــــ

[بزر نق]ش شد سكه چار[يا]ر

[ضـــر] . . . .

Ringed. Pl. VI. AR 1·, Wt. 69·5

ṢAFAVIS.

XI.—'ABBÁS III.

A.H. 1144—1148=A.D. 1731—1736.

DISTICH.

سکه بر زر زد بتوفیق الهی در جهان
ظل حق عباس ثالث ثانی صاحبقران

GOLD.

205

Iṣfahán, 1145.

Obv. Area, لا اله الا الله
محمد
رسول الله علی و
لی الله

Margin, علی حسن حسین علی محمد جعفر موسی علی
محمد علی حسن محمد

Rev. سکه بر زر زد بتوفیق الهی
در جهان ظل حق عباس ثا
لث
ثانی صاحبقران ۱۱۴۵
ضر صفهان
ا

Pl. VI. AV 95, Wt. 52·8

206

Similar, but صاحبقران ۱۱۴ه

AV ·9, Wt. 19·5

207

Tabríz, 1146.

Similar to (205), but تبريز ١١٤٦

AV ·95, Wt. 53·8

SILVER.

208

Iṣfahán, 1145.

Similar to (205), but rev. صاحبقران ١١٤٥

Pl. VI. AR 1·1, Wt. 83·8

209

Resht, 1145.

Similar, رشت

AR 1·05, Wt. 77·2

210

Ḳazvín, 1145.

Similar, [قز]وين

AR ·75, Wt. 19·

211

Iṣfahán, 1146.

Similar to (206), but ٦ for ٥.

Pierced. AR 1·05, Wt. 77·9

212

Mint obliterated, 1147.

Similar, but ٧ for ٦.

Pierced. AR 1·1, Wt. 78·8

With name of Imám 'Alee er-Rizá.

DISTICH.

از خراسان سکه بر زر شد بتوفیق خدا
نصرت و امداد شاه دین علی موسی رضا

GOLD.

213

, Mesh-hed, 1148.

Obv.
لا اله الا الله
محمد
رسول الله علی و
لی الله

Rev.
از خراسان سکه [بر] زر
شد
بتوفیق خدا نصر و امداد
شاه دین علی موسی رضا
ضرب مقدس ۱۱۴۸
مشهد

Ringed. Pl. VI. N° 9, Wt. ·55

SILVER.

213*a*

Same mint and date.

EFSHÁRIS.

I.—NÁDIR.

A.H. 1148—1160=A.D. 1736—1747.

DISTICHS.

سکه بر زر کرد نام سلطنت‌را در جهان
نادر ایران زمین و خسرو گیتی ستان

هست سلطان بر سلاطین جهان
شاه شاهان نادر صاحبقران

Motto.

(Chronogram.)

الخیر فیما وقع

GOLD.

214

Shíráz, 1150.

Obv.
بر زر کرد نام
سکه
را در جهان نادر
سلطنت
ایران زمین وخسرو گیتی ستان
ضر شیراز ۱۱۵۰

Rev.
مانوس الخیر فیما وقع
میمنت
تاریخ جلوس ۱
۱۱۴۸

Pl. VII. *N* 7, Wt. 532

215

Lahór, 1151.

Obv. نادر
السلطا
ن

Rev. [ا]لله
خلد ملكه
دار السلطنة لاهور
ب
ضر ١١٥١

Ringed. Pl. VII. AV 1·1, Wt. 366·

216

Iṣfahán, 1152.

Obv. شاهان نادر صاحبقران
شاه
سلطان بر سلاطين جهان
هست

Rev. صفهان
دار السلطنة
١١٥٢
ضرب

AV ·7, Wt. 53·3

217

Iṣfahán, 1153.

Similar, ١١٥٣

AV ·9, Wt. 153·2

218

Similar; varied in ornaments.

Pl. VII. AV ·9, Wt. 169·2

219

Iṣfahán, 1158.

Similar to (218), ١١٥٨ ; but obv., date of accession, سلاطين ١١ ٤

N ·8, Wt. 170

220

Similar ; but obv , date of accession, [ه]ا ٨ ٤١ ١ شـ

N ·8, Wt. 160·8

SILVER.

221

Mint obliterated, 1148.

Obv.

بر زر کرد نام که

[را در] جهان نادر ایران

[سلـ]طنت

[زمین] وخسرو گیتی ستان

ضر ١١٤٨

. . . . .

Rev. بتاريخ الخير فيما وقع arranged in monogram : ق carrying point of خ ; date off field.

Pl. VII. AR ·75 Wt. 41·7

222

Iṣfahán, 1149.

Obv. similar to (214) ; but

ضرب صفهان ١١٤٩

Rev. similar to (214); but enclosed in border of many foils, and at foot ١١٤٨

Pl. VII. AR ·95, Wt. 82·5

223

Mesh-hed, 1149.

Obv. similar to (214); مشهد, no date.

Rev. as (221), but points ∴ between خ and ق of monogram; beneath, ١١۴٩

Pierced. AR ·9, Wt. 60·2

224

Iṣfahán, 1150.

Obv.

نـــادر
السلطا
ن

Rev.

الله
خــــلـد
ملکه اصفهان
ب
ضرب ١١٥٠

AR ·75, Wt. 103·7

225

Similar; but ن of اصفهان in form of ر

AR ·65, Wt. 79·8

226

Tiflís, 1150.

Similar; but تفلیس
١١٥٠

AR ·75, Wt. 105·6

227

Shíráz, 1150.

Similar to (226); شيراز ضر ١١٥٠

[I.O.C.] Æ ·7, Wt. 106·3

228

Ḳandahár, 1150.

Similar; قندهار

Æ 1·1, Wt. 350·8

229

Similar; but ١١٥ (very fine work).

Pl. VII. Æ ·9, Wt. 104·8

230

Similar to (228) (ordinary work).

Æ ·8, Wt. 105·7

231

Mesh-hed, 1150.

Obv. similar to (221) ضر مشهد ١١٥٠

Rev. similar to (223).

[I.O.C.] Æ 1·, Wt. 80·5

232

Obv. as (214), مشهد but no date.

Rev. in eightfoil border, as (214), but جلوس ١ ١٥

Æ ·9, Wt. 70·0

233

Similar; varied in points.

Æ 1·, Wt. 70·8

234

Similar to (224); مشهد

Æ ·8, Wt. 107·3

235

Similar, varied in points.

Æ ·75, Wt. 104·4

236

Isfahán, 1151.

Similar to (224); ن of السلطان and اصفهان in form of ر;

ضرا ١١٥

Æ ·7, Wt. 106·

237, 238

Similar, both varied in points.

[I.O.C.] Æ ·7, Wt. 106·2
[I.O.C.] Æ ·65, Wt. 106·7

239, 240

Similar to (236), but ضرا ١١٥ ; both varied in points.

[I.O.C.] Æ ·65, Wt. 107·8
Æ ·65, Wt. 107·

241

Tabríz, 1151.

Similar to (224); but obv. within border of many foils, and

rev. خلد الله
ملكه تبريز
١١٥١
ضر

(ر and ز in Tabríz in form of د).

Æ ·75, Wt. 107·7

242

Similar to (241), but obv. dotted border and ضرب ۱۱۰۱

AR ·75, Wt. 106·2

243

Shíráz, 1151.

Similar, شیراز ; rev. ends ضرب ۱۱۰۱

AR ·75, Wt. 106·5

244

Ganja, 1151.

Obv. similar.

Rev. ۱۱۰۱
گنجه
ضرب

AR ·75, Wt. 70·3

245

Mesh-hed, 1151.

Obv. شاهان نادر صاحبقر[ا]ن شاه
بر سلاطین ن جهان هست
سلط (*sic*) ۱۱۰۱

Rev. مقدس
مشهد
ضرب

AR ·9, Wt. 174·

246

Same mint and date.

Similar to (234); ۱۱۰۱

AR ·75, Wt. 105·

247

Nádirábád, 1151.

Similar to (246) ; نـادرابـاد

Pl. VII. AR 1·05, Wt. 353·

248

Similar; but obv. varied in points; rev. same die.

AR 1·1, Wt. 351·6

249

Tabríz, 1152.

Similar to (241); but obv., ن of سلطان in form of ر ;

border plain; and rev. ضرب ١١٥٢

AR ·65, Wt. 106·2

250

Tiflís, 1152.

Obv.

شاهان نـادر صاحبقران؛
شـــــــــــــاه[ه]
بـــر سـلاطـيـن جـهـان
هـــــــــــــــ
سلطان

Rev.

١١٥٢
تـفـلـيس
ضرب

AR ·9, Wt. 178·6

251

Same mint and date.

Similar to (241) ; but obv. border plain, and تفليس ١١٥٢

AR ·55, Wt. 18·

252

Sháhjehánábád (Dehlí), 1152.

Obv. similar to (250).

Rev. خلد الله ملكه
١١٥٢
شاهجهان اباد
ضرب
دار الخلافة

Pl. VII. AR ·8, Wt. 175·7

253

Iṣfahán, 1153.

Similar to (217).

AR 1, Wt. 177·0

254

Tabríz, 1153.

Obv. similar.

Rev. دار السلطنة
ضر تبريز ١١٥٣
ب

AR ·9, Wt. 170·6

255

Same mint and date.

Obv. similar to (250).

Rev. similar to (254).

AR ·9, Wt. 178·

256

Same mint and date.

Obv. similar to (255).

Rev. تبريز

دار السلطنة

١١٥٣

ضرب

[I.O.C.] AR ·9, Wt. 175·3

257

Mesh-hed, 1153.

Obv. similar to (216); at base, ١١٥٣

Rev. مقدس

ضر مشهد

AR ·95, Wt. 177·8

258

Tabríz, 1154.

Similar to (254); but rev., date at base, ١١٥٤

AR 1·, Wt. 176·5

259

Same mint and date.

Similar to (254), but date ١١٥٤

AR ·55, Wt. 17·6

260

Ganja, 1154.

Obv. similar.

Rev. ضر گنجه

١١٥٤

Pierced. AR ·55, Wt. 17·

261

Mesh-hed, 1156.

Obv. similar to (254); but at base, ١١٥٦

Rev. مقدس
مشهد
ضرب

Æ 1·, Wt. 178·7

262

Işfahán, 1157.

Similar to (253), ١١٥٧

Æ ·9, Wt. 179·2

263

Sind, 1157.

Obv. similar to (217); but date at base ١١٥٧

Rev. سند
ضرب

Pl. VII. Æ ·8, Wt. 177·5

264

Mesh-hed, 1157.

Similar to (261), ١١٥٧

Æ ·95, Wt. 179·7

265

Işfahán, 1158.

Similar to (262), ١١٥٨

Æ ·85, Wt. 179·7

266

Tabríz, 1158.

Similar to (254), ١١٥٨

Æ ·9, Wt. 178·8

266*a*

Sind, 1158.

Obv. [هــان نــا]در صـ[ـاحــبـقـران]
شـ

[سـ]لطان [بـر سـ]لاطـين جهان شا[ه]
هـ

..٥٨

Rev. سـنـد
ضـرب

AR ·75, Wt. 175·6

267

Iṣfahán, 1159.

Similar to (265), ١١٥٩

AR ·9, Wt. 177·8

268

Tabríz, 1159.

Similar to (266), ١١٥٩

AR ·9, Wt. 178·5

269

Same mint and date.

Similar, varied in ornaments; obv. countermarked جاو

AR 1, Wt. 178·5

270

Tabríz, 1160.

Similar to (268), ١١٦٠

AR ·9, Wt. 178·3

271

Similar, ١١٦٠.

AR ·55, Wt. 17·6

272

Pesháwar, date wanting.

Obv. similar to (250).

Rev. خلد الله ملکه
ضرب
پشاور

PL. VII. AR ·9, Wt. 173·5

COPPER.

273

Bhukkur, 1156.

Obv. نادر شاهی
فلوس

Rev. بهکر
۱۱۵۶
ضرب

Æ ·85

274

Similar.

Æ ·95

274a

1158.

Similar, ۱۱۵۸

Æ ·8

ṢAFAVIS.

SÁM.

PRETENDER.

A.H. 1160=A.D. 1747.

SILVER.

275

Tabríz, 1160.

Obv.

لا اله الا الله

محمد

[ر]سول الله علی ولی الله

Rev.

بنده شاه ولا

یت

سام سلطان حسین

بن ضرب تبریز

PL. VIII. AR ·9×·55, Wt. 68·5

276

Same mint and date.

Similar; but obv. [ر]سول الله علی ولی الله

AR ·9×·6, Wt. 73·4

EFSHÁRIS.

II.—'ÁDIL SHÁH.

A.H. 1160—1161=A.D. 1747—1748.

With name of Imám 'Alí-er-Riẓá.

DISTICH.

گشت رایج بحکم لم یزلی

سکهٔ سلطنت بنام علی

277

Iṣfahán, 1160.

Obv.

لا اله الا الله

محمد

رسول الله علی و

لی الله

Rev.

رایج بحکم لم یزلی

گشت

سکه سلطنت بنام علی

ضرب صفهان ۱۱

(لم یزلی is written لمیزلی, and the ی is united with the ت of گشت)

Pl. VIII. AR ·9, Wt. 70·3

278

Similar; but ۱۱۶ علی

[I.O.C.] AR ·9, Wt. 70·7

279

Similar to (278); but rev. ضرب اصفهان ۱۱۶۰

Pierced. [I.O.C.] AR ·9, Wt. 69·6

280

Similar; but لمیزلی separate from گشت

[I.O.C.] AR 1·, Wt. 68·7

281

Tabríz, 1160.

Obv. Area as (277).

Margin, علی حسن حسین. . . . . [مو]سی علی محمد علی حسن محمد

Rev. گشت رایج بحکم لم یزلی
سکه سلطنت بنام علی
ضرب تبریز ۱۱۶۰

Pierced and ringed. AR ·85, Wt. 72·5

282

Mesh-hed, 1160.

Obv. similar to (277); rev. ۱۱۶۰ علی and مشهد

AR ·9, Wt. 66·

283

Similar; rev.

علی ۱۱۱ and ضرب مشهد

AR ·9, Wt. 70·3

284

Mesh-hed, 1161.

Obv. similar to (277).

Rev.

بحکم لم یز سکه بنام
سلطنــــــت
رایج لـی علی ۱۱۶۱
گشـــــــت
ضرب مشهد

[I.O.C.] *Pierced.* AR ·95, Wt. 69·7

285

Herát, 116x.

Obv. as (277).

Rev.

[را]یج بحکم لم یزلی
گشـــــــت
[سک]ه بنام علی
سلطنــــــت
[ضر] هرات
[ب] ۱۱۶

(لم یزلی as on (277).

AR ·9, Wt. 69·2

III.—IBRÁHÍM.

A.H. 1161—1162=A.D. 1748—1749.

DISTICH.

سکهٔ صاحبقرانی زد بتوفیق اله

همچو خورشید جهان افروز ابراهیم شاه

SILVER.

286

Tiflís, 1162.

Obv. سکه صاحبقر زد بتوفیق [اله] ان

[همچو] خورشید جهان افروز ابراهیم شاه

Rev. ۱۱۶۲

تفلیس

ضرب

Ꜷ 1·05, Wt. 213·5

287

Same mint and date.

Obv. ابرا

هیم

[ال]سلطان

Rev. as (286).

Pl. VIII. *Ringed.* Ꜷ ·6, Wt. 17·5

288

Ḳazvín, 1162.

Obv. as (286), differently arranged.

Rev. within wavy border,

دار السلطنة

ضرب قزوین ١١٦٦

(٦ in date for ٢)

Pl. VIII. Ꜷ 1·05, Wt. 215·4

With name of Imám 'Ali-er-Rizá.

DISTICH.

زفیض حضرت باری و سرنوشت قضا
رواج یافت بزر سکهٔ امام رضا

289

Tabríz, 1161.

Obv. Area, لا اله الا الله
محمد
رسول الله علی و
لی الله

Margin, علی حسن حسین علی محمد جعفر موسی علی محمد
علی حسن محمد

Rev. زفیض حضرت باری و سرنو قضا
شت
رواج یا بزر سکه امام رضا
فت

ضر تبریز ۱۱۶۱
[ب]

[I.O.C.] AR ·9, Wt. 70·

290

Similar, points varied.

Pierced. [I.O.C.] AR ·9, Wt. 69·4

291

Similar; points of obv. varied.

Rev. same die.

Pl. VIII. [I.O.C.] AR ·85, Wt. 70·7

EFSHÁRIS.

IV.—SHÁH RUKH.

First Reign.

A.H. 1161—1163=A.D. 1748—1750.

DISTICHS.

[بزر تا ؟] شاهرخ زد سکهٔ صاحبقانی را
[دو] باره (؟) دولت ایران گرفت از سر جوانی را

سکه زد در جهان بحکم خدا
شاهرخ کلب استان رضا

GOLD.

292

Mesh-hed, 116x.

Obv. از سر

[ف]ـــــــــــــــــــ

[دو] باره (؟) دولت ایران گر جوانی را

[بزر تا ؟] شاهرخ [ز]د سکهٔ صاحبقرانی ر[ا]

Rev. مقدس

مشهد

ضرب

Pl. VIII. AV 8, Wt. 166.5

SILVER.

293

Mesh-hed, 1161.

Obv.

خ
السلطا
هـر ن
شـــا

Rev

الله
خـــلـد
ملكه مقد
مشهد س
١١٦١
ب
ضر

ن of السلطان in form of ر

Pl. VIII. Æ 1·, Wt. 350·2

294

Herát, 1161.

Obv.

خـــدا رضـــا
ســـــــــــكه
جهان شاهرخ بحكم ن
[ا]ســــــــتــا
زد در ١٦١
[كـلـــب]

Rev.

هرا
ت
دار السلطنة
ضـرب

Pl. VIII. Æ ·9, Wt. 176·

295

Mesh-hed, 1162.

Similar to (293); but ١١٦٢ ب ضر

Æ 1·, Wt. 359·

296

Similar to (295), varied.

Pierced. AR 1·2, Wt. 344·4

297

Tabríz, 1162.

Obv. Area, لا الـه الا الـلـه
مـحـــــمـــد
رسول الله علی و
لی الله

Margin, جعفر موسے علی[ ]
. . . .

Rev. سکه[زد] در جهان خدا
[بـحـ]ـکـم
شـاه رخ اسـتـان رضـا
کلـب

ضرب تبریز ۱۱۶۲

[I.O.C.] *Pierced.* AR ·9, Wt. 69·7

298

Shiráz, 1162.

Obv. Area similar; no margin.

Rev. خدا [ر]ضا
[بـحـ]ـکـم
ن شـاهرخ استان
کلـب
سـکه زد در جـهـا

ضرب شـیـراز ۱۱۶۲

299

Similar to (298); but ضرب شیراز ۱۱۶۲

Pierced. AR ·9, Wt. 70·1

300

Mesh-hed, 1162.

Obv.

خدا رضا
سکه
جهان شاهرخ ن بحکم
ستا
زد در ۱۱۶۲
کلب

Rev.

مقدس
مشهد
ضرب

AR ·9, Wt. 177·8

301

Similar; زد در۲۶۲

AR ·9, Wt. 170·8

302

Tabríz, 1163.

Similar to (297), but ۱۱۶۳

AR ·85, Wt. 71·

303

Ganja, 1163.

Similar; but mint and date, گنجه ۱۱۶۳

AR ·8, Wt. 72·

304

Mesh-hed, 1163.

Similar to (293); but ضرب ١١٦٣

[I.O.C.] AR 1·1, Wt. 358·

305

Mesh-hed, 116$\frac{2}{5}$.

Similar; but ب ٢ ١١٦ [ضـ]ـرب

AR ·5, Wt. 18·1

306

Tiflís, 116x.

Obv. as (297).

Rev. سكه ز[د بـ]ـحكم [خدا]
[در جهـ]ـــــــــا[ن]
شاه رخ كلب ستان رضا
ضر تفليس
[ب]

AR ·5, Wt. 17·8

307

Similar; تفليس ١١ ; obv. varied.

Rev. same die.

Pierced. AR ·55, Wt. 15·6

308

Ḳazvín, date wanting.

Obv. similar; no margin.

Rev. similar to (297), but mint قزوين

Pierced and ringed. AR ·85, Wt. 63·2

With name of Imám 'Alí-er-Rizá.

INVOCATION.

يا على بن موسى الرضا

SILVER.

309

Resht, 1161.

Obv. Area, لا اله الا الله
محمد
رسول الله علی و
لی الله

Margin, علی موسی ....
.... محمد علی

Rev. يا علی
بن موسی الر[ضا]
ضرب رشت
١١٦١

Pierced. AR ·8, Wt. 72·

310

Ḳazvín, 1161.

Obv. Area similar; no margin.

Rev. similar; mint and date قزوين ١١٦١

PL. VIII. *Pierced.* AR ·9, Wt. 70·5

311

Similar; points varied.

[I.O.C.] *Ringed.* AR ·9, Wt. 78·

312

Mesh-hed, 1161.

Obv. similar to (311).

Rev.

مو
ضــا
یا علی بن ا سی لر
ضر مشــهـد
۱۱۶۱

Pl. VIII AR ·9, Wt. 175·5

ṢAFAVIS (maternally).

(XII.)—SULAIMÁN II.

A.H. 1163 = A.D. 1749-50.

DISTICHS.

زد از لطف حق سکهٔ کامرانی
شه عدل گشته سلیمان ثانی

وارث ملك شد سليمان بن سادات شاه
بر فروزد روی (؟) زمی چون طلوع مهر وماه

SILVER.

313

Mázandarán, 1163.

Obv.

لا اله الا الله
محمد
رسول الله علی و
لی الله

Rev.

[ز]د از لط[ف] حق سکه ک[ا]مرانی
۱۱۶۳
سه عدل گشته سلیمان ثانی

ضر مازندر[ا]ن

PL. VIII. *Pierced.* AR ·9, Wt. 65·3

314

Kazvín ? date obliterated.

Obv. Area as (313).

Margin, ... محمد علی حسین حسن علی

. . . . . . محمد

Rev. [ب]ر [ف]روز[د] ر[وی] زمی چون طلوع مهر [وماه] ین ؟

[و]ارث ملك شد سلیمان بن ساد[ا] شا[ه] . . .

. . . .

Pl. VIII. *Ringed.* Æ ·65, Wt. 69·2

EFSHÁRIS.

IV.—SHÁH RUKH.

Third Reign.

A.H. 1168—1210=A.D. 1755—1796.

DISTICHS.

سکه زد در جهان بحکم خدا
شاهرخ کلب آستان رضا

سکه زد از سَعیِ نادر ثانی صاحبقران
کلب سلطان خراسان شاهرخ [شاه] جهان

SILVER.

315

Tiflís, 1170.

Obv. Area

لا اله الا الله
محـــــــمد
رسول الله علی و
لی الله

Margin, حسن حسین علی محمد جعفر موسی علی محمد
حسن محمد (*sic*)

Rev. بحکم [زد] سکه [د]ر جهان خد[ا]

شاه رخ استان رضا

کلب

ضر تفلیس ۱۱۷

ب

Pl. IX. AR ·8, Wt. 71·5

316

Mesh-hed, 1195.

Obv. سلطان خراسان [شا]هرخ [شاه] جهان

کلب

سکه [زد] از سعی نادر ثانی صاحبق[را]ن

۱۱۹۵

Rev., in border of many foils,

مقدس

ب

مشهد

ضر

Countermark on rev. رایج ۱۱۹۸

Pl. IX. AR 1·, Wt. 170·4

317

Mesh-hed, date wanting.

Similar; countermark on rev. رایج

Pierced. AR ·55, Wt. 17·2

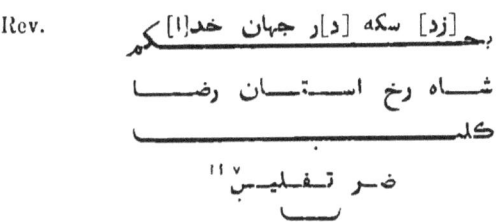

ṢAFAVIS (maternally).

(XIII.)—ISMA'ÍL (III).

A.H. 1163—1169=A.D. 1750—1756.

A. Under tutelage of 'Alí Merdán Khán, A.H. 1163 = A.D. 1750.

B. Under tutelage of Kerím Khán, A.H. 1165=A.D. 1752.

C. Under tutelage of Muḥammad Ḥasan Khán, A.H. 1165—1169=A.D. 1752—1756.

SILVER.

A. Under tutelage of 'Alí Merdán Khán.

318

Iṣfahán, 1163.

Obv.

لا الـــه الا اللـه

مـحـــــــــــمد

رسول الله علی و

لی الله

Rev.

شـــاه ولا

یـــــــــــت

۱۱۶
بـنده اسمعیل
۳

بـــــــــــب

ضر [اصفـ]ـهان

Pl. IX. *Twice pierced.* [I.O.C.] AR ·5, Wt. 17·7

C. Under tutelage of Muḥammad Ḥasan Khán.

319

Resht, 1166.

Obv. لا اله الا الله
محـــــــمد
رسول الله علی و
لی الله

Rev. شاه ولا
یــــــــــت
بنده اسمعیل رشت
ـــــــــــــــ
ضر ١١٦٦

AR ·95, Wt. 172·3

320

Mázendarán, 1166.

Obv. similar.

Rev. شاه ولا
یــــــــــت
١١٦٦
بنده اسمعیل ن
ـــــــــــــــ
ضـــر مازندرا

Pl. IX. AR ·95, Wt. 177·8

321

Máẓendarán, 1167.

Obv. similar to (320).

Rev. شاه ولا

يـــــــــ

بنده اسمعيل مازنـدران

ـــــــــ

ضر ۱۱٦۷

AR ·95, Wt. 172·5

322

Same mint and date.

Similar; but ۱۱٥۷

AR 1·, Wt. 170·7

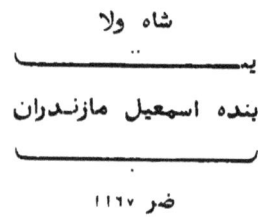

ZANDS.

I.—KERÍM KHÁN.

A.H. 1163—1193=A.D. 1750—1779.

With title of Imám Muḥammad el-Mahdí.

DISTICHS.

تا زر و سیم در جهان باشد
سکهٔ صاحب الزمان باشد

شد آفتاب و ماه زر و سیم در جهان
از سکهٔ امام بحق صاحب الزمان

INVOCATIONS.

یا کریم
یا صاحب الزمان

A. Period of divided rule, A.H. 1163—1172=A.D. 1750—1759.

For coins of Muḥammad Ḥasan Khán Ḳájár see below, p. 127 and Ázád Khán Afghan, p. 130.

GOLD.

323

Iṣfahán, 1167.

Obv. تا زر و سیم در جهان باشد
سکه صا الزمان باشد

Rev., within border of many foils,

صفهان
دار السلطنة
ضرب ۱۱۶۷

Pl. IX. AV ·95, Wt. 169·9

324

Iṣfahán, 1169.

Obv

شـد افـتـا و مـاه

زر و سيم در جهان از سكه

امام بحق صا الزمان

Rev. similar to (323); four fleurons outside border, date ١١٦٩

Pl. IX. AV ·95, Wt. 168·8

325

Army (جلو) mint, 1172.

Obv.

شـد افـتـا ومـاه

زر و سيم در جهان جلو از سكه امام

بحق صا الزمان

Rev., within elongated quatrefoil, fleuron above and below,

جلو

١١٧٢

ضر

Pl. IX. AV ·95, Wt. 169·4

SILVER.

326

Ḳazvín, 1167.

Obv. Area

لا اله الا لله

محمد

رسول الله علی ولی الله

Margin, علی حسن حسین علی محمد جعفر موسی علی
محمد علی حسن محمد

Rev. similar to (323); but

ضرب قزوین ۱۱۶۷

Pl. IX. Ꭿ ·95, Wt. 70·4

327

Same mint and date.

Obv. Area

لا اله الا الله

محمد

رسول الله علی ولی الله

Margin as (326); but Imáms' names enclosed in four borders.

Rev. similar to (326), order of words and letters varied; date ۱۱۶۷

Ꭿ ·95, Wt. 70·3

B. Period of sole rule, A.H. 1172—1193 = A.D. 1759—1779.

GOLD.

328, 328a

Shíráz, 1176.

Obv. similar to (325); but كريم in place of جلو

Rev., within pattern formed of two squares, one superimposed diagonally on the other

هو
دار شيراز
العلم ١١
٧٦
ضرب

PL. IX. 𝒩 ·85, Wt. 169·8
(Same die.) 𝒩 ·95, Wt. 169·5

(كريم on obv. and هو on rev. seem to represent the phrase يا ايمن هو بمن رجاه كريم See Introd. § Inscriptions; ال of العلم in ligature.)

329

Same mint and date.

Obv. similar, but no additional word.

Rev. within similar border, surrounded by fleurons,

دار شيراز
٧٦ العلم
ضرب
١١

𝒩 ·9, Wt. 169·7

330

Same mint and date.

Obv. similar.

Rev., within border of many foils.

دار شيراز
ولعلم
١١٧
ضرب

𝒩 ·9, Wt. 170·3

(ا of شيراز united with extremity of ب of ضرب).

331

Tabríz, 1185.

Obv. لا اله الا الله
محمد
رسول الله علی و
لی الله

Rev. یا کریم
تبریز
دار
ب
لسلطنة ا
ضر
۱۱۸۵

(یا کریم in leaf-border, date outside circle).

Pierced. $\mathcal{N}$ ·9, Wt. 40·4

332

Same mint and date.

Similar, varied in points; two fleurons outside obv. border, one at each side.

Twice pierced and ringed. $\mathcal{N}$ ·85, Wt. 41·

333

Tabríz, 1187.

Similar to (331), varied in points; date ۱۱۸۷

Ringed. $\mathcal{N}$ ·85, Wt. 42·9

334

Yazd, 1187.

Obv. similar to (324).

Rev., within flower of eight petals,

یا کریم

دار یزد

العباده

١١٨٧
ضرب

(العباده forms pattern enclosing دار and یزد)

Pl. IX. *AV* ·9, Wt. 40·9

335

Similar; obv. same die, rev. flower varied.

[I.O.C.] *Ringed.* *AV* ·85, Wt. 41·5

336

Khoï, 1189.

Obv. similar to (331); ا of اله, ل of رسول and of ولی all united in one stroke.

Rev. یا کریم

خو

ضرب

١١٨٩

(یا کریم in leaf-border.)

AV ·9, Wt. 41·8

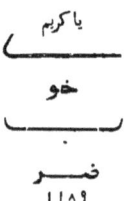

337

El-Baṣreh, 1190.

Obv. similar (to 331).

Rev. يا كر (*sic*)

لبصر

البلاد

ضر فى ام

ب

١١٩٠

Pl. IX. AV ·75, Wt. 84·

(يا كر[يم] in border springing from circle.)

338

Resht, 1190.

Obv. similar to (324).

Rev., within broad quatrefoil,

يا كريم

شت

ضر دار المرز ر

ب

١١٩٠

(يا كريم and ١١٩٠ within ornamented borders springing from pattern.)

Pl. IX. AV ·7, Wt. 79·9

339

Obv. similar, varied; rev. same die.

AV ·7, Wt. 81·6

340

Yazd, 1190.

Similar to (334); but rev. enclosed in arabesque pointed oval, date ١١٠٩ at foot.

I.O.C. AV ·8, Wt. 41·4

341

Khoï, 1192.

Obv. similar to (329); م of سیمر united with ل of الزمان

Rev. یا کریم

ضر خوی

ب

۱۱۹۲

(یا کریم in leaf-shaped border.)

Pl. IX. AV ·7, Wt. 42·3

342

Yazd, 1192.

Similar to (340); but rev. enclosed in eightfoil, date in lowest leaf, ۱۱۹۲

AV ·9, Wt. 42·5

343

Same mint and date.

Similar to (340); but rev. varied in border, یا کریم omitted, pattern of العباده varied, and date ۱۱۹۲ ضرب

[I.O.C.] AV ·9, Wt. 41·2

SILVER.

344

Mázendarán, 1173.

Obv. لا اله الا الله

محمد

رسول الله علی و

لی الله

Rev. شد افتا و ماه زر و سیم در

جهان از سکه امام بحق ص۷ا الزمان ن ۳ ۱۱

حم

ضر مازندرا

ب

PL. X. Æ ·95, Wt. 175·

345

Same mint and date.

Obv. similar.

Rev. شد افتا و ماه زر [و]سیم د[ر]

جهان از سکه امام بحق ص۷ا الزمان ۳ ۱۱

جم

ضر مازندران

ب

Æ ·9, Wt. 171·4

346

Mázendarán, no date.

Similar; order of words on rev. varied and without date.

Æ ·95, Wt. 173·6

347

Shíráz, 1174.

Obv. شد افتا و م[اه]

زر و سیم در جهان از سکه اماه

[بحق]صا [ا]لزمان

Rev. شیراز

لعلم

دارا

ضرب ۱۱۷۴

Twice pierced and ringed. Æ ·85, Wt 70·2

348

Káshán, 1174.

Obv. similar to (324).

Rev., within ornamented lozenge,

دار المومنین

ضرب ۱۱۷۴

کاشان

Æ ·8, Wt. 70·2

349

Mázendarán, 1175.

Obv. similar to (344); but date ۱۱۷۵ محمد; rev., die of 1173 same as (345).

[I.O.C.] Æ 1·1, Wt. 177·5

350

Shíráz, 1176.

Obv. similar to (347); varied in arrangement of words.

Rev. دار شيراز

ضرب

العلم ١١

ضر

PL. X. AR ·95, Wt. 71·5

351

Same mint and date.

Similar; varied in ornaments.

Pierced. AR ·9, Wt. 66·

352

Same mint and date.

Similar; varied in ornaments.

AR ·85, Wt. 17·6

353

Army-mint (Ẓarráb-khána-i-rikáb) 1176.

Obv. similar to (331).

Rev. يا كريم

ضرابخانه

ضرب

مباركه ركا

ب

١١٧٦

سنة

PL. X. AR ·75, Wt. 70·1

354

Shíráz, 1177.

Similar to (350); varied in ornaments; date ١١٧٧

[I. O. C.] AR 1·, Wt. 67·5

354a

Resht, year 16, 1178(?).

Obv. similar to (331); rev. similar to (338), but in lower border, ١٦

AR ·9, Wt. 47·2

355

Iṣfahán, 1179.

Obv. similar to (324).

Rev., within border of many foils, elongated above and below,

يا كريم
صفهان
دار السلطنة
ضرب
١١٧٩

AR ·8, Wt. 66·6

356

Tabríz, 1179.

Obv. similar to (329).

Rev. دار تبريز ا
لسلطنة
ب
ضر ١١٧
٩

(ر of تبريز in form of ن)

AR ·85, Wt. 70·7

357

Ṭehrán, 1179.

Obv. as (324).

Rev., within pear-shaped border,

يا كريم
طهران
ب
٩ ٧ ضر
١١

AR ·75, Wt. 70·4

358

Yazd, 1179.

Obv. similar to (324).

Rev., within foliate pear-shaped border,

یا کریم

یزد ٥

دار العباد

١١ ٧٩

ضرب

Pierced. AR ·85, Wt. 69·8

359

Tabríz, 1181.

Obv. similar to (329).

Rev. similar to (331), but یا کریم illegible; date in field, ضرب ١١ ٨١,
and border of quatrefoils.

AR ·95, Wt. 70·7

360

Resht, 1181.

Obv. ١١ ٨

شد افتا و ماه

زر و سیم در جهان از سکه

امام بحق صا الزمان

Rev. similar to (338); date ١١٨١

Pierced. AR ·9, Wt. 70·8

361

Shíráz, 1181.

Similar to (350); but rev. at foot, ١١ ٨١ and border of quatre-foils, having يا كريم interlaced within border above.

[I.O.C.] Æ ·95, Wt. 69·9

362

Teherán, 1181.

Obv. similar to (324).

Rev., within border of many foils, with leaf-border above and below,

ياكريم
طهران
ضرب
١١٨١

(يا كريم interlaced, طهران enclosed in two loops.)

Pl. X. Æ ·8, Wt. 70·7

363

Yazd, 1181.

Obv. similar to (324); rev. similar to (331), enclosed in border of many foils, elongated above; ياكريم interlaced; date ١١٨١

Pl. X. Æ ·85, Wt. 70·8

364

Tabríz, 1182.

Similar to (359); but rev. يا كريم legible in border above; date, ضرب ١١ ٨٢

Æ 1·, Wt. 70·4

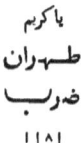

365

Tiflís, 1182 ?

Obv. شد افتا و ماه زا[ر و] سیم

در جهان از سکه امام بحق [صا] الز[مان]

[ح]

[ضرب] تفلیس

Rev. یا کریم

١١ ٨٢ (?)

(یا کریم interlaced ; unit of date obscure.)

AR ·75, Wt. 70·

366

Tiflís, 1182.

Obv. الحمد لله

ر لمین

العا

Rev., within ornamented border, surrounded by dots,

[یا کریم] in border above,

تفلیس

١١ ٨٢

ضر

AR ·75, Wt. 46·4

367

Same mint and date.

Obv., within ornamented border,

یا کریم

Rev. تفلیس

ضرب

٨٢·

(یا کریم interlaced.)

Pierced. AR ·6, Wt. 22·4

368

Tiflís, 1182.

Similar to (367); but rev. ضرب ۸۳

Pierced. AR ·6, Wt. 13·4

369

Ganja, 1182.

Obv. similar to (329).

Rev. Area

یاکریم
گنجه ۱۱۸۲
ب
ضر

Margin, لا اله الا الله محم[د ر]سول الله علی ولی الله

Pierced. AR ·1, Wt. 58·1

370

Same mint and date.

Obv. similar, varied in ornaments.

Rev., within ornamented border,

یا کریم
۱۱۸۲
گنجه
ب
ضر

(یا کریم interlaced in a border.)

AR ·1, Wt. 57·5

371

Nakhchuván, 1182.

Obv. similar, varied in ornaments.

Rev., within border of quatrefoils,

نخجوان
ب
ضر ۱۱
۸۲

(ن of نخجوان in form of ر. Border above obliterated.)

AR 1·, Wt. 70·5

372

Tabríz, 1183.

Similar to (364); but date ضرب ١١٨٣

Pierced. AR 1·05, Wt. 68·

373

Tiflís, 1183.

Similar to (366), date ضرب ١١٨٣

PL. X. AR ·8, Wt. 47·

374

Nakhchuván, 1183.

Similar to (371); but date,

ب
ضرب ١١٨٣

PL. X. AR 1·05, Wt. 70·7

375

Tabríz, 1184.

Similar to (331), date ١١٨٤

Pierced. AR ·9, Wt. 17·7

376

Tiflís, 1184.

Similar to (366), date ضرب ١١٨٤

AR ·8, Wt. 42·6

377

Ganja, 1184.

Similar to (370), date ١١٨٤

Pierced and broken. AR 1·05, Wt 51·6

378

Tabríz, 1187.

Similar to (375), date ١١٨٧

AR ·9, Wt. 17·8

379

Tabríz, 1188.

Similar to (378), date ١١٨٨

Æ ·9, Wt. 17·4

380

Kermán, 1188.

Obv. similar to (324), [ا]مام بحق (Die of previous year.)
١١ ٨٧

Rev. یاکریم

دار الامام کرمان

ضر
١١٨٨

م of امام, and ن of کرمان in form of ر, ک in form of ا

Æ ·9, Wt. 142·

381

Tiflís, 1189.

Obv. (interlaced), یا کریم

Rev. تفلیس
ضر
١٨٩
ب ١

Pl. X. Æ ·65, Wt. 25·2

382

Shamákhí, 1189.

Obv., within border of rays,

یا صا الزمان
حب
٣ ٣

Rev., within leaf-border, with smaller border beneath,

شماخ
ب
١١٨٩
ضر

Æ ·8, Wt. 48·3

383

Kermán, 1189.

Similar to (380); obv. same die of 1187, rev. date ۱۱۸۹

Pl. X. Æ ·9, Wt. 141·7

384

Ganja, 1189.

Obv. similar to (370).

Rev., within ornamented border,

یا کریم
گنجه
ب
ضرب ۱۱۸۹

Ringed. Æ ·1, Wt. 50·2

385

Same mint and date.

Similar; obv. same die, rev. varied in ornaments; countermark on obverse, رایج

Æ 1·, Wt. 47·1

386

Same mint and date.

Obv., within quatrefoil,

الزمان
صاحب
یا صا

Countermark رایج

Rev., in quatrefoil, within ornamented border,

یا کریم
گنجه
ضرب
۱۱۸۹

Æ ·95, Wt. 47·6

387

Mint obliterated, 118x?

Obv. [شـ]ـد [ا]فـتـا وماه زر و سیم

[در جـ]ـهان از [سکه] امام بحق الز[ما]ن

[حـ]

. . . . . .

Rev. [ا]لله یمر

کر

[م]ـلـکـه

خـلـد یا

AR ·8, Wt. 70·7

388

Similar; varied in ornaments.

AR ·8, Wt. 68·1

389

El-Başreh, 1190?

Obv. similar to (337).

Rev. (date outside circle), یا کریم

بصر

ده

ام البلا فی

ضر

۱۱۹۰

یا کریم in leaf-border, date outside circle.

AR ·9, Wt. 71·

390

Tiflís, 1190.

Similar to (366); but rev. within circle, around which ornamented border; and at foot ۱۱۹۰

AR ·85, Wt. 71·

391

Same mint and date.

Similar to (366); but date at foot ١١٩٠

AR ·75, Wt. 46.1

392

Same mint and date.

Similar; but date ضرب ١١٩

AR ·75, Wt. 16·8

393

Same mint and date.

Similar; but date ضرب ١١٩

AR ·75, Wt. 17·5

394

Shamákhí, 1190.

Obv., in border of many foils, within wreath,

يا صا الزما

Rev., within border of many foils; above, fleuron, around, three pellets,

شماخی

١١٩٠ ضرب

Pierced. AR ·9, Wt. 46·6

395

Ganja, 1190.

Obv. similar to (386).

Rev., within quatrefoil, ١١٩٠

گنجه یا کریم

ضرب

AR ·95, Wt. 44·1

396

Same mint and date.

Similar; date ١١٩٠

AR ·1, Wt. 47·1

397

Ganja, 1190.

Similar to (396); obv. same die, rev. countermark رايج

AR ·9, Wt. 46·6

398

Same mint and date.

Similar; obv. same die, rev. same countermark, date ١١٩

AR ·9, Wt. 47·

399

Same mint and date.

Similar; date ١١٠٩

Pierced. AR ·1, Wt. 47·7

400

Shamákhí, 1191.

Similar to (394); but obv. inner border plain; rev. no fleuron or pellets, date

١١٩١
ضرب

Pierced. AR ·9, Wt. 42·7

401

Ganja, 1191?

Similar to (395); but date ١٢١١, and countermark رايج

Pierced. AR 1·05, Wt. 40·6

402

Ganja, 1192.

Similar obv. and rev.; around, four pellets; obv. same countermark; rev. date ١١٩٢

Pl. X. AR ·1, Wt. 46·7

403

Shamákhí, 119x.

Similar to (394); but obv. in circle, within wreath.

Rev., no pellets; date, ضرب ١١٩

Pierced. AR 1·, Wt. 44·7

ḲÁJÁRS.

I.—MUḤAMMAD ḤASAN KHÁN.

A.H. 1163—1172=A.D. 1750—1759.

With name of Imám 'Ali-er-Riẓá.

DISTICH.

بزر سکه از میمنت زد قضا
بنام علی بن موسی الرضا

GOLD.

404

Iṣfahán, 1169.

Obv. لا اله الا الله
محمد
رسول الله علی و
لی الله

Rev. بزر سکه از زد قضا
میمنت
بنام علی بن موسی الرضا

ضرب اصفهان ۱۱۶۹

Pl. XI. AV ·95, Wt. 170·1

405

Same mint and date.

Similar; obv. varied in points; rev., same die.

AV ·9, Wt. 168·6

406

Tabríz, 1170.

Similar to (404); but obv., fleuron on either side, rev. ends

ضر تبريز ١١٧

PL. XI. *Pierced.* *N* ·75, Wt. 42·0

407

Yazd, 1170.

Similar to (404); but rev. ends

ضر يزد ١١٧

PL. XI. *N* ·95, Wt. 169·7

408

Iṣfahán, 1171.

Similar to (404); but obv., fleuron above, rev. ends

ضر صفهان
١١٧١

N ·9, Wt. 169·3

SILVER.

409

Tabríz, 1170.

Similar to 404; but rev. ends

[ضر] تبريز ١١٧٠

AR ·9, Wt. 177·6

410

Resht, 1170.

Similar; but rev. ends

١١٧
بنام على ابن موسى الرضا
ضر
[ر]شت

AR 1·, Wt. 176·6

411

Mázendarán, 1170.

Similar to (404) ; but rev. الرضا ۱۱۷۰ ; ضرب forms one line.

Pl. XI. Æ 1·15, Wt. 179·8

412

Same mint and date.

Similar, varied.

Æ ·9, Wt. 176·2

413

Mázendarán, 1171.

Similar ; but rev. date بنام علی ابن موسی الرضا ۱۱۷۱

Æ 1·05, Wt. 175·2

414

Similar, varied.

I.O.C.] Æ ·9, Wt. 177

415

Asterábád, date wanting.*

Obv. similar to rev. of (404), without mint.

Rev., within ornamented lozenge,

دبا
ا
سترا
دار المومنين
ف
ب
ضر

Pierced and ringed. Æ ·8, Wt. 68·4

---

* This coin may be of Aḳa Muḥammad Khán during his period of divided rule ; see p. 144.

AFGHÁN.

ÁZÁD KHÁN.

A.H. 1166—1169=A.D. 1753—1756.

With name of Azád Khán and title of Imám Muḥammad el-Mahdí.

DISTICH.

تا که آزاد در جهان باشد
سکهٔ صاحب الزمان باشد

SILVER.

116

Tabríz, 1168.

Obv., within border of many foils, pointed above and below,

لله
لا اله الا ا
محمد
رسول الله

Rev. [تا] که ازاد در جهان باشد
حب
سکه صا الزمان باشد
ضرب
تبریز ۱۱۶۸

Pl. XI AR ·95, Wt. 68·2

KHÁN OF GANJA.

With name of Nádir Sháh.

SILVER.

417

Ganja, 1176.

Obv., within border of many foils,

نادر
السلطا
ن

Rev., as obv.,

١١٧٦
گنجه
ضرب

Pl. XI. AR ·85, Wt. 70·2

418

Ganja, 1177.

Similar; but rev.,

١١٧٧
گنجه
ب
ضر

Pierced. AR ·65, Wt. 17·2

419

Ganja, 1178.

Similar; date ١١٧٨

AR ·75, Wt. 71·5

420

Ganja, 1187.

Similar, ١١٨٧

Twice pierced. AR ·75, Wt. 69·9

421

Ganja, 1188.

Similar, ١١٨٨

Pl. XI. AR ·8, Wt. 67·7

ZANDS.

II.—ABU-L-FAT-Ḥ KHÁN.

A.H. 1193=A.D. 1779.

With title of Imám Muḥammad el-Mahdí.

DISTICH.

شد آفتاب و ماه زر و سیم در جهان
از سکهٔ امام بحق صاحب الزمان

A. Abu-l-Fat-ḥ Khán with Muḥammad 'Alí Khán as colleague, A.H. 1193=A.D. 1779.

(No coins.)

B. Abu-l-Fat-ḥ Khán alone, A.H. 1193=A.D. 1779.

GOLD.

122

Yazd, 1193.

Obv.
شـــد افـتـا و مـــاه
بـــــــــــــــــ
زر و سیم در جهان از سکه
حـ]ـــــــــــب
[امام] بحق صا الزمان

Rev. within border of many foils, pointed above and below,

ابو الفتح
دار یـــزد
الــعــبـاده
۱۱۹۳
ضرب

(العباده forms pattern enclosing دار and یزد)

Pl. XII. AV 85, Wt. 42·3

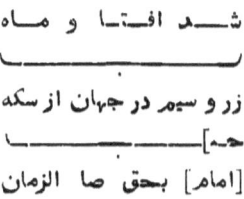

III.—ṢÁDIḲ KHÁN.

A.H. 1193—1196=A.D. 1779—1782.

With title of Imám Muḥammad el-Mahdí.

DISTICH.

شد آفتاب و ماه زر و سیم در جهان

از سکهٔ امام بحق صاحب الزمان

INVOCATION,

یا کریم

GOLD.

423

Yazd, 1194.

Obv. شـــد افـتـــا و مـــاه

[زر]و سیم در جهان از سکه

حـ

امام بحق صا الـزمـان

Rev., within border of many foils, pointed above and below,

یا کریم

دار یـــزد

الـــعـــباده

ضرب ۹۴ ۱۱

(العباده forms pattern enclosing دار and یزد)

AV ·8, Wt. 41·5

424

Shiráz, 1195.

Obv.

شد افتا و ماه

ب

زر و سیم در جهان از سکه امام

ح

بحق صا الزمان

Rev.

یا کریم

شیراز

دار العلم

ضرب

۱۱۹۵

(یا کریم in leaf-border.)

Pl. XII. AV ·85, Wt. 161·4

SILVER.

425

Tabríz, 1194.

Obv.

لا اله الا الله

محمد

رسول الله علی و

لی الله

Rev.

یا کریم

تبریز

دار

ب

لسلطنة

ضر

۱۱۹۴

(یا کریم in leaf-border; date outside circle.)

AR 1·05, Wt. 18·3

426

Shíráz, 1194.

Similar to (424); obv. same die; rev. date ١١٩٤

PL. XII. AR ·85, Wt. 174·5

427

Tabríz, 1195.

Similar to (425); but rev. date ١١٩٥

PL. XII. AR ·95, Wt. 18·

428

Khoï, 1195.

Obv. similar to (424).

Rev. خوى
ضرب
١١٩٥

AR ·95, Wt. 169·4

429

Shíráz, 1195.

Obv. similar.

Rev. similar to (424); ضرب ١١٩٥

AR ·85, Wt. 178·6

IV.—'ALÍ MURÁD KHÁN.

A.H. 1193—1199=A.D. 1779—1785.

With title of Imám Muḥammad el-Mahdí.

DISTICH.

شد آفتاب و ماه زر و سیم در جهان
از سکهٔ امام بحق صاحب الزمان

INVOCATION.

یا علی

GOLD.

430

Shíráz, 1197.

Obv. لله
لا الـــه الا ا
مـــحـــــــــــــمـــد
رسول الله علی و ا لی لله

Rev. یا علی
شـــیـــراز
دار العلم
ضرب
۱۱ ۹۷

(یا علی in leaf-border.)

PL. XII. AV ·85, Wt. 167·9

431

Yazd, 1197.

Obv. شـــد افـــتـــا ومــــاه

ـــــــــــــــــ

زر و سیم در جهان از سکه

ـــــــــــــــــ

امــام بحق صــا الــزمان

Rev., within border of many foils, pointed above and below,

یا علی

دار یـــزد

الـعـبـاده

ضرب ۱۱۹۷

العباده forms pattern enclosing دار and یزد

PL. XII. A/ ·85, Wt. 42·4

432

Shiráz, 1198.

Obv. الله

لا الـــه الا ا علی

محمد رسول ال لله

و الله

Rev. similar to (430); but date ۱۱۹۸ in border at foot; fleuron on each side.

A/ ·85, Wt. 170·2

433

Káshán, 1198.

Obv.

شـــد افـــتـــا و مـــاه

زر و سیم در جهان از سکه امام

بـــحـــق صـــا الـــزمـــان

Rev.

يا على

منين

دار لمو كاشان ا

ضـــر

۱۱۹۸

Margin enclosed in four arches.

Pl. XII. AV ·95, Wt. 42·4

434

Káshán, date obliterated.

Obv. similar to (431).

Rev., within border of many foils,

يا على

كاشان

دار المومنين

ضرب

(يا على in leaf-border.)

Pierced. AV ·8, Wt. 41·3

SILVER.

435

Iṣfahán, 1198.

Obv. similar to (433); but ا for از

Rev. يا على
صفهان
دار السلطنة
ضرب
١١٩٨
سنة

(يا على in border; date in field below.)

Pl. XII. AR ·95, Wt. 178·1

436

Shíráz, 1198.

Obv. similar to (433).

Rev. similar to (430); but date below, in border, ١١٩٨; on either side, fleuron.

AR ·9, Wt. 177·4

437

Same; same die.

[I.O.C.] AR ·9, Wt. 176·5

V.—JAA'FAR KHÁN.

A.H. 1199—1203=A.D. 1785—1789.

INVOCATION.

يا امام جعفر الصادق

GOLD.

438

Shíráz, 1201.

Obv.

دق
لـــصـــا
جـــعـــفـــر
ا يا مامر ا

Rev. in circle, around which four fleurons,

شـــيـــراز
دار العلمر
ضرب
۱۲۰۱

PL. XII. AV 1·, Wt. 170·

439

Shíráz, 1202.

Similar; rev. date ضرب ۱۲۰۲

AV ·1, Wt. 160·8

SILVER.

440

Iṣfahán, 1199.

Obv.

الصادق
جـعـفـر
يا امامر ا

Rev. صـــفـــهـــان
دار لسلطنة
۱۱۹۹
ضرب

Æ ·8, Wt. 177·

441

Same mint and date.

Obv. similar; varied.

Rev. صفهان
۱۱
دار لسلطنة
۱ ۹ ۹
ضرب

Pl. XII. [I.O.C.] Æ ·85, Wt. 171·9

442

Shíráz, 1199.

Obv. similar to (440).

Rev. similar to (438); date ضرب ۱۱۹۹; fleurons above and below.

Æ ·9, Wt. 179·7

443

Same mint and date.

Similar; but date on obv. at base ۱۱ ۹۹; none on rev.; above, fleuron.

[I.O.C.] Æ ·85, Wt. 178·7

444

Shíráz, 1202.

Similar to (438); but rev. ضرب ۱۲ ۲۰; below, in margin, س: around, four pellets.

Æ 1·, Wt. 172·4

VI.—LUṬF-'ALÍ KHÁN.

A.H. 1203—1209=A.D. 1789—1794.

DISTICH.

گشت زده سکه بر زر
لطفعلی بن جعفر

GOLD.

115

Kermán, 1208.

Obv.

ز لطفعلی
د بن جعفر
۱۲۸۰
گشت
سکه بر زر

Rev.

لطفعلی
مان کرمان
ب
ضر دارالا
۱۲۸

(لطفعلی in leaf-border.)

PL. XII. AV ·85, Wt. 30·6

ḲÁJÁRS.

II.—AḲA MUḤAMMAD KHÁN.

A.H. 1193—1211=A.D. 1779—1797.

DISTICHS.

With name of Imám 'Alí-er-Riẓá.

بزر سکه از میمنت زد قضا
بنام علی ابن موسی الرضا

With title of Imám Muḥammad-el-Mahdí.

تا زر و سیم در جهان باشد
سکهٔ صاحب الزمان باشد

تا زر و سیمرا نشان باشد
سکهٔ صاحب الزمان باشد

بر زر و سیم تا نشان باشد
سکهٔ صاحب الزمان باشد

شد آفتاب و ماه زر و سیم در جهان
از سکهٔ امام بحق صاحب الزمان

INVOCATION.

یا محمد

A. Period of divided rule, A.H. 1193—1209=A.D. 1779—1794.

For coins of the contemporary Zand Kháns see above, p. 132 seqq.

SILVER.

446

Iṣfahán, 1199.

Obv.
بزر سكه از زد قضا
ميمنت ب
بنام علي ابن موسى الرضا

Rev.
صفهان
دار السلطنة
ضرب ١١٩٩

PL. XIII. AR ·95, Wt. 176·5

B. Period of sole rule, A.H. 1209—1211=A.D. 1794—1797.

GOLD.

447

Káshán, 2 Rejeb, 1209.

Obv.
تا زر و سيمرا نشان با
شد
سكه صا الزمان
جب
باشد

Rev., within octagon, having four arched compartments springing from it, containing invocation and date,

يا محمد
كاشان
ضرب
١٢٠٩
سنة

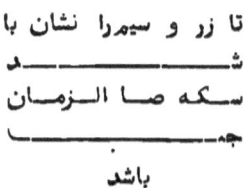

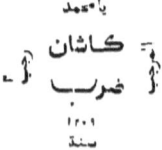

SILVER.

448

Shíráz, 1209.

Obv.

تا زر و سیم

شـــــــــــد

در جهان با سکه صا

حـــــــــــب

الزمان باشد

Rev. within border of many foils, having four leaf-borders springing from it, containing invocation and dates,

یا محمد

شـــیراز

دار العلم

ضرب

١٢٠٩

Pl. XIII. Æ ·95, Wt. 177·5

449, 450

Same mint and date.

Obverses same die, reverses varied in ornaments.

Æ ·95, Wt. 171·5

Æ ·95, Wt. 177·6

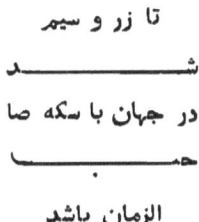

451

Khoï, 1210.

Obv. لله

لا الــــه الا علٰى

محمد رسول الى لله

و الله

Rev., within ornamented lozenge,

یا محمد

خــــو ۱۲۱۰

ضر

PL. XIII. AR ·95, Wt. 193·9

452

Resht, 1211.

Obv. شــــد [ا]فـــتــــا [ومــــاه]

زر و سیم در جهان از س[که امام]

حـ

بــحــق [صــ]ــا الــــــزمــــان

Rev., within border of dots surrounded by cusps, in the upper and lower of which, invocation and date,

[یا محمد]

شــــــ ر

[دا]ر الــمــرز

ضــر

۱۲۱۱

(م of سیم united with ل of الزمان)

PL. XIII. AR ·85, Wt. 190·5

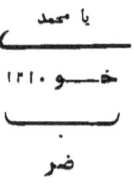

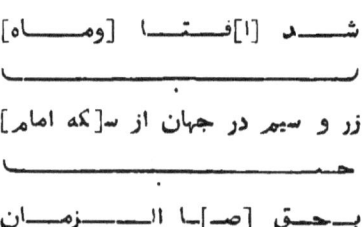

453

Same mint and date.

Obv. varied in ornaments; rev. same die.

Æ ·85, Wt. 182·8

454

Iṣfahán, date wanting.

Obv.

بر زر و سیم تا نشا

شـــــــد

با ن صا سکه الز

حـــــــــا

[با] مان شد

Rev., within border of foils,

يا محمد

صـفـهـان

دار لسلطنه

ضرب

(ا serves for دار and ال)

Pl. XIII. Æ (base) ·75, Wt. 182·4

455

Same: same die.

Æ (base) ·75, Wt. 166·6

III.—FET-Ḥ-'ALÍ (BÁBÁ KHÁN).

A.H. 1211—1250=A.D. 1797—1834.

MOTTOES.

الملك لله

العزة لله

A. Period before Proclamation, A.H. 1211—1212=A.D. 1797—1798, as Sulṭán.

BÁBÁ KHÁN.

SILVER.

456

Shíráz, 1212.

Obv.

لملك لله

ا خا

ن بابا ن

السلطا

Rev., within double border, around which, four fleurons alternating with pyramids of dots,

شيراز

دار العلم

ضرب

١٢ ١٢

(Date outside borders.)

Pl. XIII. Æ 1·05, Wt. 170·7

457

Ṭeherán, [1212.*]

Obv. لله

لا الـه الا ا علی

محمد رسول ا لى لله

و الله

Rev., within double border, around which, four pyramids of dots alternating with fleurons,

لسلطا بابا

ا خا

ن ن ن

ضر طهرا

PL. XIII. Æ 1·1, Wt. 174·7

---

* See Introduction, § Chronology.

FET-Ḥ-'ALÍ SHÁH.

B. Period after Proclamation, A.H. 1212—1250=A.D. 1797—1834.

GOLD.

458

Iṣfahán, 1213.

Obv.

قاجار

شاه فتحعلی

السلطان

۱۲۱۳

Rev., within ornamented octagonal border,

لله

العزة

صفهان

ضر دار ا ا

لسلطنه

ب

(One ا superfluous, l. 4.)

Pl. XIII. AV ·85, Wt. 95·1

459

Láhíján, 1213.

Obv. as (458).

Rev., within circle, arched above,

لله

العزة

لاهیجان

ب

ضر

AV ·8, Wt. 91·

460

Yazd, 1214.

Obv. similar to (458), with same date, ۱۲۱۳, 1213 (die of previous year).

Rev., within ornamented octagonal border,

لله
العزة
يـزد ر
ده د
الـعـباا
ضـرب
۱۲۱۴

(i.e. ضرب دار العباده يزد)

AV ·9, Wt. 94·0

461

Iṣfahán, date obliterated.

Obv. similar to (458).

Rev. inscription similar to (458) without superfluous ا: plain border, upper part of circle arched.

AV ·8, Wt. 94·4

462

Ṭeherán, date obliterated.

Obv. similar to (458), but date not legible.

Rev.

لله
العزة
دار طهران
بـــــــ
لسلطنـه ا
ضر

(العزة لله in leaf-border.)

AV ·85, Wt. 95·4

463

Tabríz, 1220.

Obv.

شاه قاجار
فتحعلی
السلطا السلطا
ا
ن بن ن

Rev.

دار السلطنه
ب
ضر تبریز
سنة ۱۲۲۰

AV ·7, Wt. 36·9

464

Iṣfahán, 1222.

Obv.

شاه قاجار
فتحعلی
السلطا لسلطا
ا ا
ن بن ن

(On either side, scroll.)

Rev.

اصفهان
السلطنه
ضر دار
ب
۱۲۲۲

(Around, four scrolls.)

AV 1·, Wt. 70·2

465

Tabríz, 1224.

Obv. similar to (464); no scrolls.

Rev. as (463); date سنة ۱۲۲۴

AV ·75, Wt. 34·9

466

Tabríz, 1225.

Similar; date سنة ۱۲۲۵

AV ·7, Wt. 42·1

467

Káshán, 1227.

Obv. similar to (464).

Rev. كاشان
دار المومنين
ضرب
۱۲۲۷

AV ·8, Wt. 54·8

468

Iṣfahán, 1228.

Similar to (461), but obv.

السلطا اسلطا
ا
ن بن ن

Rev., Scroll above only; date ۱۲۲۸

AV ·95, Wt. 74·2

X

469

Tabríz, 1228.

Similar to (463), but rev. سنة ١٢٢٨

AV ·7, Wt. 37·3

470

Shíráz, 1228.

Obv. similar to (464).

Rev.

شيراز
لعلم
دار ا
ضرب
١٢٢٨

Above, scroll.

AV ·9, Wt. 73·5

471

Khoï, 1232.

Obv. similar to (467).

Rev., within border, surrounded by eight fleurons,

ب
ضر خوى
سنة ١٢٣٢

AV ·85, Wt. 70·4

472

Khoï, 1234.

Similar, date ١٢٣٤

AV ·95, Wt. 70·5

473

Kermánsháhán, 1234.

Obv. similar.

Rev.

ن ن
شــهــا
دار الدوله كرما
ــــــــــــــ
۱۲۳۴
ضر ســنة

N ·95, Wt. 71·5

474

Yazd, 1234.

Obv. similar.

Rev.

يزد
العــبـــا
ضر دار دهٔ
ــــــ
۱۲۰۳۴

Around, four scrolls.

N 1·05, Wt. 70·8

475

Tabríz, 1236.

Similar to (465), but ۱۲۳ سـنة

N ·9, Wt. 70·9

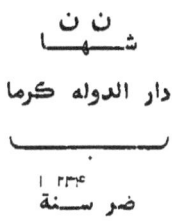

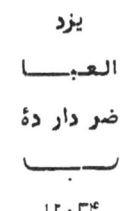

476

Zenján, 1236.

Obv. The Sháh crowned and armed with lance and sabre, on horse at full gallop l.; behind, in arabesque border,

شاه

فتحعلی

سلطان

beneath, laurel-branches.

Rev. زنجان

دار السعاده

ضرب

۱۲۳۶

Pl. XIII. *N* ·9, Wt. 70·7

477

Zenján, 1239.

Obv. Similar type r., Sháh armed with lance; behind, in arabesque border,

شاه

فتحعلی

السلطا

ن

Rev. similar; date ۱۲۳۹

Pl. XIV. *N* 1·2, Wt. 211·8

478

Ṭeherán, 1242.

Obv. شه
سكه فتحعلى
خسرو صاحبقران

Rev. طهران
لخلافه
ضر دار ا
ب
١٢٤٢

AV ·85, Wt. 70·6

479

Tabríz, 1244.

Obv. similar ; arrangement of words varied.

Rev. similar to (463), but سنة ١٢ ٤ ٤

PL. XIV. AV ·8, Wt. 70·9

480

Same mint and date.

Similar, but rev. سنة ١ ٢٤ ٤

AV ·85, Wt. 71·5

481

Ḳazvín, 1246.

Obv. شه
سكه فتحعلى
كشور ستان
خسرو

Rev.

لسلطنة
دار ا
ب
ضر قزوين
۱۲ ۴ ۶
سنة

N ·75, Wt. 53·5

482

Hamadán, 1246.

Obv. similar.

Rev., within circle, surrounded by scrolls,

همذان
طيبه
ضر بلده
ب
۱۲۴۶

N ·8, Wt. 52·9

483

Kermán, 1248.

Obv. similar; arrangement of words varied.

Rev., within double border, around which four pyramids of dots,

دار الا كر
ما ما
ضر ن ن
ب
۱۲۴۸

(Legend reads ضرب دار الامان كرمان)

N ·7, Wt. 52·9

484

Iṣfahán, 1249.

Obv. The Sháh crowned and armed with sabre, seated on throne, facing, towards l.; to l., in arabesque border,

شاه
فتحعلی
۱۲۴۸

(Die of year preceding.)

Rev., within ornamented label, above and below which, arabesque scrolls,

دار السلطنه اصفهان
ضرب ۱۲۴۹

Pl. XIV. AV ·85, Wt. 63·2

485

Ṭeherán, 1249.

Obv. similar to (481).

Rev. طهران
الخلافه
ضرب دار ۱۲۴۹

Pl. XIV. AV ·75, Wt. 53·1

486

Resht, 1250.

Obv. similar.

Rev. رشت
ضرب دار المرز
۱۲۵۰

AV ·7, Wt. 53·1

487

Hamadán, 1250.

Obv. similar to (481).

Rev. similar to (482); date ١٢٥٠

AV ·75, Wt. 53·

SILVER.

488

Iṣfahán, 1213.

Obv. similar to (458), date ١٢١٣

Rev. similar to (461), upper part of circle arched.

Pl. XIV. *AR* ·9, Wt. 160·

489

Ṭeherán, 1213.

Obv. similar.

Rev.

لله
العزة
طهران
ضر دار
السلطنه
ب

Ringed. *AR* ·75, Wt. 26·

490

Shíráz, 1214.

Obv. similar to (458); date ١٢١٤

Rev., within octagonal border,

شيراز
دار العلم
ضرب

Pl. XIV. *AR* ·85, Wt. 158·6

491

Ganja, 1214.

Obv., within double border, surrounded by pyramids of dots,

لا اله الا الله

محـــــــمد

رسول الله علی و

لی الله

Rev. گنجه

ـــــــ

ضرب ۱۲۱۴

Pl. XIV. AR 1·05, Wt. 231·4

492

Yazd, 1214.

Obv. similar to (490), date ۱۲۱۴

Rev., within dotted border of many foils, arched above,

العزة لله

دار يـــــزد

الــعبــا

ـــــــ

ضرب ده

AR 1·1, Wt. 160·3

493

Same mint and date.

Same as (460); same dies.

PL. XIV. AR ·95, Wt. 159·9

494

Shíráz, 1215.

Obv. similar to (458); date ١٢١٥

Rev., within border arched above,

[لله]

العزة

شـيـــر

دار از

بـــــب

العـــلم

ضر

AR 1·06, Wt. 159·1

495

Ṭeherán, 1215.

Obv. similar; date ١٢١٥

Rev., within border arched above, similar to (489).

AR ·95, Wt. 161·5

496

Eriván, 1216.

Obv. similar to (458); no date legible.

Rev., within square,

وان
ب
ضرايز

Margin in segments; above, العزة لله; beneath, ١٢١٥; on sides, scrolls.

AR ·95, Wt. 158·9

497

Yazd, 1216.

Obv. similar; no date legible.

Rev., within square,

ر يزد
ب
ضـر ده
دا لعبا

Margin similar; date ١٢١٥

AR ·1, Wt. 154·3

498

Tabríz, 1217.

Obv. similar; no date legible.

Rev., within square,

تبريز ر
ب
ضـــر دا
السلطنه

Around in four arched borders, above, العزة لله, and ١٢١٧ thrice.

AR ·95, Wt. 159·0

499

Tabríz, 1221.

Similar to (465); but obv., scroll on either side; rev. ends

١٢ ٢١
سـنة

PL. XIV. Æ 1·, Wt. 159·

500

Resht, 1222.

Obv. similar to (458), with date ١٢٢١ of year preceding.

Rev.

شـت
دار الـمـرز ر
ب
ضـر ١٢٢٢

Æ ·75, Wt. 78·

501

Mesh-hed, 1222.

Obv.

شاه قاجا[ر]
فتحعلى
١٢ ٢٢
[ا]لسلطا السلط[ا]
ن بن ن

Rev.

مقدس
مشهد
ضرب
١٢٢٢

Æ ·9, Wt. 158·0

502

Iṣfahán, 1223.

Obv. شاه قاجار
فتحعلى
السلطا لسلطا
ا ا
ن بن ن

Rev. ن
صفها
ا
لسلطنه
دار ا ۱۲۲۳
ضرب

AR ·8, Wt. 20·2

503

Kermánsháhán, 1223.

Obv. similar to (464).

Rev. ن
بلده كرمانشاها
ضرب
۱۲۲۳

AR 1·, Wt. 160·7

504

Kermán, 1224.

Obv. similar to (468).

Rev. كر ۱۲۲۴
ضر
ما

(ضر and ما in ligature.)

AR ·65, Wt. 37·3

505

Iṣfahán, 1225.

Similar to (502) ; date ١٢٢٥

AR ·7, Wt. 19·9

506

Same mint and date.

Obv. similar to (464).

Rev.
صفهان
السلطنه
دار ١٢٢٥
ضرب

AR ·7, Wt. 19·8

507

Tabríz, 1225.

Same as (466) ; obv. copied ; rev. same die.

AR ·7, Wt. 38·7

508

Eriván, 1226.

Obv. as (463), but perhaps بن for ابن as (513).

Rev.
ايروان
ضرب
ضر حجور سعد
ء
١٢٢

Outside border, ornaments.

AR ·7, Wt. 28·6

509

Iṣfahán, 1226.

Obv. as (463), but لسلطا لسلطا
ان بن ن ا

Rev. صفهان
السلطنه
دار ۱۲۲۶
ضرب

AR ·7, Wt. 20·

510

Same mint and date.

Obv. similar to (502).

Rev. similar to last.

AR ·75, Wt. 19·9

511

Same mint and date.

Obv. same die.

Rev. صفهان
السلطنه
دار ۱۲۲۶
ضرب

(ا superfluous).

AR ·7, Wt. 19·8

512

Same mint and date.

Similar; rev. same die.

[I.O.C.] AR ·75, Wt. 19·8

513

Khoï, 1226.

Obv. similar to (463), but

السلطا السلطا

ن بن ن

Rev.

ب

ضر خوى

١٢٢٦

سنة

AR ·75, Wt. 18·4

514

Ḳazvín, 1226.

Obv. similar to (463), but

لسلطا لسلطا

ان بن ن

Rev.

قزوين

دا لسلط[نه]

را

ضرب

١٢٢٦

AR ·75, Wt. 18·7

515

Shiráz, 1227.

Obv. similar to (463), but

السلطا السلطا

ن بن ن

Rev.

شيراز

لعلم

دارا

ضرب

١٢٢٧

AR ·9, Wt. 19·5

516

Mesh-hed, 1230?

Obv. similar to (463), but

لسلطا لسلـ[طا]
ا ا
ن بن ن

on either side, scroll.

Rev., within ornamented border, as (501); but ضرب
١٢ ٣

AR ·8, Wt. 160·4

516*a*

Kermánsháhán, 1231.

Obv. similar to (163), but

لسلطا لسلطا
ا ا
ن بن ن

Rev.

ن
نشـــا
بلده كرما ها
ضرب
١٢٣١

(Formerly plated?)

Æ ·7, Wt. 59·7

517

Asterábád, 1232.

Obv. similar to (464).

Rev.

استرابـاد
مـنـين
دار المو
ضرب
١٢٣٢

AR 1·05, Wt. 110·5

518

Kermánsháhán, 1232.

Obv. similar to (517).

Rev.

ما ها
ن ن
شـــــا
دار الدوله كر
ب
١٢٣٢
ضـــر بـــنة

Æ 1·, Wt. 141·7

519

Yazd, 1232.

Similar to (474); date ١٢٣٢

Æ 1·, Wt. 141·2

520

Same mint and date.

Similar to (474); outside rev. border, dots; date ١٢٠٣٢

Pierced. Æ ·6, Wt. 29·

521

Kazvín, 1233.

Obv. similar to (464).

Rev. similar to (514): outside border, scrolls; date ١٢٣٣

Æ ·9, Wt. 140·4

522

Mesh-hed, 1234.

Obv. similar to (516).

Rev.

اقـــدس
ب
ارض ١٢٣٤
ضر

Æ 1·, Wt. 138·3

523

Ṭcherán, 1235.

Obv. similar to (464).

Rev. طـهـران
لخـلافـه
ضـر دار ا
ب
١٢٣٥

AR ·9, Wt. 141·2

524

Tabríz, 1238.

Similar to (465); date ١٢٣٨

AR 1·, Wt. 141·9

525

Hamadán, 1240 ?

Obv. شه
سـكه فـتحعلى
خسرو صاحبقران

Rev. هـمـذان
بلده طيبهٔ
ضرب
١٢٤

Pl. XIV. AR ·85, Wt. 106·2

526

Iṣfahán, 1241.

Obv. similar.

Rev. لسلطنـه
دار ا
ضرب
صفـهان
١٢٤١ ا

AR ·85, Wt. 105·

527

Zenján, 1241.

Obv. similar to (525).

Rev. similar to (476); date ١٢٤١

AR ·9, Wt. 105·

528

Kashán, 1241.

Obv. similar.

Rev.

كاشان
مغين
دار المو
ضرب
١٢٤١

AR ·85, Wt. 105·6

529

Kermánsháhán, 1241.

Obv. similar to (525).

Rev.

نشهان
دار الدوله كرما
ضرب
١٢٤١

AR ·8, Wt. 101·1

530

Kermánsháhán, 1242.

Similar, but date ١٢٤٢

AR ·85, Wt. 101·1

531

Hamadán, 1244.

Obv. similar to (525).

Rev., within ornamented border, similar to (482); date ١٢٤٤

AR ·85, Wt. 106·5

532

Yazd, 1244.

Obv. similar to (525).

Rev.

يزد
ب
دار ا ده
١٢٤٤
لعبا
ضر

AR ·8, Wt. 103·5

533

Tabríz, 1245.

Obv. similar to (525).

Rev. similar to (465); date ١٢٤٥ سنة

AR ·75, Wt. 106·4

534

Hamadán, 1245.

Similar to (531); date ١٢٤٥

AR ·8, Wt. 104·6

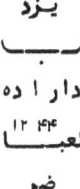

535

Yazd, 1245.

Similar to (532); date ١٢٤٥.

AR ·8, Wt. 109·2

536

Shíráz, 1246.

Obv. similar to (525).

Rev. شيراز
العلم
ضر دار ا
ب
١٢٤٦

AR ·85, Wt. 104·9

537

Yazd, 1247.

Obv. similar to (525).

Rev. يزد
العبا
ضر دار ا ده
ب
١٢٠٤٧

AR ·8, Wt. 106·7

538

Yazd, 1248.

Similar; pyramid of dots in rev. border above; date ١٢٠٤٨

AR ·75, Wt. 102·2

539

Same mint and date.

Similar; but rev. within ornamented border.

Æ ·75, Wt. 104·6

540

Kermán, 1249 ?

Obv. similar to (481).

Rev. ضر کرمان

١٢٤٩ (?)

(unit of date doubtful, possibly ٥)

Æ ·75, Wt. 30·3

541

Yazd, date off field (early in reign).

Obv. similar to (492).

Rev., within wreath of single leaves,

العز[ة] لله

دار یــزد

الـعـبـا

ضر ه د

(دار العباده یزد)

[I.O.C.] Æ ·85, Wt. 158·8

542—544.

Pattern; no mint or date.

Obv. شــاه قاجـار

فـتـحـعـلـى

الســلطا لسلطا

ا ا

ن بن ن

Rev. Shield, arms of Persia; lion couchant gardant; behind him, sun, rayed; supporters, lion rampant and wyvern, collared; crest, plumed crown; on riband beneath, motto اسد الغالب

الله

beneath, B (Bain, die-engraver).

Pl. XIV. *Milled.* Bil. ·85, Wt. 79·7
Milled. Bil. ·85, Wt. 70·2
Milled. Bil. ·85, Wt. 74·2

MUḤAMMAD SHÁH.

A.H. 1250—1261=A.D. 1835—1848.

MOTTO.

شاهنشه انبیآ محمد

GOLD.

545

Resht, 1255.

Obv., within border, surrounded by arches,

ا محمد
نبـــیا
شاهنشه

Rev. as obv.,

المرز ر
شــت
ضرب دار
١٢٥٥

I.O.C.] $\mathcal{N}$ ·7, Wt. 53·1

546

Resht, 1262.

Obv., within border, surrounded by wreath; similar.

Rev. similar; but within arches, above, below, and on each side, شاه, date ضرب دار ١٢٦٢

$\mathcal{N}$ ·76, Wt. 53·

547

Tehrán, 1262.

Obv. Lion l., sabre in r. fore-paw; behind, sun; above, plumed crown; all within laurel-wreath.

Rev., within square, around which, scrolls,

شاهنشه انبيا محمد

ضرب دار لخلافه طهران

۱ ۱ ۲۶۲

(between lines of inscription, ornament.)

Pl. XV. AV ·8, Wt. 52·9

SILVER.

548

Tehrán, 1250.

Obv. similar to (545); broad plain border.

Rev.

طهران

لخلا

دار ا فه

ضرب

۱۲ ۵

Pl. XV. AR ·55, Wt. 22·3

549

El-Mesh-hed, 1251.

Obv. similar; around, scrolls.

Rev.; around, scrolls,

المقدس

ب

۱۲۵۱

ضرا فی امشهد

AR ·85, Wt. 105·3

550

Same mint and date.

Obv. similar ; above border, quatrefoil only.

Rev. similar ; around, stars.

Æ ·8, Wt. 107·

551

Yazd, 1251.

Obv.

محمد

نبـــــــيا

شاهنشه

Rev.

يزد

لعبـــــــا

ضرب دار العبادهٔ

۱۲۵۱

Æ ·75, Wt. 89·8

552

Tabríz, 1252.

Obv. as (545) ; around, wreath.

Rev

لسلط[نه]

دار ا

ضرب تبريز

۱۲ ۵۲

سـ[نـة]

Æ ·75, Wt. 89·1

553

Shíráz, 1252.

Obv. similar to (545); border of dots.

Rev.

شـــيـــراز
لـعـــلـم
ضـر دار ا
ب
١٢٥٢

AR ·5, Wt. 9·5

554

Kermánsháhán, 1252.

Obv. as (549).

Rev. within circle, in square, around which, scrolls,

نشـــهـــان
دار الدوله كرما
ضـرب
١٢ ٥٢

AR ·75, Wt. 88·5

555

Same mint and date.

Similar; no scrolls around obv.; date ضرب ١٢٥٢

AR ·75, Wt. 88·

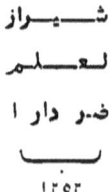

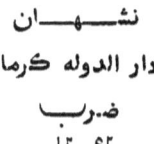

556

Kermánsháhán, 1253.

Obv. similar.

Rev., within double circle,

۱۲۵۳
نشـــهـــان
دار الدوله کرما
ضرب
۱۲ ۵۳

Pierced. Æ ·55, Wt. 10·9

557

Yazd, 1253.

Obv. similar to (545), rev. similar to (551), date ۱۲ ۵۳; around obv. and rev. four pyramids of dots.

Æ ·75, Wt. 89·7

558

Shíráz, 1254.

Obv. within border, around which, pyramids of dots, similar.

Rev. as obv., دار العلم
۱۲۵۴
ضرب
شـــيـراز

Æ ·75, Wt. 88·0

559

Resht, 1255.

Obv. as (549).

Rev., within ornamented octagonal arabesque border,

شـــت
دار المرز ر
ضرب
۱۲ ۵۵

560

Ṭeherán, 1255.

Obv. similar.

Rev.

طهرن فه
الخلا
دار
ضرب
١٢٥ ٥

AR ·7, Wt. 84·

561

Ṭaberistán, 1257.

Obv.; around, scrolls,

انبيا
محمد
شاهنشه

Rev.; around, scrolls,

طبرستان
دار
الملك
١٢٥٧
ضرب

AR ·8, Wt. 83·8

562

Ṭeherán, 1258.

Obv. similar to (547).

Rev. similar to (547), varied; date at foot, ١٢ ٥٨

PL. XV. AR ·75, Wt. 79·8

563

Mesh-hed, 1258.

Obv. similar to (549).

Rev. as obv., مقدس
مشهد
ضرب
١٢٥٨

Pl. XV. Æ ·75, Wt. 83·4

564

Ṭeherán, 1259.

Obv. similar to (547).

Rev. similar to (547), varied; date ضرب ١٢٥٩

Æ ·76, Wt. 92·

565

Mesh-hed, 1260.

Similar to (563); but both obv. and rev. border surrounded by arches; date ضرب ١٢٠

Æ ·75, Wt. 83·5

566

Ṭeherán, 1261.

Similar to (547); date ضرب ١٢٦١

Æ ·9, Wt. 93 1

567

Ṭeherán, 126x.

Similar; varied; date ١٢٦

Æ ·75 Wt. 8

568

Ṭeherán, 1262.

Similar to (567); varied, ضـرب
١ ٢٦٢

AR ·75, Wt. 83·

569

Tabríz, 1263.

Obv. similar to (552); border surrounded by arches.

Rev. as obv., سلطنه
دار ا
ب
ضر تبريز
١ ٢ ٦ ٣
سـنة

AR ·75, Wt. 82·

570

Ṭeherán, 1263.

Similar to (566); date ١٢ ضرب ٦٣

AR ·9, Wt. 165·1

571

Similar obv.; star, in field r.; ornament dividing rev. varied.

AR ·75, Wt. 83·2

572

Mesh-hed, 1263.

Similar to (565); date ١٢٦ ٣

AR ·8, Wt. 82·6

573

Iṣfahán, date obliterated.

Obv. similar; border plain.

Rev. صفهان
السلطنه
ضر دار
ب

Æ ·45, Wt. 10·6

574

Shíráz, date obliterated.

Similar to (553); wreath-borders.

Æ ·55, Wt. 10·1

575

Kermánsháhán, 12*xx*.

Obv. similar to (561).

Rev. similar to (554), ضرب ۱۲ no square.

Æ ·7, Wt. 82·9

COPPER.

576

Irán, 126*x*.

Obv.: Lion recumbent l., head facing; behind, sun; above, star; beneath, ۱۲۷۲ سنة; around, wreath.

Rev. فلوس رايج
ممالک
محمد شه و ايران

Obv. restruck by Náṣir-ed-dín, 1272.

Pl. XV. *Serrated edge.* Æ ·05

REBELLION OF ḤASAN KHÁN SÁLÁR.

A.H. 1264—1266=A.D. 1848—1850.

GOLD.

577

Mesh-hed, 1265.

Obv., within border surrounded by arches,

ا محمد
نبيا
شاهنشه
١٢٦٥

Rev., as obv.,

مقدس
مشهد
ضرب
١٢٦٥

Pl. XV. AV ·7, Wt. 52·8

NÁṢIR-ED-DIN.

A.H. 1264=A.D. 1848 (*Regnant*).

GOLD.

578

Resht, 1265.

Obv.

ناصر الدين شاه قاجار
لسلطا لسلطا
ا ا ا
ن بن ن

Rev.; around, fleurons,

شت
دار المرز ر
ضرب
١٢ ٦٥
سنة

AV ·75, Wt. 53·3

579

Resht, 1266.

Obv. similar.

Rev., within ornamented eightfoil,

لمرز ر (*sic*)
شت
دار
ضرب
١٢ ٦ ٦

AV ·8, Wt. 54·

580

Ṭeherán, 1268.

Obv.

قاجار

ناصر الدين شاه

لسلطا لسلطا

ن ابن ان

Rev.

طهران

لخلافه

دارا

ضرب

۱۲۶۸

PL. XV. AV ·7, Wt. 26·6

581

Mesh-hed, 1268.

Obv.

ناصر الدين شاه قاجار

لسلطا لسلطا

ان بن ان

Rev., within square border, around which, scrolls,

مقدس

مشهد

ضرب

۱۲۶۸

PL. XV. AV ·8, Wt. 52·9

582

Iṣfahán, 1273.

Obv. ناصر الدين شاه قاجار
لسلطا لسلطا
ان بن ن ا

Rev. لسلطنه ١٢٧٣
دار ن
صفهـا
ا
ضرب

AV ·6, Wt. 20·7

583

Ṭabaristán, 1273.

Obv. similar to (578), but wreath-border.

Rev., within pattern of eight points,

طبرستان
لملك
دارا
ضرب
١٢٧٣

PL. XV. AV ·8, Wt. 53·6

584

Tabríz, 1275.

Obv. similar to (582) ; but بن for بن

Rev. لسلطنه
دار ا
ب
ضر تبريز
سنة
١٢٧٥

AV ·6, Wt. 27·4

585

Sarakhs, 1276.

Obv. similar to (578).

Rev., within pattern of eight points,

يه
ناصر خس سر
سلام
نصرة الا ا
ضرب ا
۲۷۶

(ا superfluous.)

~~Pl. XV.~~ AV ·7, Wt. 27·3

586

Ṭeherán, 1277.

Obv. similar to (578).

Rev.

طهران
الخلافه
ضر دار
۷۷ ب ۱۲

AV ·75, Wt. 53·1

587

Mesh-hed, 1279.

Obv., within square, around which, scrolls; similar to (578).

Rev., within pattern of eight points, in circle surrounded by laurel-wreath; similar to (581), date ضرب
۱۲ ۷۹

AV ·7, Wt. 26·1

588

Mesh-hed, 1281.

Obv., within laurel-wreath, Tughrá of

السلطان ناصر الدين شاه قاجار

above, star; to r. spray.

Rev., within laurel-wreath,

الرضا ع
مشهد
السلام
عليه في
ضرب
١٢ ٨١

Above, star.

PL. XV. AV ·95, Wt. 107·

589

Ṭabaristán, 1282.

Obv., within square; similar to (578).

Rev., within square, around which, scrolls; similar to (583),

date ضرب ١٢ ٨٢

AV ·55, Wt. 26·

590

Resht, 1283.

Obv. similar to (578).

Rev., with scrolls around border,

المرزر
شت
ضر دار
١٢ ب ٨٣

Clipped. AV ·6, Wt. 10·1

591

Ṭeherán, 1294.

Obv. as (578).

Rev. as (586); but ضرب
١٢٩ ۴

Pierced. AV ·7, Wt. 10·

592

Ṭeherán, 12xx.

Obv. Bust of Sháh l., wearing cap with aigrette; in field r. and l., within ornamented borders,

شاه ان
ناصر الدين لسلطا
١٢۶۴

beneath, two laurel-branches.

Rev., within laurel-wreath, above which lion recumbent l., and sun; similar to (586), but ضرب دار
١٢

(1264, julús-year.)

AV ·75, Wt. 52·

New Coinage.

593, 594

Ṭeherán, 1295.

Obv., within wreath of laurel and oak, lion l. holding sabre in r. fore-paw; behind, sun; above, plumed crown; below all, ١٢٩٥

Rev., within wreath, as obv.,

شاه قاجار
ناصر الدين
السلطان

beneath all, طهران

AV ·45, Wt. 9·
Same die. AV ·45, Wt. 9·

595

Ṭeherán, 1296.

Obv. similar; beneath lion, پنجهزار : beneath all, ۱۲۹۶

Rev. similar.

PL. XV. AV ·65, Wt. 22·2

596

Ṭeherán, 1297.

Ten-Túmán-Piece.

Obv. Bust of Sháh, three-quarter face l., wearing cap with aigrette.

Rev.

طهران

فخر ناصر الدين شاه قاجار

الاعظم والخاقان الا

۱۲ ۹
السلطان ۷

ده تومان

around, border of flowers and pellets, within which, mint.

PL. XVI. AV 1·4, Wt. 443·

597

Ṭeherán, 1297.

Obv. similar; but inscriptions around,

ضرب ايران در سنة ۱۲۹۷ جلوس سلطنت در سنة ۱۲۹۴

Rev. similar to (593)

(Julus-year should be ۱۲۶۴)

Milled. AV ·75, Wt. 44·2

598

Same mint and date.

Similar to (597); but obv. inscr. ١٢ ٩٧ only.

Milled. AV ·66, Wt. 22·2

599

Ṭeherán, no date.

Similar; but obv. no inscr.

Pl. XVI. *Milled.* AV ·75, Wt. 49·6

600

One-sided Nauróz piece.

ناصر الدين [شاه قا]جار

لـسـلـطا لـسـلـطـا

ا ا ا

ن بن ن

AV ·7, Wt. 9·

SILVER.

601

Tabríz, 1265.

Obv. ناصر الدين قاجار

شـــــــاه

السـلـطا السـلطا

ان بن ن

Rev. similar to (584); but date ٥ ٦ ١٢ سـنـة

Pl. XVI. AR ·65, Wt. 21·1

602

Ṭabaristán, 1265.

Obv. قاجار
ناصر الدين شاه
لسلطا لسلطا
ا ا
ن بن ن

Rev., within border of branches and flowers,

طبرستان
۱۲ ۶۵
لملک
ضر دار ا
ب

around, ornaments.

AR ·8, Wt. 84·4

603

Ṭeherán, 1265.

Obv. similar; but لسلطا لسلطا
ا ا ا
ن بن ن

Rev. طهران ۶
الخلافه
ضر دار ۱۲ ۶۵
ب

Pl. XVI. AR ·75, Wt. 70·2

604

Same mint and date.

Obv. similar.

Rev. ا
طهرن
الخلافه
دار ۱۲۶۵
ضرب

AR ·75, Wt. 82·4

605

Khoï, 1266.

Obv. ناصر الدين شاه قاجار

لسلطا لسلطا

ا
ان بن ن

Rev., within wreath-border,

خوى

ضر دار لصفا

ب

١٢٦٦

Ringed. Æ ·8, Wt. 83·5

606

Asterábád, 1272.

Obv., within ornamented lozenge of four compartments,

قاجار

ناصرلد شاه
ا ين

ن
السلطا

around, laurel-wreath.

Rev., within border of many foils pointed above,

باد

استرا

منين

دار المو

ضرب

around, laurel-wreath; above, ١٢ ٧٢

Æ ·8, Wt. 80·2

607

Ṭeherán, 1272.

Similar to (592); but obv. in r. border لسلطان / ١٢١٤, rev. لخلافه ا ;

date below ١٢ ٧٢

Æ ·6, Wt. 37·5

608, 609

Ṭeherán, 1273.

Similar; but obv. r. border, ١ of date serves for ا of السلطان ;

rev. similar to (592); date ١٢ ٧٣

Æ ·65, Wt. 37·7

Rev. same die. Æ ·65, Wt. 37·8

610

Ḳazvín, 1273.

Obv. similar to (601); but

لسلطا لسلطا

ا ا ا

ن بن ن

Rev., within square, ornaments in segments outside,

قـــزويـــن

لـسلـطـنـه

ضر ا دار

١٢ب ٧٣

Æ ·65, Wt. 82·8

611

Iṣfahán, 1274.

Obv. Within wreath-border, the Sháh seated facing, towards l., crowned and holding sabre; above, and in leaf-borders, on either side,

شا ه

ن ین
سلطا ناصرالد

beneath, branches.

Rev., within wreath-border,

لسلطنه
دار ن
صفها
ضارب
۱۲ ۷۴

AR ·65, Wt. 20·3

612

Ṭehrán, 1274.

Similar to (608); date ۱۲۷۴

AR ·6, Wt. 38·8

613

Same mint and date.

Similar; but rev. ۴ in ن of طهران

AR ·55, Wt. 39·

614

Ḳazvín, 1274.

Obv. similar to (608).

Rev., within laurel-wreath, similar to (610); date ۱۲ ۷۴

AR ·6, Wt. 38·

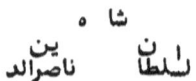

615

Káshán, 1274.

Obv. similar to (578).

Rev.

كاشان
منين
دار المو
ضرب
٧ ۴

AR ·55, Wt. 30

616

Ṭeherán, 1275.

Similar to (586) ; date ١٢ ٧٥

AR ·6, Wt. 38·

617

Similar ; varied.

AR ·6, Wt. 37·7

618

Kermánsháhán, 1275.

Obv. similar ; date at foot, ١٢٧٥

Rev., within laurel-wreath,

مان
نشهـــــا
ضر كر دار لدوله
١٢ ٧٥
ب

(i.e. ضرب دار الدوله كرمانشهان)

AR ·6, Wt. 38·2

619

Asterábád, 1276.

Obv., within three oblong labels,

شاه قاجار
نا
لسلطا صر الد
ابن ن ين
السلطان

Rev., within square, around which, ornaments,

المو استراباد
منـــــين
دار
ضرب
١٢٧٦

Pierced. AR ·65, Wt. 37·6

620

Iṣfahán, 1276.

Obv. شاه ناصر الدين قاجار
لسلطا لسلطا
ان بن نا

Rev., within square, around which, scrolls,

دار ا
لسلطنه
ضرب
صفهان
١٢ ٧٦ ا

AR ·55, Wt. 37·5

621

Ṭeherán, 1276.

Similar to (608); date ١٢ ٧٦

AR ·65, Wt. 38·

622

Ṭeherán, 1277.

Similar; but obv. السلطان, rev. date ١٢٧٧
١٢٦٤

AR ·6, Wt. 38·2

623

Yazd, 1277.

Obv. similar to (601), but

لسلطا لسلطا
ان بن ن[ا]

Rev. يزد
لعبـــــا
ضر دار ا د[ه]
ب
١٢٧٧

AR ·55, Wt. 38·1

624

Mesh-hed, 1278.

Similar to (587); but obv. within wreath; rev. within square, around which, scrolls; date

ضرب
١٢٧٨

AR ·75, Wt. 76·2

625

Mesh-hed, 1279.

Similar; but obv. and rev. in circles, around which, stars; date ضرب
١٢٧٩

AR ·8, Wt. 76·4

626

Resht, 1280?

Similar to (590); but rev. with stars around border, and

ضر دار
ب ۸
۱۲

Æ ·7, Wt. 77

627

Asterábád, 1282.

Obv. similar to (602), within laurel-wreath, but

لسلطا لسلطا
ا ا ا
بن ن ن

Rev., within border of double arches,

استراباد
منـين
دار المو
ضرب
۱۲ ۸۲

Æ ·7, Wt. 61·5

New Coinage.

628

Teherán, 1281.

Obv., within wreath of laurel and oak, lion l., holding sabre with r. fore-paw; behind, sun; above, plumed crown; beneath, دو هزار دينار: beneath all, ۱۲۸۱

Rev., within wreath, as obv.,

شاه قاجار
ناصر الدين
السلطان

beneath, طهران

629

Same mint and date.

Obv. same; but beneath lion, یکهزار دینار

Milled. Æ ·9, Wt. 85·1

630

Same mint and date.

Same; but beneath lion, دینار ۵..

Milled. Æ ·75, Wt. 45·

631

Same mint and date.

Same; but beneath lion, ربعی

Milled. Æ ·5, Wt. 22·9

Old Coinage.

632

Iṣfahán, 1283.

Obv. similar to (578).

Rev. ا ن
صفها
دا ر
السلطنه
۱۲۸۳
ضرب

633

Iṣfahán, 1284.

Obv. شاه

الدين قا

صر ر

نا السلطا

السلطا جا

ن ن ن

(ا throughout written ﺪ)

Rev., within arched border,

ب

دار ا

ضر صفها

لسلطنه

١٢٨٤

ن

AR ·65, Wt. 70·4

634

Kermán, 1284.

Obv. similar to (578).

Rev. ن د ر

كــــــــر

ضـر ن

١٢٨٤

ب

ا ما لا ما ا

(Inscription reads ضرب دار الامان كرمان)

AR ·75, Wt. 75

635

(Mesh-hed), Arẓ-i-ḳuds, 1287.

Obv. Tughrá composed of ناصر الدين شاه قاجار ; beneath, and on either side,

لسلطا بن السلطا
ان ۱۲۸۷ ان

in field right, spray.

Rev. ضر عليه السلام

ارض قدس امام

PL. XVI. AR ·85, Wt. 76·4

636

Ṭeherán, 1288.

Obv. similar to (578),

Rev. similar to (586) ; date ۱۲ ۸۸

AR ·95, Wt. 76·5

637

Same mint and date ?

Similar.

(Unit of date obscure.)

AR ·7, Wt. 19·5

638

Ḳazvín, 12⅞8 ?

Obv., within laurel-wreath, similar to (578) ; inscr. imperfect.

Rev. as obv., similar to (614) ; but ضرب ۸

AR ·55, Wt. 37·1

639

(Ṭeherán) Náṣirí, 1292.

Obv., within laurel-wreath; lion and sun and crown as (628).

Rev. area

ناصری
دار الخلافه
ضرب ۱۲
۹۲

Margin, السلطان بن السلطان ناصر الدین شاه قاجار

AR ·75, Wt. 41·5

New Coinage.

640

Ṭeherán, 1294.

Same as (631); but date ۱۲۹۴

Milled. AR ·6, Wt. 17·

Old Coinage.

641

Ṭeherán, 1295.

Obv. similar to (578).

Rev., within laurel-wreath, with plumed crown above,

طهران فه
الخلا
ضر دار ا
ب
۱۲۹۵

AR ·75, Wt. 76·5

New Coinage.

642

Ṭeherán, 1296.

Same as (628); but date ١٢٩۶

Milled. AR 1·05, Wt. 142·

643

Same mint and date.

Same as (629); but date ١٢٩۶

Milled. AR ·8, Wt. 70·

644

Same mint and date.

Same as (631); but date ١٢٩۶

Milled. AR ·6, Wt. 17·6

Old Coinage.

645

Asterábád, date effaced.

Obv. similar to (580); border ornamented, within it above, سا

Rev.
استراد
با
منين
دار المو
ضرب

(A surfrappe: on rev. is seen two-headed eagle, above which, crown.)

AR ·7, Wt. 76·

COPPER.

New Coinage.

646

Ṭeherán, 1281.

Obv., within wreath of laurel and oak, sun rayed; above, plumed crown; beneath all, ۱۲۸۱

Rev., within wreath with crown, as obv.,

رایج مملکت ایران

۵۰ دینار

beneath wreath, طهران

PL. XVI. Æ 1·2, Wt 154

647

Same mint and date.

Same; but rev. ۲۵ دینار

Æ 1·, Wt. 77·1

648, 649

Ṭeherán, 1295.

Same; but obv. ۴ ۱۲۹۵ ۴; rev. ۵۰ دینار

Æ 1·, Wt. 77·4
Æ 1·, Wt. 75·6

650

Same mint and date.

Same; but rev. ۲۵ دینار

Æ ·8, Wt. 39·3

UNCERTAIN.

SILVER.

651

(Time of Isma'íl I. or Ṭahmasp I.)

No mint or date.

Obv. Mill-sail pattern formed of علی repeated, the ع making a rosette in centre, and each angle enclosing و الله, the لی of ولی being included in علی, (علی ولی الله)

Rev. . . .

اللهم محمد و
علی حسن حسین
جعفر الصادق
. . . م

AR ·45, Wt. 32·

VASSAL KING.

I.—TÍMÚRÍ.

BÁBER.

UNDER ISMA'ÍL I.

Transoxiana, A.H. 917—920=A.D. 1511—1514.

GOLD.

652

Obv. Area, within square formed by prolonged letters of lines in margin, lozenge formed by على repeated,

لاا
له الله
محمد رسو
ل الله على
الله لى
و

Around,
مو
.... سى محمد
حسين على [حسـ]ن على جعفر على حسن على

Margin,
[نـاد علـيا مظهر العجائب]
[تجده عونالك فى النوائب]
كل هم وغم سينجلى
ب[ولايتك يا على يا على يا عل]ى

Rev. نصر من الله و[فتح قریب]

السلطان العادل الكامل

الوا ا ای بو المظفر اسمعیل شاه

...... الصفوی خلد الله

ملکه وسلطانه ضرب . .

[س]لطا[ن] محمد ه

(Obv. الا implied; rev. ا of العادل serves also for that of اسمعیل)

Pl. XVI. *N* ·7, Wt. 51·

AUTONOMOUS COPPER.

IRÁN.

1

1260

Obv. Lion recumbent l., head facing, and sun.

Rev. [ف]لو ایرا
س ن
۶۲

Æ ·9

2

Obv. Same type r.

Rev. ایرا
فلوس ن

Æ ·65

3

1260 ?

Obv. Lion rampant l.

Rev., within ornamented label, scrolls above and below,
فلو ایرا
۱۲
س ن ۶

Æ ·9

See also Tabríz, no. (82).

ABÚ-SHAHR.

a. With name Abú-shahr.

4

1122

Obv. Two lions rampant facing one another, behind each, sun ; beneath all, leaf.

Rev.

شهر
بوا ١١٢٢
ضر

PL. XVII. Æ ·9

5

Obv., within ornamented border, similar : no symbol.

Rev.

شهر
ابو
رايج

Æ 1·

6

1267 ?

Obv. Lion l.

Rev.

شهر
بو
ا رايج
ضر ١٢٦٧

Æ ·9

7

1270

Obv. Lion r.

Rev. شهر
ضر ابو
ب
۱۲۷۰

PL. XVII. Æ ·6

8

1214 ?*

Obv. Sun rayed.

Rev. بوا شهر
ضرب
۱۱۱۴

(Restruck; traces of previous type, obv., peacock (?) l.)

PL. XVII. Æ ·9

9

1239

Obv. Peacock r., around, arabesque.

Rev. ابو شهر
فلوس
۱۲۳۹

PL. XVII. Æ ·9

10

12xx

Obv. Two peacocks, back to back.

Rev. شهر
ابو
ضرب
۱۲

Æ ·9

---

* Conjecturally dated from style.

11

Obv. Ship l.

Rev. شـــهـــر
ضر ابو
بــــب

PL. XVII. Æ ·8

12, 13

Obv. Ornamented label, enclosing quatrefoil.

Rev., within square, ابـو شهر
ضرلـــب

PL. XVII. Æ 1·2 × ·85
Æ 1·15 × ·75

14

Obv. similar.

Rev., within circle, ا شهر
بو ب
ضـــر

Æ 1·15 × ·7

b. With name Bandar-Abú-shahr.

15

Obv. Lion l., looking back.

Rev. بو[ا]
شـــهر
بـنـدر
ضرب

(Restruck.)

Æ 1·1

16

1211 ?

Obv. Lion r.

Rev.

[اب]و شهر

بنــــــدر

فــلــوس

١١

[ضرب]

Æ ·8

17

Obv. Same type.

Rev. similar ; no date legible.

Æ ·8

18

Obv. Same type.

Rev.

بندر

[اب]و شهر

فـلـوس

[را]يـج

Æ ·9

19

1221 ?

Obv. Lion r.: border of pellets.

Rev.

ابو ١٢١ شهر

ضر بـنـدر

ب

Pl. XVII. Æ ·85

20

1221 ?

Obv. Fish l.

Rev. Same; same die.

PL. XVII. Æ ·9

ARDEBÍL.

21

1123

Obv. Peacock r.; around, branches.

Rev. [ا]ردبیل

[فـلو]س
١١٢٣

PL. XVII. Æ ·95

URÚMÍ.

22

1249

Obv. Lion recumbent l., and sun; beneath, ١٢٤٩

Rev. area, ضرب
ارو

Margin, [ف . ل . و] . س . ض . ر . ب

PL. XVIII. Æ 1·

23

Date obscure.

Obv. Dragon coiled r., looking back.

Rev., within ornamented border,

ضر

ب

ا فلوس

رومى

. . .

Pl. XVIII. Æ 1·2

24

122x

Obv. Bird l., wings open: around, ornaments.

Rev.

رومى

فلوس ا

ب

١٢٢

ضر

Pl. XVIII. Æ 1·15

25

Obv. Turtle r.; above, سر; beneath, ضرب

Rev.

س

فلو اروى

Pl. XVIII. Æ ·85

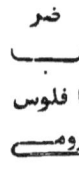

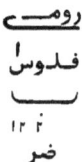

IṢFAHÁN.

26

1120

Obv. Lion r., and sun ; in field, foliage.

Rev.

ن
اصفها
فلوس
ب
ضر ١١٢٠

Pl. XVIII. Æ 1·15

27

Same date.

Similar.

Æ ·95

28

Similar ; date obliterated.

Æ 1·1

29

Similar ; date obliterated.

Æ 1·

30

Obv. Same type as (29), l.

Rev. Similar to (29).

Æ ·95

31

Same type r.

Rev. similar to (26) ; date not visible.

Æ ·7

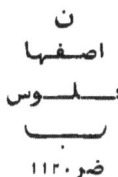

32

1246, 1247

Lion r., and sun; beneath, ١٢٤٧

Rev.

١٢٤٦

اصفها

ب

ضرن

(Restruck on Russian two copek-piece 1813?)

Æ 1·2

33

Obv. Lion seizing stag r.; in field, foliage.

Rev.

ضر

ب

ن

اصفها

فلوس

Pl. XVIII. Æ 1·1

34

Obv. similar.

Rev.

ن

اصفها

فلوس

ب

[ضر]

ERIVÁN.

35

1084

Obv. Lion l., and sun; around, foliage.

Rev. ایـروان
فلـوس
۱۰۸۴
ب
ضر

Æ ·9

36

1120

Similar; rev. order of letters varied; date ۱۱۲۰.

Pl. XVIII. Æ 1·05

37

1160

Obv. Same type; no foliage.

Rev. *
فـــلـــوس
۱۱۶
[ضـــر]ب
[ایر]وان مـو(؟)

Æ ·5

38

Same date.

Same; same die.

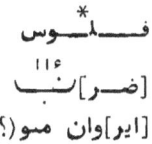

39

1176?

Similar to (38); rev. no star, date ٧٦?

Æ ·8

40

1180

Obv. Same type.

Rev.
ايروان
فلوس
١١٨٠
سب
ضر

PL. XVIII. Æ 1·×·7

41

1187

Obv. Same die.

Rev. Similar; date ١١٨٧

Æ ·9×·65

42

1232

Obv. Same type r.

Rev.
ان و
ضر ير
سب
١٢٣٢

Æ ·9

43

Obv. Similar.

Rev.

ا ا
و ن
ب
ضرير

Struck on coin with types of (45); date ۱۲۴

(Double-struck.)

Æ ·9

44

Obv. Similar.

Rev. Similar.

Æ ·75

45

124x

Obv. Lion recumbent r., and sun.

Rev. Similar; date ۱۲۴

Æ ·9

46

1130

Obv. Sun, rayed.

Rev.

ن
ايروا
فلوس
۱۱۳۰
ب
ضر

Pl. XVIII. Æ ·8

47

1136

Obv. Lion and cub r.; above, foliage.

Rev. Similar to (46), date ١١٣٦ ضرب

PL. XVIII. Æ ·9

48

Same date.

Same; same dies.

Æ ·9

49

1057

Obv. Elephant r.; around, arabesque.

Rev. وان
ایسر ٥٧٠
فلوس
ضرب

PL. XIX. Æ 1·2 × ·85

50

1132

Obv. Elephant l.; above and below, foliage.

Rev. Similar to (46); date ١١٣٢

Æ ·85

51

Obv. Same; same die.

Rev. similar; arrangement of letters varied.

Æ ·9

52

Similar; obv. varied, beyond elephant, tree (?); rev., date obliterated.

Æ ·95

53

1133

Obv. Camel r.; around, foliage.

Rev. similar to (50); but date, ١٣٣

Pl. XIX. Æ ·9

54

Obv. Ibex recumbent; around, foliage.

Rev. Similar to (35), date obscure.

Pl. XIX. Æ ·85

55

1127

Obv. Ape r., in tree, looking back.

Rev.

يــروان

[١]فلوس

١١٢٧

ضــر [ ]

Æ ·8

56

1128

Similar; date ١١٢٨

Pl. XIX. Æ ·95

57

Obv. Hare l.

Rev.

ايـــــر[وا]

[فلـ]وس ن

Pl. XIX. Æ ·8

58

Obv. Cock l.; above, flower; in front, branch.

Rev. Similar to (36); date obliterated.

PL. XIX. Æ ·9

59

١٢٢٤

Obv. Goose r.; around, arabesque.

Rev.

يـــروان
ا ب فلوس
ضر ۴

PL. XIX. Æ ·9

BORUJIRD.

60

No date.

Obv. Bird l. looking back, seated on capital; in field r., flower.

Rev.

و د
بر جر
فلوس

BAGHDÁD.

61

[10]45

Obv. Horse l., bridled; beyond, tree.

Rev. بغدا[د]
فلوس
ب
[ر]خ ۱۰۴۵

Pl. XIX. Æ ·9

62

Obv. Bird l.

Rev. ب
ضرب
بغد[ا]د

Æ ·55

BANDAR-'ABBÁS?

63

Obv. Lion r., and sun.

Rev. بندر
فلوس رايج

Pl. XIX. Æ ·85

64

Obv. Same type.

Rev. Similar; arrangement of letters varied; double-struck.

Æ ·8

BEHBEHÁN.

65

1256

Obv. Lion, looking back, seizing stag, r.

Rev.

ن
بهبها
ضرب
ع ١٢٥

Æ ·85

66

Same date.

Similar, but ٦ for ٢ ; around, scrolls.

Æ ·85

67

Same date.

Obv. Similar.

Rev., within ornamented eight-foil ; same inscr., but ضرب ١٢٥

Æ ·8

68

Same date.

Obv. Similar.

Rev., within eight-pointed border,

ب
ضر ن
بهبها
ع ٢٥

Æ ·9

69

12xx

Similar to (66); date ١٢ only legible.

Æ ·75

70

No date.

Similar; but rev. within double dotted border.

Pl. XIX. Æ ·8

TABRÍZ.

71

1085

Obv. Lion l., and sun.

Rev. تبريز
فلوس
٨٥
ب
ضر

Æ ·9

72

Obv. Same type r.

Rev. Similar, date obliterated.

Æ 1·

73

1126

Similar to (72); date ٢٦

Æ ·8

74

1136

Similar, date ١٣٦

Pl. XX. Æ ·85

75

1171?

Obv. Same type l.

Rev. Similar, date فلوس
١١٧١ (؟)

Æ ·7

76

117*x*

Obv. Same type r.

Rev. Similar, date فلوس ١٧

Æ ·85

77

Obv. Same type l.

Rev. Similar, date not legible.

Æ 1·

78

1224

Obv. Similar.

Rev.
تبريز
ب
ضر
١٢٢٤

79

1230

Obv. Lion recumbent l., and sun.

Rev., within arabesque border,

تبريز

ب

ضر ١٢٣

(Restruck: on rev. traces of former obv. Lion recumbent left.)

Æ 1·05

80

1235

Similar, date ب ضرب ١٢٣٥

Pl. XX. Æ 1·05

81

Same date.

Obv. Similar.

Rev., within quatrefoil, ب

تبريز

ضر

١٢٣٥

Æ ·8

82

1256

Obv. Lion recumbent r., head facing.

Rev. فلوس ایر[ا]ن

ب

ضر تبريز

٢ ٥ ٠

83

1239

Obv. Sun, rayed; wreath border.

Rev., within ornamented label; flower above, branches below,

ضر تبریز
ب
۱۲ ۳۹

Æ 1·

84

Same date.

Similar; rev. branches varied.

Æ 1·

85

Same date.

Similar; rev. branches varied.

Æ 1·

86

1240

Similar; beneath, two leaves; date ۱۲۴

Æ 1·

87

Same date.

Obv. Sun.

Rev., within ornamented label, pointed above.

تبریز
ضر
ب
۲۴

Date outside label.

Æ ·85

88

1095

Obv., within wreath-border, humped bull r.; above, branch.

Rev., within wreath-border,

تبريز
فلوس
١٠٩٥
ب
ضر

Æ ·9

89

Same date.

Obv. Same, same die; rev. similar.

Æ ·85

90

1133

Obv. Same type l.; around, branches.

Rev. Similar; date ١١٣٣

Pl. XX. Æ 1·1 × ·65

91

1134

Obv. Similar, type r.

Rev. Similar; date ١١٣٤

Æ 1·05 × ·55

92

1112

Obv. Humped bull standing on fish r.; around, branches.

Rev.

تبريز
١١١٢
فلوس
ب
ضر

Pl. XX. Æ hexagonal, 1·2

93

1051

Obv. Elephant r.; around, arabesques.

Rev. Similar to (92); date ١٠٩١ ضرب

PL. XX. Æ ·95

94

1081

Obv. Peacock l.; on back, flower.

Rev. Similar; date ١٠٨١

PL. XX. Æ ·9

TIFLÍS.

95

1014

Obv. Lion l.; above, ornaments, degradation of sun; around, arabesque.

Rev. Area, within lozenge, having ornament on each side, lion l.

Margin, ضرب فلوس | تفليس ١٠١٤ |

PL. XX. Æ 1·05

96

Same date.

Obv. Similar.

Rev. Same; same die.

Æ 1·05

97

1075

Obv. Sun, rayed.

Rev. ١٠٧٥
تفليس
فلوس
ضرب

Æ 1·

98

1148

Obv. Lion seizing bull r.

Rev. فلوس
ب
ضر ١١٤٨
تفليس

Æ 1·

99

Same date.

Similar, but ب ١١٤٨ ضر

Æ ·95

TÚÏ.

100

No date.

Obv. Elephant l., harnessed; around, arabesques.

Rev. توی
ب
ضر
فلوس

Pl. XX. Æ ·85

TÍRA?

101

No date.

Obv. Lion l.; around, arabesques.

Rev. Fish r., between ?[تـ]یری and ضرب

Pl. XX. Æ ·75

102

No date.

Obv. Elephant l.; around, arabesques.

Rev. Similar.

Pl. XX. Æ ·9

KHOÏ.

103

1189

Obv. Lion l. and sun; around, ornaments: countermark, star.

Rev.

خوی

فلوس

ضرب

۱۱۸ ۹

ضر

Pl. XXI. Æ 1·

104

1191

Obv. Similar: similar countermark.

Rev. Similar, but date ۱۱ضرب۹۱

Æ 1·

105

1209

Obv. Similar type.

Rev. Similar, date ۹ضرب
۱۲۰

Æ 1·05

106

No date.

Obv. Hare r.; around, arabesque.

Rev., within lozenge, rounded above and below,

ب

ضرب

خو

around, arabesque border.

Pl. XXI. Æ ·8

107

1241

Obv. Within arabesque border, bird l.

Rev., within arabesque border,

خوی

۴۱

۱۲........

ضرب

(Restruck.)

PL. XXI. Æ 1·25

DEMÁVEND.

108

Obv. Lion r., and sun ; around, ornaments.

Rev.

دماوند

ب

ضر

فلوس

PL. XXI. Æ 1

RESHT.

109

1233

Obv. Lion r., looking back.

Rev

ر

شت

۱۲۳۳

ب

ضر

PL. XXI. Æ 1·2

110

Same date.

Similar.

Æ 1·25

111

Obv. Parrot r., head lowered.

Rev.

ر
شت
فلوس
ب
ضر

Pl. XXI. Æ 1·05

RA'NÁSH.

112

1030

Obv. Lion r., and sun.

Rev.

ش
عنا ۱۰۳۰
ر فلوس
ب
[ضر]

Pl. XXI. Æ ·85

113

1034

Similar; date ۱۰۳۴

SÁ-ÚJ BULÁGH.

114

No date.

Obv. Two geese, facing one another.

Rev., within ornamented border,

بلاغ
ساوج
ضرب

PL. XXI. Æ 1·

SHEMÁKHÍ.

115

1117

Obv. Lion l., and sun.

Rev.

شماخی
١١١٧
فلوس
ب
ضر

PL. XXI. Æ ·95

116

1120

Obv. Horse walking l.; around, floral ornaments.

Rev. Similar, but date ب
ضر ١١٢٠

Æ 1·

117

1110

Obv. Peacock l.; around, branches.

Rev. Similar to (115); date ١١١٠.

Æ ·95

118

Same date.

Similar.

Æ 1·1

SHÍRÁZ.

119

1097

Obv. Ibex running r.; around, foliage.

Rev.
ز ا
شـــيـــر
فـــلـــوس
ب
[ضـ]ـر ١٠٩٧

Æ ·95

120

Obv. Similar.

Rev. Effaced.

Æ 1·

ṬEHERÁN.

121

Obv. Lion l., and sun.

Rev.
طـهـران
فـلـوس
[ضـرب]

Æ 1·

122

1143

Obv. Lion seizing stag r.; above stag's head, ط; around, foliage.

Rev.
طهران
١١٤٣
فـلوس
ضـرب

PL. XXI. Æ 1·25

123

1222

Obv. Peacock l.; behind, ١٢٢٢

Rev.
ن
رایج طهرا
١٢٢٢

PL. XXI. Æ ·9

124

Obv. Goose r., wings open.

Rev. Similar to (121).

(Restruck.)

Æ 1·

ḲAZVÍN.

125

1130

Obv. Lion r., and sun.

Rev. ١١٣
فلوس
ب
ضر قزوين

Æ ·95

126

1182

Obv. Same type l.

Rev. قزوين
[فـ]ـلوس
١١٨٢
ب
[ضـ]ـر

Æ 1·05 × ·65

127

Same (same die).

Æ 1· × ·65

128

1..3

Obv. Horse galloping r., and sun; beneath, floral ornament.

Rev. قزوين
فلوس
٣
ب
ضر

Pl. XXII. Æ ·85

129

Obv. Lion l.

Rev. Similar to (125), date obliterated.

(Restruck.)

Æ ·85

130

1114

Obv. Ibex walking l.

Rev. Similar to (126); date ضرب ۱۴

Æ ·9

ḲANDAHÁR.

131

1058

Obv. Lion l, and sun.

Rev. قندهار
فلوس
۱۰۵۸
ضرب

Pl. XXII. Æ ·9

132

Same date.

Similar.

133

1107

Obv. Same type r.

Rev. فلوس

ضرب

قندهار ١١٠٧

Æ ·8

134

1085

Obv. Lion l.

Rev. قندهار

فلوس

١٠٨٥

ضرب

Æ ·95

135

1086

Similar; date ١٠٨٦ ضرب

Æ 1·

136

Same date.

Similar; date ١٠٨٦

Æ 1·2

137

1059

Obv. Lion l., seizing stag r.

Rev. Similar to (136); date ١٠٥٩

Æ 1·05

138

1080

Obv. Horse galloping r.; above, floral ornament.

Rev. Similar; date ١٠٨٠ ب ضر

Pl. XXII. Æ ·9

139

Same date.

Obv. Same type l.; above, floral ornament.

Rev. Similar; date ١٠٨٠ ب ضر

Æ ·9

140

1082

Obv. Camel l.

Rev. Similar; date ١٠٨٢

Pl. XXII. Æ ·9

141

Same date.

Similar.

Æ 1·

142

Same date.

Obv. Same type r.

Rev. Similar.

Æ 1

143

1083

Similar; date ١٠٨٣

Æ ·9

144

Obv. Stag l.; around, floral ornaments.

Rev. فلوس
قندها[ر]

Pl. XXII. Æ ·75

145

Two-dínár-piece.

957

Obv. Antelope running l.; above, سنة ٩٥٧

Rev., within quatrefoil,
ر
قند
ها ر
دو دنا (*sic*)
ضرب

Æ 1·15

146

Same date.

Similar to (145).

Æ 1·2

147

Same date.

Similar.

Æ 1·2

148

Similar; but obv., around, branch; date effaced; rev. دینار and ضرب

Æ 1·1

149

No date.

Obv. Similar type.

Rev., within lozenge,

قند
هـــار
دو دینار
ضر
ب

Æ 1·05

150

No date.

Obv. Peacock l.

Rev.

س
فلو
قندهار

Pl. XXII. Æ 1·05

151

Similar.

Æ 1·05

152

No date.

Obv. Within wreath, two fishes l. and r.; between them, star in circle.

Rev. قند ر
ها
فلوس
ب
[ضر]

Pl. XXII. Æ ·9

153

Similar.

Æ ·9

154

No date.

Obv. Flower.

Rev. ب
ضر
فلوس
قندهار

Across field, sabre r.

Æ 1·

155

1097

Obv. Two-bladed sabre (Zu'l-fiḳár) l.; around, floral ornaments.

Rev. Similar to (152); date, ب ١٠٩٧ [ضر]

Æ 1·1

156

Obv. Same type as no. (155) r.

Rev. Similar; date effaced.

PL. XXII. Æ 1·1

157

Obv. Sabre l.; around, floral ornaments.

Rev. قندهار
فلوس
ضرب

Æ ·7

158

Similar.

Æ ·95

KERMÁNSHÁHÁN.

159

Obv. Lion r.

Rev. ن
ما ها
كر نشا
فلوس
. . .

PL. XXII. Æ ·9

160

1172

Obv. Boar r.? above lion l.

Rev.

ن
کر
ها ..
نشا

١٧٢

PL. XXII. Æ ·55

161

1258

Obv. Elephant l. with rider; in field, ٨٥ ٢١

Rev.

ن
نشها
ضر کرما
ب
١٢٥١

(die of 1251.)

Æ ·9

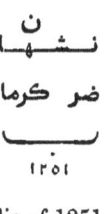

KÁSHÁN.

162

1111 ?

Obv. Lion r., and sun.

Rev.

ن

[ك]اشا

[فلـ]وس

١١١

ضـ[ر]

Æ ·9

163

1132

Similar; date ١١٣٢

ضر

Æ 1·

164

1137

Obv. Similar.

Rev.

ن

كاشـ[ـا]

فلوس

ضر

Æ ·9

165

1160 ?

Obv. Similar.

Rev.

س
فلو
كاشان
ب
ضر[ب] ١١٦٠

Æ ·95

166

Obv. Sun, rayed.

Rev. Similar to (162); date effaced.

Pl. XXIII. Æ ·9

167

Obv. Peacock l.

Rev. Similar; date effaced.

Pl. XXIII. Æ 1·05

GANJA.

168

1106

Obv. Lion l., and sun.

Rev.

گنجه
فلوس
١١٠٦
ب
ضر

Æ ·95

169

1149

Similar to (168); but rev. date, ۱۱۴۹ گنجه

Æ ·9

170

1123

Obv. Lion r.; beyond, tree.

Rev. Similar to (168); date ۱۱۲۳

Æ ·95

171

1181

Obv. Lion r.

Rev. Similar to (169); date ۱۱۸۱

Æ ·9

172

Date obliterated.

Obv. Sun;

Countermark leaf-shaped, بز
العز
عبد

Rev. گنجه
ب
ض[ر]

Æ 1·15

173

1132

Obv. Horse walking l.; above, and in front, branch; beneath, flower.

Rev. Similar to (168); date ١٣٢

Pl. XXIII. Æ ·9

174

Same date.

Similar; mint-name off field.

Æ ·85

175

1158?

Obv. Similar type; around, arabesque.

Rev. Similar; date فلوس ١١٥

Pl. XXIII. Æ ·85

176

118x

Similar; obv., type r.; rev., date فلوس ١١٨

Æ ·8

177

1106

Obv. Ibex r.; above, and in front, branch; beneath, flower.

Rev. Similar to (168); date ١ ۶

Æ 1·05

178

Same date.

Similar to (177); date ۱۱۰۶

Æ 1·05

179

1116

Obv. Similar.

Rev. گنجه
فلوس
ـــب
ضرب ۱۱۱

Æ 1·

180

1207

Obv. Duck l.

Rev. Similar to (172); date ۱۲۰۷ گنجه

(Restruck.)

Pl. XXIII. Æ ·8

181

1215

Obv. Two-bladed sabre (Zu-l-fikár) l.

Rev. Similar; date ۱۲۱۵

Pl. XXIII. Æ ·7

MÁZANDERÁN.

182

1138

Obv. Lion r., and sun.

Rev. فلوس ضر

ب

١١٣

مازندران

Pl. XXIII. Æ ·95

183

Date obliterated.

Obv. Similar.

Rev. مازندرا[ن]

ب

فلوس [ضر]

Æ ·1

184

1140?

Obv. Lion seizing stag r.

Rev. فلوس ضر

ب

١١٤

مازندران

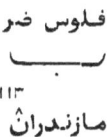

185

1140?

Obv. Similar.

Rev. ما[ز]ند[را]ن
فلوس ضرب ۱۱۴۰

Æ 1·

186

Date obliterated.

Similar.

Æ 1·

187

1159

Obv. Similar type, lion l., stag r.

Rev. [ماز]ند[ران]
فلوس
۱۱۵۹
ضرب

Pl. XXIII. Æ 1·×·7

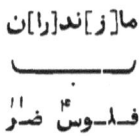

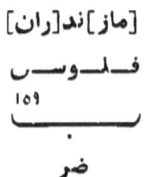

MESH-HED.

188

Obv. Lion l., and sun.

Rev.

مقد[س]

مشهد

ب

فلوس ضر

Æ ·95

189

Obv. Sun, rayed.

Rev.

مقدس

ب

ضر مشهد

Æ ·8

190

1205

Obv. Elephant l., and driver; countermark رایج

Rev.

مقدس

مشهد

١٢٠٥

ب

فلوس ضر

Æ 1·

191

1246

Obv. Same type as (190) r., beneath, ١٢٤٦

Rev. Similar to (190); no date.

Æ ·9

192

Similar; no date visible.

Pl. XXIII. Æ ·85

193

Obv. رايج in monogram.

Rev. Similar; no date visible.

(Restruck.)

Æ ·85

HERÁT.

194

1131

Obv. Horse galloping l.; above, سنة ١١٣١

Rev.

هرات

فلوس ضرب

Between lines, two-bladed sabre (Zu-l-fiḳár) l.

Æ 1·

HAMADÁN.

195

1054

Obv. Eagle r. devouring partridge?

Rev. همذان

فلوس

١٠٥٤

ب

[ضر]

Pl. XXIII. Æ 1·

YAZD.

196

Obv. Lion l., and sun.

Rev. يزد

فلوس

ضرب

Pl. XXIII. Æ 1·2

MEDALS.

GOLD.

1

REWARD OF VALOUR.

1297

Obv. Within wreath of laurel and oak, on base, lion l. holding sabre with r. fore-paw; behind, sun.

Rev. Area

شاه قاجار
ناصر الدين
السلطان
۱۲۹۷

Margin, هر شيردل كه دشمن شه‌را عيان گرفت
از آفتاب همّت ما اين نشان گرفت

Pl. XXIV. 𝒩 1·4, Wt. 222·

SILVER.

2

1273

Obv. ناصر الدين شاهنشاه

Bust of Sháh r., in uniform.

Rev. به فخر دولت عليهٔ ايران

Within wreath of laurel and oak, lion and sun, as (1); above, plumed crown; in ex., ۱۲۷۳

Pl. XXIV. Æ 1·1, Wt. 150·

3

1293

30th year of reign, and centenary of Ḳájár Dynasty.

Obv. Same as (1): same die.

Rev. Within laurel-wreath,

هو الناصر
بیادگار قرن جُلوس
همایُون که قرین سال صدُم
سَلطنت قاجار اَست در ضرّا
بخانهٔ دولتی ضرب شد
۱۲۹۳

(vowelled, قرنُ جُلوس : last ، probably is intended for صدُم)

In border, P F

PL. XXIV. AR 1·4, Wt. 352·

SUPPLEMENT.

ISMA'ÍL I.

SILVER.

12*

Nímrúz, 9¦2.

Obv. Area

لا اله الا الــلــه
محمدل
ل الــلــه الــلــه
سو علی و
ر

Margin, in cartouches,

| [علی حسن حسین] | [علی] محمد جعفر | موسی علی محمد | علی [محمد] حسن |

Rev. Area

[السلطان العادل]
بو
[ال]ها[د]ی ا المظفر
[ا]شاه در
[سم]عیل بهاخان
الله نه
... ملکه وسلطا

In centre, within hexagon,

ضرب
نیمر
وز

AR ·9, Wt. 59·7

M M

12a

Herát, 927.

Obv. Area similar to (12*), varied.

Margin,

علی ... حسن حسین | علی جعفر محمد | موسی علی محمد |
علی حسن محمد

Rev. Area similar to (12*), but ends الله ملک ۲۷ خلد .

In centre, within six-foil,

هراة
ضرب

AR 1·, Wt 71·9

15a

Nímrúz, 928.

Obv. Similar to (12*); margin more complete.

Rev. Area similar to (12*); date ۹۲۸ [اس]معیل

In centre, within hexagon,

وز
نیمر
ضرب

AR ·85, Wt. 59·1

15b

Tabríz, 929.

Obv. Area similar to (11), varied.

Margin, in cartouches,

علی محمد حسین | علی موس[ی] جعفر | [علی محمد حسن] |
علی محمد حسن

Rev. similar to (15); but order of words varied, and in centre, within quatrefoil,

تبريز
ضرب
سنة
٩٢٩

AR ·9, Wt. 121·

17*a*

Ardebíl, date off field.

Obv. similar to (17), in circle, على and ولى united: margin almost entirely wanting.

Rev. similar to (15); but ends

[الص]فوى خلد الله
ملكه

In centre, within sixfoil,

بيل
ارد
ضرب

AR ·85, Wt. 120·

18*b*

Mint and date obliterated.

Obv. Area as (17*a*).

Margin, ... تقى ... كاظ[م ... صادق .... سجاد ....

Rev. Area, within eightfoil,

السلطان شا[ه]
اسمعيل
بهادر خا[ن]
بلا بن[ده] (؟)
شا[ه] كر (؟)

AR ·9, Wt. 119·4

ṬAHMÁSP I.

SILVER.

27*

Mint and date obliterated.

Obv. similar to (25).

No traces of marginal inscr.

Rev.

[ا]لسلطا[ن] العا[د]ل

[ا]لكا[م]ل الها[د]ى

[ابو] خا[ن](؟)

. . . . . ۀ . . . .

In centre, within ornamented quatrefoil,

بهادر

طهماسب

شاه

AR ·8, Wt. 121·

27**, 27***

Similar.

AR ·85, Wt. 119·

AR ·85, Wt. 120·

MUḤAMMAD KHUDABANDA.

GOLD.

27a *

Iṣfahán, 987.

Obv. Area similar to (27a); but رسول الله

Margin, within cartouches,

| | | علی جعفر | |
| | | ... م | |

Rev. Area م‍‍‍‍‍ح‍‍‍‍‍م‍‍‍‍‍د ال‍‍‍‍‍س‍‍‍‍‍ل‍‍‍‍‍[ا]م‍ر آبآئه
[غ]ـلام امـام مـهـدی عـلـیـه و
مـحـمـد   ملـکـه
[سل]ط[ا]ن   الحسینی خلا[د]
[ابو المظفر] باد [شاه بن] طهماسب [شاه]

In centre, within circle,

ن
اصفہا
۹۸۷
ضـرب

N ·65, Wt. 71·4

27a **

Ḳazvín, 987.

Obv. Area, within border of many foils, similar to (27a*).

Margin, within cartouches,

علی حسین(؟) | علی جعفر | موسی علی محمد |
علی حسن(؟) | [محمد] |
علی محمد حسن

Rev. Area similar (to 27a *);

ابـ[و] المظفر بادشاه بن طهماسب شا[ه] legible.

In centre, within circle,

قزوین
ضـرب
۹۸۷

27*a****

Ḳazvín, fifth year, 989.

Obv. Area similar to (27*a*).

Margin, traces of names of Imáms.

Rev. Area,

[غ]لا[م ا]مام محمد مهدی ....و .... [با]د [شاه الس]لطا[ن]
الحسین[ی]

In centre, within border of many foils,

قزوین
ب ۹۸۹ ه
ضر

N ·75, Wt. 71·4

'ABBÁS II.

SILVER.

36*b*

Iṣfahán, 1064.

Obv. Area

لله
لا اله الا اعلى
سو لله
محمد رل الى و
الله

Margin as (36).

Rev. similar to (36), differently arranged, but ends

١٠٤٦
ضر اصفهان
ب

Æ 1·55, Wt. 56·1

38*a*

Ardebíl, 1067.

Similar to (36); but rev., differently arranged, ends

٦٧
اردبيل

Æ 1·3, Wt 137·6

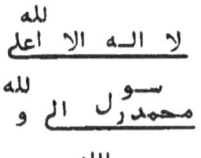

SULAIMÁN I. (SAFÍ II.)

SILVER.

74*

Eriván, 1104.

Obv. similar to (74).

Rev. Similar to (62); but | ون ایر ۱۱۰۴ |

Æ 1·, Wt. 113·

SULṬÁN ḤUSAIN.

SILVER.

101*a*

Tabríz, 1125.

Obv. similar to (88), rev. to (101); but ب
ضر تبریز

Æ ·9, Wt. 104·3

MAḤMÚD.

197*a*

Ḳandahár, date wanting.

Obv. area, within square,

لا اله الا الله
الله
محـــــــمد
رســول

Margin, in segments,

ابا بكر | عمر | عثمان | عل[ى]

Rev.

[زد ا]ز [م]شرق [اي]ر[ا]ن چ[و]
ســــــــــــــــــــــكه
[قر]ص آفتاب محمود جهانگير ه
شــــــــــــــــــــــا
ا[نـ]ـــاب قـــنـــدهـــار
ــيا[د]ت

Æ 9, Wt. 164

NÁDIR.

GOLD.

216*a*

Iṣfahán, 1152.

Similar to (236); but date ١١٥٢

AV ·55, Wt. 53·

SILVER.

260*a*

Iṣfahán, 1156.

Similar to (253); but date ١١٥٦

AR ·85, Wt. 170·8

I. INDEX OF YEARS.

A. H.	Metal.	MINT.	DYNASTY.	PRINCE.	NO.	Page.
908	AR		Ṣafavis	Isma'íl I.	4	3
911?	"	Ámul	"	"	17	9
9$\frac{1}{2}$2	"	Nímrúz	"	"	12*	265
9$\frac{1}{2}$5	"	Merv	"	"	10	5
915	"		"	"	12	6
916	AV	Herát	"	"	1	1
922	"	Shíráz	"	"	2	2
927	AR	Herát	"	"	12*a*	266
928	"	Aberkúh	"	"	13	7
"	"	Shíráz	"	"	14	7
"	"	Káshán	"	"	15	8
"	"	Nímrúz	"	"	15*a*	266
929	"	Tabríz	"	"	15*b*	266
"	"		"	"	16	9
938	"	Hamadán	"	Ṭahmásp I.	20	13
949	"	Iṣfahán	"	"	21	14
955	"	"	"	"	22	14
957	Æ	Ḳandahár			145-7	247-8
976	AR	Mesh-hed	"	"	23-4	15
985	AV	Iṣfahán	"	Muḥammad Khuda-banda	27*a*	19
987	"	"	"	"	27*a**	269
"	"	Ḳazvín	"	"	27*a***	269
989	"	"	"	"	27*a****	270
997	"	Iṣfahán	"	'Abbás I.	28	21
1014	Æ	Tiflís			95-6	234
1017?	AR	Ḥuwaiza	"	"	32	23
1030	Æ	Ra'násh			112	239
1034	"	"			113	239
1038	AR	Eriván	"	Ṣafí I.	34	24
1039	"	Iṣfahán	"	"	34*a*	25
103$\frac{8}{9}$	"	"	"	"	35	25
1045	Æ	Baghdád			61	227
1051	"	Tabríz			93	234
1054	AR	Ḥuwaiza	"	'Abbás II.	48	
"	Æ	Hamadán			195	261
1057	"	Eriván			49	224
1058	"	Ḳandahár			131	244
1059	AR	Tabríz	"	"	36	26
"	Æ	Ḳandahár			137	246

A.H.	Metal.	MINT.	DYNASTY.	PRINCE.	NO.	Page.
1062	Æ	Tabríz	Ṣafavis	'Abbás II.	36a	27
1064	,,	Iṣfahán	,,	,,	36b	271
1065	,,		,,	,,	37	27
1066	,,	Tabríz	,,	,,	38	27
1067	,,	Ardebíl	,,	,,	38a	271
1069	,,	Tabríz	,,	,,	39	27
1070	,,	,,	,,	,,	40	27
1071	,,		,,	,,	41	27
1072	,,		,,	,,	42	28
1072?	,,	Ḥuwaiza	,,	,,	49	29
1072	Æ	Kermánsháhán			160	251
1073	Æ		,,	,,	43	28
1075	,,	Eriván	,,	,,	44	28
,,	Æ	Tiflís			97	235
107x	Æ	,,	,,	,,	45	28
1080	Æ	Ḳandahár			138	246
1081	,,	Tabríz			94	234
1082	Æ	Iṣfahán	,,	Sulaimán I.	50	30
,,	Æ	Ḳandahár			140	246
1083	,,	,,			143	247
1084	Æ	Ḥuwaiza	,,	,,	77-8	37
,,	Æ	Eriván			35	221
1085	Æ	Ḥuwaiza	,,	,,	79-81	37
,,	Æ	Tabríz			71	229
,,	,,	Ḳandahár			134	245
1086	Æ	Ḥuwaiza	,,	,,	82	38
,,	,,	Ganja	,,	,,	51	31
,,	Æ	Ḳandahár			135-6	245
1087	Æ	Tabríz	,,	,,	52	31
,,	,,	Ḥuwaiza	,,	,,	83	38
1088	,,	,,	,,	,,	84	38
1089	,,	,,	,,	,,	85	38
1090	,,	Iṣfahán	,,	,,	53	31
1092	,,	Tabríz	,,	,,	55	32
1093	,,	Iṣfahán	,,	,,	56	32
1095	Æ	Tabríz			88	233
1096	Æ	Iṣfahán	,,	,,	57	32
,,	,,	Nakhchuván	,,	,,	58-60	33
1097	,,	Iṣfahán	,,	,,	61	33
,,	,,	Nakhchuván	,,	,,	62-65	33-4
,,	,,	Hamadán	,,	,,	66	34
,,	Æ	Shíráz			119-20	241
,,	,,	Ḳandahár			155	249
1098	Æ	Resht	,,	,,	67	34
1099	,,	Iṣfahán	,,	,,	68-9	34-5
,,	,,	Tabríz	,,	,,	70	35
109x	,,	Iṣfahán	,,	,,	71	35
1101	,,	Nakhchuván	,,	,,	72	35

A.H.	Metal.	MINT.	DYNASTY.	PRINCE.	NO.	Page.
1103	AR	Ganja	Ṣafavis	Sulaimán I.	73	36
1104	,,	Iṣfahán	,,	,,	74	36
,,	,,	Eriván	,,	,,	74*	272
1105	,,	Ganja	,,	,,	74*a*	36
1106	Æ	,,			168	253
,,	,,	,,			177	255
1107	AR	Tiflís	,,	Sultán Ḥusain	89	40
,,	Æ	Ḳandahár			133	245
1110	AR	Tabríz ?	,,	,,	90	40
,,	,,	Ganja	,,	,,	90*a*	41
,,	,,		,,	,,	91	41
,,	Æ	Shemákhí			117-8	241
1111 ?	,,	Káshán			162	252
1112	AR		,,	,,	92	41
,,	Æ	Tabríz			92	233
1113	AR	Iṣfahán	,,	,,	93	42
,,	,,		,,	,,	94-5	42
1114	Æ	Ḳazwín			130	244
1116	,,	Ganja			179	256
1117	,,	Shemákhí			115	240
1118	AR	Iṣfahán	,,	,,	96	42
1120	Æ	,,			26-7	219
,,	,,	Eriván			36	221
,,	,,	Shemákhí			116	240
1121	AR	Iṣfahán	,,	,,	97	43
1122	Æ	Abú-Shahr			4	213
1123	AR	Iṣfahán	,,	,,	98-9	44
,,	Æ	Ardebíl			21	217
,,	,,	Ganja			170	254
1124	AR	Mesh-hed	,,	,,	100	44
1125	,,	Eriván	,,	,,	101	44
,,	,,	Tabríz	,,	,,	101*a*	272
1126	Æ	,,			73	230
1127	AR	Iṣfahán	,,	,,	102-4	45
,,	,,	Eriván	,,	,,	105*a*	46
,,	Æ	,,			55	225
1128	,,	,,			56	225
1129	AR	Iṣfahán	,,	,,	106	46
,,	,,	Tabríz	,,	,,	107-8	46-7
1130	,,	Iṣfahán	,,	,,	109-10*a*	47
,,	,,	Tabríz	,,	,,	111-111*a*	47-8
,,	,,	Tiflís	,,	,,	112-112*a*	48
,,	,,	Ḳazvín	,,	,,	113	48
,,	,,	Ḳáshán	,,	,,	114-114*a*	48
1130 ?	,,	Mesh-hed	,,	,,	115	49
1130	,,	Nakhchuván	,,	,,	116-116*a*	49
,,	Æ	Eriván			46	223
,,	,,	Ḳazvín			125	243

A.H.	Metal.	MINT.	DYNASTY.	PRINCE.	NO.	Page.
1131	AR	Iṣfahán	Ṣafavís	Sultán Ḥusain	117–117*a*	49-50
,,	,,	Eriván	,,	,,	117*b*	50
,,	,,	Tabríz	,,	,,	118	50
,,	,,	Tiflís	,,	,,	119-21	50
,,	,,	Ḳazvín	,,	,,	122	50
1132	,,	Iṣfahán	,,	,,	123-125	51
,,	,,	Eriván	,,	,,	126-7	51
,,	,,	Resht	,,	,,	127*a*	51
,,	,,	Ḳazvín	,,	,,	128	52
,,	Æ	Eriván			50-51	224
,,	,,	Káshán			163	252
,,	,,	Ganja			173-4	255
1133	AR	Iṣfahán	,,	,,	129-30	52
,,	,,	Tabríz	,,	,,	131-131*a*	52
,,	,,	Tiflís	,,	,,	132	53
,,	,,	Nakhchuván	,,	,,	133	53
,,	Æ	Eriván			53	225
,,	,,	Tabríz			90	233
1134	AV	Iṣfahán	,,	,,	88	39
,,	AR	Tabríz	,,	,,	134-40	53-54
,,	,,	Tiflís	,,	,,	141	54
,,	Æ	Tabríz			91	233
,,	,,	Herát			194	260
,,	AV	Ḳazvín	,,	Ṭahmásp II.	145	55
,,	AR	Tabríz	,,	,,	149	56
1135	,,	,,	,,	Sultán Ḥusain	142	54
,,	,,	Iṣfahán	Afgháns	Maḥmúd	193-97	64-65
[1135-7]	,,	Ḳandahár	,,	,,	197*a*	273
1135	,,	Tabríz	Ṣafavís	Ṭahmásp II.	150-8	56-57
,,	,,	Ḳazvín	,,	,,	159	57
1136	AV	Tabríz	,,	,,	146	55
,,	AR	,,	,,	,,	160-4	57
,,	Æ	Eriván			47-8	224
,,	,,	Tabríz			74	230
1137	AR	,,	,,	,,	165	57
,,	AV	Iṣfahán	Afgháns	Ashraf	198	66
,,	Æ	Káshán			164	252
1138	AR	Mázenderán	Ṣafavís	Ṭahmásp II.	166	58
,,	Æ	,,			182	257
1139	AR	Resht	,,	,,	167	58
,,	,,	Láhíján	,,	,,	168	58
,,	,,	Mázenderán	,,	,,	168*a*	58
,,	,,	Mesh-hed	,,	,,	169-71	58
1140	,,	,,	,,	,,	172-73	59
,,	AV	Iṣfahán	Afgháns	Ashraf	199	67
,,	AR	,,	,,	,,	200	67
1140?	Æ	Mázenderán			184-85	257-8
1141	AR	,,	Ṣafavís	Ṭahmásp II.	174	59
,,	,,	Mesh-hed	,,	,,	175	59

A.H.	Metal.	MINT.	DYNASTY.	PRINCE.	NO.	Page.
1141	Æ	Iṣfahán	Afgháns	Ashraf	201	67
114x	,,	,,	,,	,,	202	68
1142	N	,,	Ṣafavis	Ṭahmásp II.	147-8	56
,,	Æ	,,	,,	,,	176-80	59-60
,,	,,	Mázenderán	,,	,,	181	60
1143	,,	Tabríz	,,	,,	182	60
,,	,,	Mázenderán	,,	,, ('Ali Riẓa)	184-5	61-2
,,	,,	Mesh-hed	,,	,, (,,)	186-90	62-3
,,	Æ	Ṭeherán			122	242
1144	Æ	Tabríz	,,	,,	183	61
,,	,,	Mázenderán	,,	,, ('Ali Riẓa)	191	63
1145	N	Iṣfahán	,,	'Abbás III.	205-6	69
,,	Æ	,,	,,	,,	208	70
,,	,,	Resht	,,	,,	209	70
,,	,,	Ḳazvín	,,	,,	210	70
1146	N	Tabríz	,,	,,	207	70
,,	Æ	Iṣfahán	,,	,,	211	70
,,	,,		,,	,,	212	70
1148	N	Mesh-hed	,,	,, ('Ali Riẓa)	213	71
,,	Æ	,,	,,	,, (,,)	213a	71
,,	Æ	Tiflís			98-9	235
,,	Æ		Efsháris	Nádir	221	74
1149	,,	Iṣfahán	,,	,,	222	74
,,	,,	Mesh-hed	,,	,,	223	75
,,	Æ	Ganja			169	254
1150	N	Shíráz	,,	,,	214	72
,,	Æ	Iṣfahán	,,	,,	224-5	75
,,	,,	Tiflís	,,	,,	226	75
,,	,,	Shíráz	,,	,,	227	76
,,	,,	Ḳandahár	,,	,,	228-30	76
,,	,,	Mesh-hed	,,	,,	231-5	76-7
1151	N	Lahór	,,	,,	215	73
,,	Æ	Iṣfahán	,,	,,	236-40	77
,,	,,	Tabríz	,,	,,	241-2	77-8
,,	,,	Shíráz	,,	,,	243	78
,,	,,	Ganja	,,	,,	244	78
,,	,,	Mesh-hed	,,	,,	245-6	78
,,	,,	Nádirábád	,,	,,	247-8	79
1152	N	Iṣfahán	,,	,,	216-216a	73, 274
,,	Æ	Tabríz	,,	,,	249	79
,,	,,	Tiflís	,,	,,	250-1	79
,,	,,	Sháhjehánábád (Dehlí)	,,	,,	252	80
1153	N	Iṣfahán	,,	,,	217-18	73
,,	Æ	,,	,,	,,	253	80
,,	,,	Tabríz	,,	,,	254-6	80-81
,,	,,	Mesh-hed	,,	,,	257	81
1154	,,	Tabríz	,,	,,	258-9	81
,,	,,	Ganja	,,	,,	260	81

A H.	Metal.	MINT.	DYNASTY.	PRINCE.	NO.	Page.
1156	Æ	Işfahán	Efsháris	Nádir	260a	274
"	"	Mesh-hed	"	"	261	82
"	Æ	Bhukkur	"	"	273-4	84
1157	Æ	Işfahán	"	"	262	82
"	"	Sind	"	"	263	82
"	"	Mesh-hed	"	"	264	82
1158	AV	Işfahán	"	"	219-20	74
"	Æ	"	"	"	265	82
"	"	Tabríz	"	"	266	82
"	"	Sind	"	"	266a	83
"	Æ	Bhukkur	"	"	274a	84
1158 ?	"	Ganja			175	255
1159	Æ	Işfahán	"	"	267	83
"	"	Tabríz	"	"	268-9	83
"	Æ	Mázenderán			187	258
1160	Æ	Tabríz	"	"	270-71	83
"	Æ	Eriván			37-8	221
1160 ?	"	Káshán			165	253
1160	Æ	Tabríz	Safavís	Sám	275-6	85
"	"	Işfahán	Efsháris	'Ádil Sháh ('Ali Riza)	277-80	86-7
"	"	Tabríz	"	" (")	281	87
"	"	Mesh-hed	"	" (")	282-3	87
1161	"	"	"	" (")	284	88
116?	"	Herát	"	" (")	285	88
1161	"	Tabríz	"	Ibrahím (")	289-91	90
"	"	Mesh-hed	"	Sháh Rukh	293	92
"	"	Herát	"	"	294	92
"	"	Resht	"	" (")	309	96
"	"	Ķazvín	"	" (")	310-1	96
"	"	Mesh-hed	"	" (")	312	97
1162	"	Tiflís	"	Ibrahím	286-7	89
"	"	Ķazvín	"	"	288	89
"	"	Tabríz	"	Sháh Rukh	297	93
"	"	Shíráz	"	"	298-9	93-4
"	"	Mesh-hed	"	"	295-6	92-3
"	"	"	"	"	300-301	94
1163	"	Tabríz	"	"	302	94
"	"	Ganja	"	"	303	94
"	"	Mesh-hed	"	"	304	95
116$\frac{2}{3}$	"	"	"	"	305	95
116x	AV	"	"	"	292	91
116x	Æ	Tiflís	"	"	306-7	95
116x	"	Ķazvín	"	"	308	95
1163	"	Mázenderán	Şafavís	Sulaimán II.	313	98
[1163]	"	Ķazvín ?	"	"	314	99
1163	"	Işfahán	"	Isma'íl (III.)	318	102
1166	"	Resht	"	"	319	103
"	"	Mázenderán	"	"	320	103

A.H.	Metal.	MINT.	DYNASTY.	PRINCE.	NO.	Page.
1167	AR	Mázenderán	Ṣafavis	Isma'íl (III.)	321-2	104
"	AV	Iṣfahán	Zands	Kerím Khán	323	105
"	AR	Ḳazvín	"	"	326-7	107
1168	"	Tabríz	Afgháns	Ázád Khán	416	130
1169	AV	Iṣfahán	Zands	Kerím Khán	324	106
"	"	"	Ḳájárs	Muḥammad Ḥasan Khán	404-5	127
1170	AR	Tiflís	Efsháris	Sháh Rukh	315	100
"	AV	Tabríz	Ḳájárs	Muḥammad Ḥasan Khán	406	128
"	"	Yazd	"	"	407	128
"	AR	Tabríz	"	"	409	128
"	"	Resht	"	"	410	128
"	"	Mázenderán	"	"	411-12	129
1171	AV	Iṣfahán	"	"	408	128
"	AR	Mázenderán	"	"	413-14	129
1171?	Æ	Tabríz			75	230
1172	AV	Army-mint (Julú)	Zands	Kerím Khán	325	106
"	Æ	Kermánsháhán			160	251
1173	AR	Mázenderán	"	"	344-5	112-3
1174	"	Shíráz	"	"	347	114
"	"	Káshán	"	"	348	114
1175	"	Mázenderán	"	"	349	114
1176	AV	Shíráz	"	"	328-30	108
"	AR	"	"	"	350-52	115
"	"	Army-mint (Ẓarráb-khána-i-rikáb)	"	"	353	115
"	"	Ganja		Khán of Ganja	417	131
1176?	Æ	Eriván			39	222
1177	AR	Shíráz	"	Kerím Khán	354	115
"	"	Ganja		Khán of Ganja	418	131
1178	"	"		"	419	131
1178?	"	Resht	"	Kerím Khán	354a	116
1179	"	Iṣfahán	"	"	355	116
"	"	Tabríz	"	"	356	116
"	"	Ṭeherán	"	"	357	116
"	"	Yazd		"	358	117
117x	Æ	Tabríz			76	230
1180	"	Eriván			40	222
1181	AR	Tabríz	"	"	359	117
"	"	Resht	"	"	360	117
"	"	Shíráz	"	"	361	118
"	"	Ṭeherán	"	"	362	118
"	"	Yazd	"	"	363	118
"	Æ	Ganja			171	254
1182	AR	Tabríz	"	"	364	118
"	"	Tiflís	"	"	366-8	119-20

A.H.	Metal.	MINT.	DYNASTY.	PRINCE.	NO.	Page.
1182?	AR	Tiflís	Zands	Kerím Khán	365	119
1182	,,	Ganja	,,	,,	369-70	120
,,	,,	Nakhchuván	,,	,,	371	120
,,	Æ	Kazvín			126-7	243
1183	AR	Tabríz	,,	,,	372	121
,,	,,	Tiflís	,,	,,	373	121
,,	,,	Nakhchuván	,,	,,	374	121
1184	,,	Tabríz	,,	,,	375	121
,,	,,	Tiflís	,,	,,	376	121
,,	,,	Ganja	,,	,,	377	121
1185	AV	Tabríz	,,	,,	331-2	109
1187	,,	,,	,,	,,	333	109
,,	,,	Yazd	,,	,,	334-5	110
,,	AR	Tabríz	,,	,,	378	121
,,	,,	Ganja		Khán of Ganja	420	131
,,	Æ	Eriván			41	222
1188	AR	Tabríz	,,	Kerím Khán	379	122
,,	,,	Kermán	,,	,,	380	122
,,	,,	Ganja		Khán of Ganja	421	131
1189	AV	Khoï	,,	Kerím Khán	336	110
,,	AR	Tiflís	,,	,,	381	122
,,	,,	Shemákhi	,,	,,	382	122
,,	,,	Kermán	,,	,,	383	123
,,	,,	Ganja	,,	,,	384-6	123
,,	Æ	Khoï			103	237
1190	AV	El-Baṣreh	,,	,,	337	111
,,	,,	Resht	,,	,,	338-9	111
,,	,,	Yazd	,,	,,	340	111
1190?	AR	(El-)Baṣreh	,,	,,	389	124
1190	,,	Tiflís	,,	,,	390-3	124-5
,,	,,	Shemákhí	,,	,,	394	125
,,	,,	Ganja	,,	,,	395-9	125-6
1191	,,	Shemákhí	,,	,,	400	126
1191?	,,	Ganja	,,	,,	401	126
1191	Æ	Khoï			104	237
1192	AV	,,	,,	,,	341	112
,,	,,	Yazd	,,	,,	342-3	112
,,	AR	Ganja	,,	,,	402	126
1193	AV	Yazd	,,	Abu-l-fat-ḥ Khán	422	132
1194	,,	,,	,,	Ṣádiḳ Khán	423	133
,,	AR	Tabríz	,,	,,	425	134
,,	,,	Shíráz	,,	,,	426	135
1195	,,	Mesh-hed	Efsháris	Sháh Rukh	316	101
,,	AV	Shíráz	Zands	Ṣádiḳ Khán	424	134
,,	AR	Tabríz	,,	,,	427	135
,,	,,	Khoï	,,	,,	428	135
,,	,,	Shíráz	,,	,,	429	135
1197	AV	,,	,,	'Alí Murád Khán	430	136

A.H.	Metal.	MINT.	DYNASTY.	PRINCE.	NO.	Page.
1197	AV	Yazd	Zands	'Alí Murád Khán	431	137
1198	,,	Shíráz	,,	,,	432	137
,,	,,	Káshán	,,	,,	433	138
,,	AR	Iṣfahán	,,	,,	435	139
,,	,,	Shíráz	,,	,,	436-7	139
1199	,,	Iṣfahán	,,	Jaa'far Khán	440-41	140-41
,,	,,	Shíráz	,,	,,	442-3	141
,,	,,	Iṣfahán	Ḳájárs	Aḳa Muḥammad Khán	446	144
1201	AV	Shíráz	Zands	Jaa'far Khán	438	140
1202	,,	,,	,,	,,	439	140
,,	AR	,,	,,	,,	444	141
1205	Æ	Mesh-hed			190	259
1207	,,	Ganja			180	256
1208	AV	Kermán	,,	Luṭf-'Alí Khán	445	142
1209	,,	Káshán	Ḳájárs	Aḳa Muḥammad Khán	447	144
,,	AR	Shíráz	,,	,,	448-50	145
,,	Æ	Khoï			105	237
1210	AR	,,	,,	,,	451	146
1211	,,	Resht	,,	,,	452-3	146-7
1211 ?	Æ	Bandar-Abú-Shahr			16	216
1212	AR	Shíráz	,,	Bábá Khán (Fet-ḥ-'Alí)	456	148
[1212]	,,	Ṭeherán	,,	,,	457	149
1213	AV	Iṣfahán	,,	Fet-ḥ-'Alí	458	150
,,	,,	Lahíján	,,	,,	459	150
,,	AR	Iṣfahán	,,	,,	488	160
,,	,,	Ṭeherán	,,	,,	489	160
1214	AV	Yazd	,,	,,	460	151
,,	AR	Shíráz	,,	,,	490	160
,,	,,	Ganja	,,	,,	491	161
,,	,,	Yazd	,,	,,	492-3	161-2
1214 ?	Æ	Abú-Shahr			8	214
1215	AR	Shíráz	,,	,,	494	162
,,	,,	Ṭeherán	,,	,,	495	162
,,	Æ	Ganja			181	256
1216	AR	Eriván	,,	,,	496	163
,,	,,	Yazd	,,	,,	497	163
1217	,,	Tabríz	,,	,,	498	163
1220	AV	,,	,,	,,	463	152
1221	AR	,,	,,	,,	499	164
1221 ?	Æ	Bandar-Abú-Shahr			19-20	216-7
1222	AV	Iṣfahán	,,	,,	464	152
,,	AR	Resht	,,	,,	500	164
,,	,,	Mesh-hed	,,	,,	501	164
,,	Æ	Ṭeherán			123	242
1223	AR	Iṣfahán	,,	,,	502	165
,,	,,	Kermánsháhán	,,	,,	503	165

A.H.	Metal.	MINT.	DYNASTY.	PRINCE.	NO.	Page.
1224	AV	Tabríz	Ḳájárs	Feṭ-h-'Alí	465	153
"	AR	Kermán	"	"	504	165
"	Æ	Tabríz			78	230
1225	AV	"	"	"	466	153
"	AR	Iṣfahán	"	"	505-6	166
"	"	Tabríz	"	"	507	166
1226	"	Eriván	"	"	508	166
"	"	Iṣfahán	"	"	509-12	167
"	"	Khoï	"	"	513	168
"	"	Ḳazvín	"	"	514	168
1227	AV	Káshán	"	"	467	153
"	AR	Shíráz	"	"	515	168
1228	AV	Iṣfahán	"	"	468	153
"	"	Tabríz	"	"	469	154
"	"	Shíráz	"	"	470	154
122x	Æ	Urúmí			24	218
1230	"	Tabríz			79	231
1230 ?	AR	Mesh-hed	"	"	516	169
1231	Æ	Kermánsháhán	"	"	516a	169
1232	AV	Khoï	"	"	471	154
"	AR	Asterábád	"	"	517	169
"	"	Kermánsháhán	"	"	518	170
"	"	Yazd	"	"	519-20	170
"	Æ	Eriván			42	222
1233	AR	Ḳazvín	"	"	521	170
"	Æ	Resht			109-10	238-9
1234	AV	Khoï	"	"	472	154
"	"	Kermánsháhán	"	"	473	155
"	"	Yazd	"	"	474	155
"	AR	Mesh-hed	"	"	522	170
1235	"	Ṭeherán	"	"	523	171
"	Æ	Tabríz			80	231
1236	AV	"	"	"	475	155
"	"	Zenján	"	"	476	156
1238	AR	Tabríz	"	"	524	171
1239	AV	Zenján	"	"	477	156
"	Æ	Abú-Shahr			9	214
"	"	Tabríz			83	232
1240 ?	AR	Hamadán	"	"	525	171
1241	"	Iṣfahán	"	"	526	171
"	"	Zenján	"	"	527	172
"	"	Káshán	"	"	528	172
"	"	Kermánsháhán	"	"	529	172
"	Æ	Khoï			107	238
1242	AV	Ṭeherán	"	"	478	157
"	AR	Kermánsháhán	"	"	530	172
1244	AV	Tabríz	"	"	479-80	157
"	AR	Hamadán	"	"	531	173

A.H.	Metal.	MINT.	DYNASTY.	PRINCE.	NO.	Page.
1244	AR	Yazd	Ḳájárs	Feṭ-h-'Alí	532	173
1245	,,	Tabríz	,,	,,	533	173
,,	,,	Hamadán	,,	,,	534	173
,,	,,	Yazd	,,	,,	535	174
1246	AV	Ḳazvín	,,	,,	481	157
,,	,,	Hamadán	,,	,,	482	158
,,	AR	Shíráz	,,	,,	536	174
,,	Æ	Mesh-hed			191	260
1246-7	,,	Iṣfahán			32	220
1247	AR	Yazd	,,	,,	537	174
1248	AV	Kermán	,,	,,	483	158
,,	AR	Yazd	,,	,,	538-9	174-5
1249	AV	Iṣfahán	,,	,,	484	159
,,	,,	Ṭeherán	,,	,,	485	159
,,	Æ	Urúmí			22	217
1249 ?	AR	Kermán	,,	,,	540	175
124x	Æ	Eriván			43-45	223
1250	AV	Resht	,,	,,	486	159
,,	,,	Hamadán	,,	,,	487	160
,,	AR	Ṭeherán	,,	Muḥammad	548	178
1251	,,	Mesh-hed (El-)	,,	,,	549-50	178-9
,,	,,	Yazd	,,	,,	551	179
1252	,,	Tabríz	,,	,,	552	179
,,	,,	Shíráz	,,	,,	553	180
,,	,,	Kermánsháhán	,,	,,	554-5	180
1253	,,	,,	,,	,,	556	181
,,	,,	Yazd	,,	,,	557	181
1254	,,	Shíráz	,,	,,	558	181
1255	AV	Resht	,,	,,	545	177
,,	AR	,,	,,	,,	559	181
,,	,,	Ṭeherán	,,	,,	560	182
1256	Æ	Behbehán			65-68	228
,,	,,	Tabríz			82	231
1257	AR	Ṭaberistán	,,	,,	561	182
1258	,,	Ṭeherán	,,	,,	562	182
,,	,,	Mesh-hed	,,	,,	563	183
,,	Æ	Kermánsháhán			161	251
1259	AR	Ṭeherán	,,	,,	564	183
1260	,,	Mesh-hed	,,	,,	565	183
,,	Æ	Irán			1	212
1260 ?	,,	,,			3	212
1261	AR	Ṭeherán	,,	,,	566	183
1262	AV	Resht	,,	,,	546	177
,,	,,	Ṭeherán	,,	,,	547	178
,,	AR	,,	,,	,,	568	184
1263	,,	Tabríz	,,	,,	569	184
,,	,,	Ṭeherán	,,	,,	570-1	184
,,	,,	Mesh-hed	,,	,,	572	184

A.H.	Metal.	MINT.	DYNASTY.	PRINCE.	NO.	Page.
126x	Æ	Irán	Ḳájárs	Muḥammad	576	185
1265	AV	Mesh-hed		Ḥasan Khán Sálár (Rebel)	577	186
,,	,,	Resht	,,	Náṣir-ed-dín	578	187
,,	AR	Tabríz	,,	,,	601	194
,,	,,	Ṭaberistán	,,	,,	602	195
,,	,,	Ṭeherán	,,	,,	603-4	195
1266	AV	Resht	,,	,,	579	187
,,	AR	Khoï	,,	,,	605	196
1267 ?	Æ	Abú-Shahr			6	213
1268	AV	Ṭeherán	,,	,,	580	188
,,	,,	Mesh-hed	,,	,,	581	188
1270	Æ	Abú-Shahr			7	214
1272	AR	Asterábád	,,	,,	606	196
,,	,,	Ṭeherán	,,	,,	607	197
1273	AV	Iṣfahán	,,	,,	582	189
,,	,,	Ṭaberistán	,,	,,	583	189
,,	AR	Ṭeherán	,,	,,	608-9	197
,,	,,	Ḳazvín	,,	,,	610	197
,,	,,	(Medal)	,,	,,	2	262
1274	,,	Iṣfahán	,,	,,	611	198
,,	,,	Ṭeherán	,,	,,	612-3	198
,,	,,	Ḳazvín	,,	,,	614	198
,,	,,	Káshán	,,	,,	615	199
1275	AV	Tabríz	,,	,,	584	189
,,	AR	Ṭeherán	,,	,,	616-7	199
,,	,,	Kermánsháhán	,,	,,	618	199
1276	AV	Sarakhs	,,	,,	585	190
,,	AR	Asterábád	,,	,,	619	200
,,	,,	Iṣfahán	,,	,,	620	200
,,	,,	Ṭeherán	,,	,,	621	200
1277	AV	,,	,,	,,	586	190
,,	AR	,,	,,	,,	622	201
,,	,,	Yazd	,,	,,	623	201
1278	,,	Mesh-hed	,,	,,	624	201
1279	AV	,,	,,	,,	587	190
,,	AR	,,	,,	,,	625	201
1280 ?	,,	Resht	,,	,,	626	202
1281	AV	Mesh-hed	,,	,,	588	191
,,	AR	Ṭeherán	,,	,,	628-31	202-3
,,	Æ	,,	,,	,,	646-7	208
1282	AV	Ṭaberistán	,,	,,	589	191
,,	AR	Asterábád	,,	,,	627	202
1283	AV	Resht	,,	,,	590	191
1283	AR	Iṣfahán	,,	,,	632	203
1284	,,	,,	,,	,,	633	204
,,	,,	Kermán		,,	634	204
1287	,,	Arẓ-i-aḳdas (Mesh-hed)	,,	,,	635	205

A.H.	Metal.	MINT.	DYNASTY.	PRINCE.	NO.	Page.
1288	AR	Ṭeherán	Ḳájárs	Náṣir-ed-dín	636-7	205
1292	„	Náṣirí (Ṭeherán)	„	„	639	206
1293	„	(Medal)	„	„	3	263
1294	AV	Ṭeherán	„	„	591	192
„	AR	„	„	„	640	206
1295	AV	„	„	„	593-4	192
„	AR	„	„	„	641	206
„	Æ	„	„	„	648-50	208
1296	AV	„	„	„	595	193
„	AR	„	„	„	642-4	207
1297	AV	„	„	„	596-8	193-4
„	„	(Medal)	„	„	1	262

II. INDEX OF MINTS.

MINT.	Metal.	A.H.	DYNASTY.	PRINCE.	NO.	Page.
ابرقوه Aberkúh	AR	928	Ṣafavis	Isma'íl I.	13	7
ابو شهر Abú-shahr	Æ	1122			4	213
	„	1214?			8	214
	„	1239			9	214
	„	1267?			6	213
	„	1270			7	214
	„	12*xx*			10	214
	„				5	213
	„				11	215
	„				12, 13	215
	„				14	215
			See بندر ابو شهر Bandar Abú-Shahr			
اردبيل Ardebíl	AR		Ṣafavis	Isma'íl I.	17*a*	267
	„	1067	„	Abbás II.	38*a*	271
	Æ	1123			21	217
ارض اقدس Arz-i-akdas	AR	1234	Kájárs	Fet-ḥ-'Alí	522	170
ارض اقدس امام	„	1287	„	Naṣir-ed-dín	635	205

See مشهد Mesh-hed

MINT.	Metal.	A.H.	DYNASTY.	PRINCE.	NO.	Page
ارومی Urúmí	Æ	122x			24	218
	„	1249			22	217
	„				23	218
	„				25	218
استراباد Asterábád	AR		Safavis	Isma'íl I.	5	3
دارالمومنين	„		Kájárs	Muhammad Hasan ?	415	129
„	„	1232	„	Fet-h-'Alí	517	169
„	„	1272	„	Násir-ed-dín	606	196
„	„	1276	„	„	619	200
„	„	1282	„	„	627	202
„	„		„	„	645	207
اصفهان Isfahán	AR	949	Safavis	Tahmásp I.	21	14
	„	955	„	„	22	14
	AV	985	„	Muhammad Khuda-banda	27a	19
	„	987	„	„	27a*	269
	„	997	„	'Abbás I.	28	21
	AR	1039	„	Safí (I.)	34a	25
	„	103[8/9]	„	„	35	25
	„	1064	„	'Abbás II.	36b	271
	„	1082	„	Sulaimán I.	50	30
	„	1090	„	„	53	31
	„	1090 ?	„	„	54	31
	„	1093	„	„	56	32
	„	1096	„	„	57	32
	„	1097	„	„	61	33
	„	1099	„	„	68-9	34-5
	„	109x	„	„	71	35
	„	1104	„	„	74	36
	„	1113	„	Husain	93	42
	„	1118	„	„	96	42
	Æ	1120			26-7	219
	„				28-31	219
	AR	1121	„	„	97	43
	„	1123	„	„	98-9	44
	„	1127	„	„	102-4	45
	„		„	„	105	46

MINT.	Metal.	A.H.	DYNASTY.	PRINCE.	NO.	Page.
اصفهان Isfahán (*continued*)	AR	1129	Ṣafavís	Ḥusain	106	46
	,,	1130	,,	,,	109-10*a*	47
	,,	1131	,,	,,	117-17*a*	49-50
	,,	1132	,,	,,	123-5	51
	,,	1133	,,	,,	129-30	52
	AV	1134	,,	,,	88	39
	AR	1135	Afgháns	Maḥmúd	193-6	64-5
	AV	1137	,,	Ashraf	198	66
	,,	1140	,,	,,	199	67
	AR	1140	,,	,,	200	67
	,,	1141	,,	,,	201	67
	,,	114*x*	,,	,,	202	68
	,,		,,	,,	203	68
	AV	1142	Ṣafavis	Ṭahmásp II.	147-8	56
	AR	1142	,,	,,	176-80	59-60
	AV	1145	,,	'Abbás III.	205-6	69
	AR	1145	,,	,,	208	70
	,,	1146	,,	,,	211	70
	,,	1149	Efsháris	Nádir	222	74
	,,	1150	,,	,,	224-5	75
	,,	1151	,,	,,	236-40	77
دار السلطنه	AV	1152	,,	,,	216-16*a*	73, 273
,,	,,	1153	,,	,,	217-18	73
,,	AR	1153	,,	,,	253	80
,,	,,	1156	,,	,,	260*a*	273
,,	,,	1157	,,	,,	262	82
,,	AV	1158	,,		219-20	74
,,	AR	1158	,,	,,	265	82
,,	,,	1159	,,	,,	267	83
	,,	1160	,,	'Ádil Sháh	277-80	86-7
	,,	1163	Ṣafavis	Isma'íl (III.)	318	102
,,	AV	1167	Zands	Kerím Khán	323	105
,,	,,	1169	,,	,,	324	106
	,,	1169	Ḳájárs	Muḥammad Ḥasan	404-5	127
	,,	1171	,,	,,	408	128
,,	AR	1179	Zands	Kerím Khán	355	116
,,	,,	1198		'Alí Murád	435	139
,,	,,	1199	,,	Jaa'far	440-1	140-1
,,	,,	1199	Ḳájárs	Aḳa Muḥammad	446	144
,,	,,		,,	,,	454-5	147
,,	AV	1213	,,	Fet-ḥ-'Alí	458	150
,,	AR	1213	,,	,,	488	160
,,	AV	1222	,,	,,	464	152
,,	AR	1223	,,	,,	502	165
,,	,,	1225	,,	,,	505-6	166
,,	,,	1226	,,	,,	509-12	167
,,	AV	1228	,,	,,	468	153

MINT.	Metal.	A.H.	DYNASTY.	PRINCE.	NO.	Page.
اصفهان Iṣfahán (*continued*)						
دار السلطنه	AR	1241	Ḳájárs	Fet-ḥ-'Alí	526	171
	Æ	1246-7			32	220
,,	AV	1249	,,	,,	484	159
,,	,,		,,	,,	461	151
,,	AR		,,	Muḥammad	573	185
,,	AV	1273	,,	Náṣir-ed-dín	582	189
,,	AR	1274	,,	,,	611	198
,,	,,	1276	,,	,,	620	200
,,	,,	1283	,,	,,	632	203
,,	,,	1284	,,	,,	633	204
	Æ				33-4	220
آمل Ámul	AR	911 ?	Ṣafavis	Isma'íl I.	17	9
ايران Írán	Æ	1260			1	212
	,,				2	212
	,,	1260 ?			3	212
	,,	126*x*	Ḳájárs	Muḥammad	576	185
		See	Tabríz Æ, nos. 82, 1256; Ṭeherán Æ, nos. 646-7, 1281; 648-50, 1295.			
ايروان Eriván	AR	1038	Ṣafavis	Ṣafi I.	34	24
	Æ	1057			49	224
	AR	1075	,,	'Abbás II.	44	28
	Æ	1084			35	221
	AR	1104	,,	Sulaimán I.	74*	272
	Æ	1120			36	221
	AR	1125	,,	Ḥusain	101	44
	,,	1127	,,	,,	105*a*	46
	Æ	1127			55	225
	,,	1128			56	225
	,,	1130			46	223
	AR	1131	,,	,,	117*b*	50

MINT.	Metal	A.H.	DYNASTY.	PRINCE.	NO.	Page.
ايروان Eriván (*continued*)	AR	1132	Ṣafavis	Ḥusain	126-7	51
	Æ	1132			50-1	224
	,,	1133			53	225
	,,	1136			47-8	224
	,,	1160			37-8	221
	,,	1176?			39	222
	,,	1180			40	222
	,,	1187			41	222
	AR	1216	Ḳájárs	Fet-ḥ-'Alí	496	163
حجور سعد	,,	1226	,,	,,	508	166
	Æ	1232			42	222
	,,	124*x*			45	223
	,,	1*xx*4			59	226
	,,				43-4	223
	,,				54	225
	,,				57	225
	,,				58	226
بروجرد Borujird	Æ				60	226
البصره El-Baṣreh, Baṣreh ام البلاد	AV	1190	Zands	Kerím Khán	337	111
بصره ,,	AR	1190?	,,	,,	389	124
بغداد Baghdád	Æ	[10]45			61	227
	,,				62	227
بندر ابو شهر Bandar-	Æ	1211?			16	216
Abú-Shahr	,,	1221?			19-20	216-7
	,,				15	215
	,,				17-18	216

MINT.	Metal.	A.H.	DYNASTY.	PRINCE.	NO.	Page.
بندر بندر عباس ? Bandar, Bandar-'Abbás ?	Æ				63-4	227
بهبهان Behbehán	Æ	1256			65-8	228
	"	12*xx*			69	229
	"				70	229
بهكر Bhukkur	Æ	1156	Efsháris	Nádir	273-4	84
	"	1158	"	"	274*a*	84
پشاور Pesháwar	AR		"	"	272	84
تبريز Tabríz	AR	929	Ṣafavis	Isma'íl I.	15*b*	266
	"		"	"	8	4
	Æ	1051			93	234
	AR	1059	"	'Abbás II.	36	26
	"	1062	"	"	36*a*	27
	"	1066	"	"	38	27
	"	1069	"	"	39	27
	"	1070	"	"	40	27
	"		"	"	47	28
	Æ	1081			94	234
	"	1085			71	229
	AR	1087	"	Sulaimán I.	52	31
	"	1092	"	"	55	32
?	Æ	1095			88-9	233
	AR	1099	"	"	70	35
	"	1110	"	Ḥusain	90	40
	Æ	1112			92	233
	AR	1125	"	"	101*a*	272

MINT.	Metal.	A.H.	DYNASTY.	PRINCE.	NO.	Page.
تبريز Tabríz (*continued*)	Æ	1126			73	230
	AR	1129	Ṣafavis	Ḥusain	107-8	46-7
	"	1130	"	"	111-11*a*	47-8
	"	1131	"	"	118	50
	"	1133	"	"	131-31*a*	52
	Æ	1133			90	233
	AR	1134	"	"	134-40	53-4
	"	1134	"	Ṭahmásp II.	149	56
	Æ	1134			91	233
	AR	1135	"	Ḥusain	142	54
	"	1135	"	Ṭahmásp II.	150-8	56-7
	AV	1136	"	"	146	55
	AR	1136	"	"	160-4	57
	Æ	1136			74	230
	AR	1137	"	"	165	57
	"	1143	"	"	182	60
	"	1144	"	"	183	61
	AV	1146	"	'Abbás III.	207	70
	AR	1151	Efsháris	Nádir	241-2	77-8
	"	1152	"	"	249	79
دار السلطنه	"	1153	"	"	254-6	80-1
"	"	1154	"	"	258-9	81
"	"	1158	"	"	266	82
"	"	1159	"	"	268-9	83
"	"	1160	"	"	270-1	83
	"	1160	Ṣafavis	Sám (Pretender)	275-6	85
	"	1160	Efsháris	'Ádil Sháh	281	87
	"	1161	"	Ibráhím ('Ali Riẓa Series)	289-91	90
	"	1162	"	Sháh Rukh	297	93
	"	1163	"	"	302	94
	"	1168	Afghán	Ázád Khán	416	130
	AV	1170	Ḳájárs	Muḥammad Ḥasan	406	128
	AR	1170	"	"	409	128
	Æ	1171			75	230
"	AR	1179	Zands	Kerím Khán	356	116
	Æ	117*x*			76	230
"	AR	1181	"	"	359	117
"	"	1182	"	"	364	118
"	"	1183	"	"	372	121
"	"	1184	"	"	375	121
"	AV	1185	"	"	331-2	109
"	"	1187	"	"	333	109
"	AR	1187	"	"	378	121
"	"	1188	"	"	379	122
"	"	1194	"	Ṣadiḳ	425	134
"	"	1195	"	"	427	135

MINT.	Metal.	A.H.	DYNASTY.	PRINCE.	NO.	Page.
تبريز Tabríz (*continued*)						
دار السلطنه	AR	1217	Ḳájárs	Fet-ḥ-'Alí	498	163
,,	AV	1220	,,	,,	463	152
,,	AR	1221	,,	,,	499	164
,,	AV	1224	,,	,,	465	153
	Æ	1224			78	230
,,	AV	1225	,,	,,	466	153
,,	AR	1225	,,	,,	507	166
,,	AV	1228	,,	,,	469	154
	Æ	1230			79	231
	,,	1235			80-1	231
,,	AV	1236	,,	,,	475	155
,,	AR	1238	,,	,,	524	171
	Æ	1239			83-5	232
	,,	1240			86-7	232
,,	AV	1244	,,	,,	479-80	157
,,	AR	1245	,,	,,	533	173
,,	,,	1252	,,	Muḥammad	552	179
	Æ	1256			82	231
,,	AR	1263	,,	,,	569	184
,,	,,	1265	,,	Náṣir-ed-dín	601	194
,,	AV	1275	,,	,,	584	189
	Æ				72	229
	,,				77	230
تفليس Tiflís	Æ	1014			95-6	234
	,,	1075			97	235
	AR	107*x*	Ṣafavis	'Abbás II.	45	28
	,,		,,	,,	46	28
	,,	1107	,,	Ḥusain	89	40
	,,	1130	,,	,,	112-2*a*	48
	,,	1131	,,	,,	119-21	50
	,,	1133	,,	,,	132	53
	,,	1134	,,	,,	141	54
	,,		,,	,,	143	54
	Æ	1148			98-9	235
	AR	1150	Efsháris	Nádir	226	75
	,,	1152	,,	,,	250-1	79
	,,	1162	,,	Ibráhím	286	89
	,,	116*x*	,,	Sháh Rukh	306-7	95
	,,	1170	,,	,,	315	100
	,,	1182	Zands	Kerím Khán	366-8	119-20

MINT.	Metal.	A.H.	DYNASTY.	PRINCE.	NO.	Page.
تفليس Tiflís (*continued*)	AR	1182 ?	Zands	Kerím Khán	365	119
	,,	1183	,,	,,	373	121
	,,	1184	,,	,,	376	121
	,,	1189	,,	,,	381	122
	,,	1190	,,	,,	390-3	124-5
توی Túï	Æ				100	236
[ت]یری Tíra ?	Æ				101-2	236
جلو Army mint	AV	1172	,,	,,	325	106
حويزه Ḥuwaiza	AR	1017 ?	Ṣafavis	'Abbás I.	32	23
	,,		,,	,,	33	24
	,,	1054	,,	'Abbás II.	48	29
	,,	1072 ?	,,	,,	49	29
	,,	1084	,,	Sulaimán I.	77-8	37
	,,	1085	,,	,,	79-81	37
	,,	1086	,,	,,	82	38
	,,	1087	,,	,,	83	38
	,,	1088	,,	,,	84	38
	,,	1089	,,	,,	85	38
	,,		,,	,, ?	86-7	38
خوی Khoï	AV	1189	Zands	Kerím Khán	336	110
	Æ	1189			103	237
	,,	1191			104	237

MINT.	Metal.	A.H.	DYNASTY.	PRINCE.	NO.	Page.
خوی Khoï (*continued*)	AV	1192	Zands	Kerím Khán	341	112
	AR	1195	"	Ṣádiḳ	428	135
	Æ	1209			105	237
	AR	1210	Ḳájárs	Aḳa Muḥammad	451	146
	"	1226	"	Fet-ḥ-Alí	513	168
	AV	1232	"	"	471	154
	"	1234	"	"	472	154
	Æ	1241			107	238
دار الصفا	AR	1266	"	Náṣir-ed-dín	605	196
	Æ				106	237
دماوند Demávend	AR		Ṣafavis	Isma'íl I.	17*a*	10
	Æ				108	238
Dehlí			*See* شاه جهان اباد Sháhjehánábád			
رشت Resht	AR		Ṣafavis	Ṭahmásp I.	24*a*	16
	"	1098	"	Sulaimán I.	67	34
	"	1132	"	Ḥusain	127*a*	51
	"	1139	"	Ṭahmásp II.	167	58
	"	1145	"	'Abbás III.	209	70
	"	1161	Efsháris	Sháh Rukh ('Ali Riẓa Series)	309	96
	"	1166	Safavis	Isma'íl (III.)	319	103
	"	1170	Ḳájárs	Muḥammad Ḥasan	410	128
دار المرز	"	1178 ?	Zands	Kerím Khán	354 *a*	116
"	"	1181	"	"	360	117
"	AV	1190	"	"	338-9	111
"	AR	1211	Ḳájárs	Aḳa Muḥammad	452-3	146-7
"	"	1222	"	Fet-ḥ-'Alí	500	164
	Æ	1233			109-10	238-9
"	AV	1250	"	"	486	159
"	"	1255	"	Muḥammad	545	177
"	AR	1255	"	"	559	181
"	AV	1262	"	"	546	177
"	"	1265	"	Náṣir-ed-dín	578	187
"	"	1266	"	"	579	187
"	AR	1280 ?	"	"	626	202
"	AV	1283	"	"	590	191
	Æ				111	239

MINT.	Metal.	A.H.	DYNASTY.	PRINCE.	NO.	Page.
رعناش Ra'násh	Æ	1030			112	239
	,,	1034			113	239
زنجان Zenján						
دار السعاده	*N*	1236	Ḳájárs	Fet-ḥ-'Alí	476	156
,,	,,	1239	,,	,,	477	156
,,	*R*	1241	,,	,,	527	172
سرخس Sarakhs	*N*	1276	,,	Náṣir-ed-dín	585	190
ساري Sárí	*R*		Ṣafavis	Muḥammad Khudabanda	27*b*	20
	,,		,,	,,	27*c*	20
سلطانيه Sulṭáníya	,,		,,	Isma'íl I.	7	4
سند Sind	,,	1157	Efsháris	Nádir	263	82
	,,	1158	,,	,,	266*a*	83
ساوج بلاغ Sá-új Bulágh	Æ				114	240

MINT.	Metal.	A.H.	DYNASTY.	PRINCE.	NO.	Page.
شاهجهان اباد Sháhjehánábád دار الخلافه	Á	1152	Efsháris	Nádir	252	80
شماخی Shemákhí	Æ	1110			117-8	241
	"	1117			115	240
	"	1120			116	240
	Á	1189	Zands	Kerím Khán	382	122
	"	1190	"	"	394	125
	"	1191	"	"	400	126
	"	119*x*	"	"	403	126
شيراز Shíráz	Ñ	922	Ṣafavis	Isma'íl I.	2	2
	Á	928	"	"	14	7
	Æ	1097			119	241
	"				120	241
	Ñ	1150	Efsháris	Nádir	214	72
	Á	1150	"	"	227	76
	"	1151	"	"	243	78
	"	1162	"	Sháh Rukh	298-9	93-4
دار العلم	"	1174	Zands	Kerím Khán	347	114
"	Ñ	1176	"	"	328-30	108
"	Á	1176	"	"	350-2	115
"	"	1177	"	"	354	115
"	"	1181	"	"	361	118
"	"	1194	"	Ṣádik	426	135
"	Ñ	1195	"	"	424	134
"	Á	1195	"	"	429	135
"	Ñ	1197	"	'Alí Murád	430	136
"	"	1198	"	"	432	137
"	Á	1198	"	"	436-7	139
"	"	1199	"	Jaa'far	442-3	141
"	Ñ	1201	"	"	438	140
"	"	1202	"	"	439	140
"	Á	1202	"	"	444	141
"	"	1209	Ḳájárs	Aka Muḥammad	448-50	145
"	"	1212	"	Bábá Khán (Fet-ḥ-'Alí)	456	148
"	"	1214	"	Fet-ḥ-'Alí	490	160

MINT.	Metal.	A.H.	DYNASTY.	PRINCE.	NO.	Page.
شیراز Shíráz (*continued*)						
دار العلم	AR	1215	Ḳájárs	Fet-ḥ-'Alí	494	162
,,	,,	1227	,,	,,	515	168
,,	AV	1228	,,	,,	470	154
,,	AR	1246	,,	,,	536	174
,,	,,	1252	,,	Muḥammad	553	180
,,	,,	1254	,,	,,	558	181
,,	,,		,,	,,	574	185
ضرابخانهٔ رکاب Army-mint	AR	1176	Zands	Kerím Khán	353	115
طبرستان Ṭaberistán						
دار الملك	AR	1257	Ḳájárs	Muḥammad	561	182
,,	,,	1265	,,	Náṣir-ed-dín	602	195
,,	AV	1273	,,	,,	583	189
,,	,,	1282	,,	,,	589	191
طهران Ṭehrán	Æ	1143			122	242
	AR	1179	Zands	Kerím Khán	357	116
	,,	1181	,,	,,	362	118
	,,	[1212]	Ḳájárs	Bábá Khán (Fet-ḥ-'Alí)	457	149
دار السلطنه	,,	1213	,,	Fet-ḥ-'Alí	489	160
,,	,,	1215	,,	,,	495	162
,,	AV		,,	,,	462	151
	Æ	1222			123	242
دار الخلافه	AR	1235	,,	,,	523	171
,,	AV	1242	,,	,,	478	157
,,	,,	1249	,,	,,	485	159
,,	AR	1250	,,	Muḥammad	548	178
,,	,,	1255	,,	,,	560	182
,,	,,	1258	,,	,,	562	182
,,	,,	1259	,,	,,	564	183
,,	,,	1261	,,	,,	566	183
,,	AV	1262	,,	,,	547	178
,,	AR	1262	,,	,,	568	184
,,	,,	1263	,,	,,	570-1	184
,,	,,	126x	,,	,,	567	183

MINT.	Metal.	A.H.	DYNASTY.	PRINCE.	NO.	Page.
طهران Ṭeherán (*continued*)						
دار الخلافه	AR	1265	Ḳájárs	Náṣir-ed-dín	603-4	195
„	AV	1268	„	„	580	188
„	AR	1272	„	„	607	197
„	„	1273	„	„	608-9	197
„	„	1274	„	„	612-3	198
„	„	1275	„	„	616-7	199
„	„	1276	„	„	621	200
„	AV	1277	„	„	586	190
„	AR	1277	„	„	622	201
	„	1281	„	„	628-31	202-3
	Æ	1281	„	„	646-7	208
„	AR	1288	„	„	636	205
„	„	1288 ?	„	„	637	205
„	AV	1294	„	„	591	192
	AR	1294	„	„	640	206
	AV	1295	„	„	593-4	192
„	AR	1295	„	„	641	206
	Æ	1295	„	„	648-50	208
	AV	1296	„	„	595	193
	AR	1296	„	„	642-4	207
	AV	1297	„	„	596-8	193-4
„	„	12*xx*	„	„	592	192
	„				599	194
	Æ				124	242
			See ناصری Náṣirí			
قزوين Ḳazvín	? AR		Ṣafavis	Isma'íl I.	18	10
	AV	987	„	Muḥammad Khudabanda	27*a***	269
	„	989	„	„	27*a****	270
	„		„	'Abbás I.	29	22
	AR	10*xx*	„	Sulaimán I.	75	36
	Æ	1114			130	244
	AR	1130	„	Ḥusain	113	48
	Æ	1130			125	243
	AR	1131	„	„	122	50
	„	1132	„	„	128	52
	AV	1134	„	Ṭahmásp II.	145	55
	AR	1135	„	„	159	57
	„	1145	„	'Abbás III.	210	70
	„	1161	Efsháris	Sháh Rukh ('Alí Riẓa Series)	310-1	96

MINT.	Metal.	A.H.	DYNASTY.	PRINCE.	NO.	Page.
قزوين Ḳazvín (*continued*)	AR	116*x*	Efsháris	Ibráhím	308	95
دار السلطنه	"	1162		"	288	89
	? "	[1163]	Ṣafavis	Sulaimán II.	314	99
	"	1167	Zands	Kerím Khán	326-7	107
	Æ	1182			126-7	243
	"	1*xx*3			128	243
"	AR	1226	Ḳájárs	Fet-ḥ-'Alí	514	168
"	"	1233	"	"	521	170
"	AV	1246	"	"	481	157
"	AR	1273	"	Náṣir-ed-dín	610	197
"	"	1274	"	"	614	198
"	"	12?8 ?	"	"	638	205
قم (*sic* قوم) Ḳumm	AR		Ṣafavis	Ṭahmásp I.	25	16
قندهار Kandahár	Æ	957			145-7	247-8
	"	1058			131-2	244
	"	1059			137	246
	"	1080			138-9	246
	"	1082			140-2	246-7
	"	1083			143	247
	"	1085			134	245
	"	1086			135-6	245
	"	1097			155	249
	"	1107			133	245
	AR	[1135-7]	Afgháns	Maḥmúd	197*a*	273
	"	1150	Efsháris	Nádir	228-30	76
	Æ				144	247
	"				148	248
	"				149	248
	"				150-1	248-9
	"				152-3	249
	"				154	249
	"				156	250
	"				157-8	250

MINT.	Metal.	A.H.	DYNASTY.	PRINCE.	NO.	Page.
كاشان Káshán	AR	928	Ṣafavis	Isma'íl I.	15	8
	Æ	1111 ?			162	252
	AR	1130	,,	Ḥusain	114-4*a*	48
	Æ	1132			163	252
	,,	1137			164	252
	,,	1160 ?			165	253
دار المومنين	AR	1174	Zands	Kerím Khán	348	114
,,	AV	1198	,,	'Alí Murád	433	138
,,	,,		,,	,,	434	138
	,,	1209	Ḳájárs	Aḳa Muḥammad	447	144
,,	,,	1227	,,	Fet-ḥ-'Alí	467	153
,,	AR	1241	,,	,,	528	172
,,	,,	1274	,,	Náṣir-ed-dín	615	199
	Æ				166	253
	,,				167	253
كرمان Kermán						
دار الامان	AR	1188	Zands	Kerím Khán	380	122
,,	,,	1189	,,	,,	383	123
,,	AV	1208	,,	Luṭf-'Alí	445	142
	AR	1224	Ḳájárs	Fet-ḥ-'Alí	504	165
,,	AV	1248	,,	,,	483	158
	AR	1249 ?	,,	,,	540	175
,,	,,	1284	,,	Náṣir-ed-dín	634	204
كرمانشاهان Kermánsháhán	Æ	1172			160	251
بلده	AR	1223	Ḳájárs	Fet-ḥ-'Alí	503	165
,,	Æ	1231	,,	,,	516*a*	169
دار الدوله	AR	1232	,,	,,	518	170
,,	AV	1234	,,	,,	473	155
,,	AR	1241	,,	,,	529	172
,,	,,	1242	,,	,,	530	172
,,	,,	1252	,,	Muḥammad	554-5	180
,,	,,	1253	,,	,,	556	181
	Æ	1258			161	251
,,	AR	12*xx*	,,	,,	575	185
,,	,,	1275	,,	Náṣir-ed-dín	618	199
	Æ				159	250

MINT.	Metal.	A.H.	DYNASTY.	PRINCE.	NO.	Page.
گنجه Ganja	AR	1086	Ṣafavis	Sulaimán I.	51	31
	,,	1103	,,	,,	73	36
	,,	1105	,,	,,	74a	36
	Æ	1106			168	253
	,,	1106			177-8	255-6
	AR	1110	,,	Ḥusain	90a	41
	Æ	1116			179	256
	,,	1123			170	254
	,,	1132			173-4	255
	,,	1149			169	254
	AR	1151	Efsháris	Nádir	244	78
	,,	1154	,,	,,	260	81
	Æ	1158 ?			175	255
	AR	1163	,,	Sháh Rukh	303	94
	,,	1176		Khán of Ganja	417	131
	,,	1177		,,	418	131
	,,	1178		,,	419	131
	Æ	1181			171	254
	AR	1182	Zands	Kerím Khán	369-70	120
	,,	1184	,,	,,	377	121
	,,	1187		Khán of Ganja	420	131
	,,	1188		,,	421	131
	,,	1189	,,	Kerím Khán	384-6	123
	Æ	118x			176	255
	AR	1190	,,	,,	395-9	125-6
	,,	1191 ?	,,	,,	401	126
	,,	1192	,,	,,	402	126
	Æ	1207			180	256
	AR	1214	Ḳájárs	Fet-ḥ-'Alí	491	161
	Æ	1215			181	256
	,,				172	254
لاهور Láhór دار السلطنه	AV	1151	Efsháris	Nádir	215	73
لاهیجان Láhíján	AR	1139	Ṣafavis	Ṭahmásp II.	168	58
	AV	1213	Ḳájárs	Fet-ḥ-'Alí	459	150

MINT.	Metal	A.H.	DYNASTY.	PRINCE.	NO.	Page.
مرو Merv	Æ	[9½]5	Ṣafavis	Isma'íl I.	10	5
	„		„	„	9	5
مزندران Mazenderán	Æ	1138	Ṣafavis	Ṭahmásp II.	166	58
	Æ	1138			182	257
	Æ	1139	„	„	168a	58
	Æ	1140 ?			184 5	257-8
	Æ	1141	„	„	174	59
	„	1142	„	„	181	60
	„	1143	„	„ ('Alí Riza ser.)	184-5	61-2
	„	1144	„	„ *or* 'Abbás III. („)	191	63
	Æ	1159			187	258
	Æ	1163	„	Sulaimán II.	313	98
	„	1166	„	Isma'íl III.	320	103
	„	1167	„	„	321-2	104
	„	1170	Ḳájárs	Muḥammad Ḥasan	411-2	129
	„	1171	„	„	413-4	129
	„	1173	Zands	Kerím Khán	344-5	112-3
	„	1175	„	„	349	114
	„		„	„	346	113
	Æ				183	257
	„				186	258
مشهد Mesh-hed						
مشهد امام رضا	Æ	976	Ṣafavis	Ṭahmásp I.	23-4	15
	„	1124	„	Ḥusain	100	44
	„	1130 ?	„	„	115	49
مشهد مقدس	„	1139	„	Ṭahmasp II.	169-71	58
„ „	„	1140	„	„	172-3	59
„ „	„	1141	„	„	175	59
„ „	„	1143	„	„ ('Alí Riza ser.)	186-90	62-3
„ „	„	114*x*	„	„ *or* 'Abbás III. („)	192	63
„ „	N	1148	„	'Abbás III. („)	213	71
„ „	Æ	1148	„	„ („)	213a	71
	„	1149	Efsháris	Nádir	223	75
	„	1150	„	„	231-5	76-7
„ „	„	1151	„	„	245	78
„ „	„	1151	„	,	246	78
„ „	„	1153	„	„	257	81

MINT.	Metal.	A.H.	DYNASTY.	PRINCE.	NO.	Page.
مشهد Mesh-hed (*continued*)						
مشهد مقدس	AR	1156	Efsháris	Nádir	261	82
" "	"	1157	"	"	264	82
	"	1160	"	'Ádil Sháh	282-3	87
	"	1161	"	"	284	88
" "	"	1161	"	Sháh Rukh	293	92
	"	1161	"	" ('Alí Riẓa ser.)	312	97
	"	1162	"	"	295-6	92-3
" "	"	1162	"	"	300-1	94
" "	"	1163	"	"	304	95
" "	"	116$\frac{2}{3}$	"	"	305	95
" "	AV	116[1-3]	"	"	292	91
" "	AR	1195	"	"	316	101
" "	"		"	"	317	101
" "	Æ	1205			190	259
" "	AR	1222	Ḳájárs	Fet-ḥ-'Alí	501	164
" "	"	1230 ?	"	"	516	169
" "	Æ	1246			191	260
لمشهد المقدس	AR	1251	"	Muḥammad Sháh	549-50	178-9
مشهد مقدس	"	1258	"	"	563	183
" "	"	1260	"	"	565	183
" "	"	1263	"	"	572	184
" "	AV	1265		Ḥasan Khán Sálár, Rebel	577	186
" "	"	1268	"	Náṣir-ed-dín	581	188
" "	AR	1278	"	"	624	201
" "	AV	1279	"	"	587	190
" "	AR	1279	"	"	625	201
مشهد الرضا	AV	1281	"	"	588	191
مشهد مقدس	Æ				188	259
" "	"				189	259
" "	"				192-3	260
		See ارض اقدس Arẓ-i-aḳdas.				
نخجوان Nakhchuván	AR	1097	Ṣafavis	Sulaimán I.	62-5	33-4
	"	1101	"	"	72	35
	"	1130	"	Ḥusain	116	49
	"	1133	"	"	133	53
	"	1182	Zands	Kerím Khán	371	120
	"	1183	"	"	374	121
نادراباد Nádirábád	AR	1151	Efsháris	Nádir	247-8	79

MINT.	Metal.	A.H.	DYNASTY.	PRINCE.	NO.	Page.
ناصری Náṣiri دار الخلافه	Æ	1292	Ḳájárs	Náṣir-ed-dín	639	206
			See طهران Ṭeherán.			
نیمروز Nímróz	Æ	9½2	Ṣafavis	Isma'íl I.	12a	265
	,,	928	,,	,,	15a	266
هراة Herát	Æ	916	Ṣafavis	Isma'íl I.	1	1
	Æ	927	,,	,,	12b	266
	,,			Ṭahmásp I.	26	17
هرات	Æ	1134			194	260
,,	Æ	116?	Efsháris	'Ádil Sháh	285	88
دار السلطنه	,,		,,	Sháh Rukh	294	92
همذان Hamadán	Æ	938	Ṣafavís	Ṭahmásp I.	20	13
	Æ	1054			195	261
	Æ	1097	,,	Sulaimán I.	66	34
بلدهٔ طیبه	,,	1240 ?	Ḳájárs	Fet-ḥ-'Alí	525	171
,, ,,	,,	1244	,,	,,	531	173
,, ,,	,,	1245	,,	,,	534	173
,, ,,	N	1246	,,	,,	482	158
,, ,,	,,	1250	,,	,,	487	160
یزد Yazd	N	1170	Ḳájárs	Muḥammad Ḥasan	407	128
دار العباده	Æ	1179	Zands	Kerím Khán	358	117
,, ,,	,,	1181	,,	,,	363	118
,, ,,	N	1187	,,	,,	334-5	110
,, ,,	,,	1190	,,	,,	340	111
,, ,,	,,	1192	,,	,,	342-3	112
,, ,,	,,	1193	,,	Abu-l-Fet-ḥ	422	132
,, ,,	,,	1194	,,	Ṣádiḳ	423	133
,, ,,	,,	1197	,,	'Alí Murád	431	137
,, ,,	,,	1214	Ḳájárs	Fet-ḥ-'Alí	460	151

MINT.	Metal.	A.H.	DYNASTY.	PRINCE.	NO.	Page.
يزد Yazd (*continued*)						
دار العباده	AR	1214	Kájárs	Fet-ḥ-'Alí	492-3	161-2
„ „	„	1216	„	„	497	163
„ „	„	1232	„	„	519-20	170
„ „	AV	1234	„	„	474	155
„ „	AR	1244	„	„	532	173
„ „	„	1247	„	„	537	174
„ „	„	1248	„	„	538-9	174-5
„ „	„		„	„	541	175
„ „	„	1251	„	Muḥammad	551	179
„ „	„	1253	„	„	557	181
„ „	„	1277	„	Náṣir-ed-dín	623	201
	Æ				196	261

II. A. TITLES OF MINTS.

TITLE.	MINT.
ارض اقدس امام	[مشهد]
ارض اقدس	[,,]
ام البلاد	البصره , بصره
بلده طيبه	همذان
حجور سعد	ايروان
(دار الارشد)	(اردبيل
دار الامان	كرمان
(دار الايمان)	(قم
دار الخلافه	طهران
,, ,,	شاه جهان اباد (دهلی)
دار الدوله	كرمانشاهان
(دار السرور)	(بروجرد
دار السعده	زنجان
دار السلطنه	اصفهان
,, ,,	تبريز
,, ,,	طهران
,, ,,	قزوين

MINT.	TITLE.
دار السلطنه	لاهور
,, ,,	هرات
دار الصفا	خوی
دار العباده	یزد
دار العلم	شیراز
دار المرز	رشت
دار الملك	طبرستان
دار المومنین	استراباد
,, ,,	كاشان
مشهد الرضا	مشهد
مشهد امام رضا	,,
مشهد مقدس	,,
المشهد المقدس	,,

The entries enclosed in parentheses are from Fræhn, Opusc. Post. i., p. 353.

ابراهیم—

ابراهیم شاه 286, 288

السلطان ابراهیم 287

ابو الفتح 422

ابو المظفر *see* اسمعیل (I. II.), حسین, طهماسب (II.), محمد خدابنده

آزاد 416

اشرف 198, 199

اشرف شاه 200—204

اسمعیل (I.)—

السلطان العادل الکامل الهادی الوالی ابو المظفر شاه اسمعیل بهادر خان الصفوی الحسینی 17*a*, 18

السلطان العادل الکامل الهادی الوالی ابو المظفر شاه اسمعیل بهادر خان الصفوی 4, 5, 6, 7, 8, 9, 11

السلطان العادل الکامل الهادی الوالی ابو المظفر شاه اسمعیل بهادر خان 1, 2

السلطان العادل الکامل الهادی الوَلی سلطان سَمعیل شاه [بهادر] خان الصوی (*sic*) 18*a*

السطان العادل الکامل الهادی ابو المظفر شاه اسمعیل بهادر خان الصفوی 15, 15*a*

السلطان العادل الهادی ابو المظفر اسمعیل شاه بهادر خان 12*, 12*a*

السلطان العادل ابو المظفر اسمعیل شاه بهادر خان 12

السلطان العادل اسمعیل شاه بهادر خان الصفوی 10

السلطان شاه اسمعیل بهادر خان بندهٔ (؟) شاه کربلا (؟) 18*b*
السلطان الغازی فی سبیل الله ابو المظفر اسمعیل بهادر خان 13
سلطان شاه اسمعیل 14
شاه اسمعیل الصفوی 16

اسمعیل (II.)—
ابو المظفر اسمعیل شاه بن طهماسب شاه الصفوی. Introd., pp. lxvii., lxxviii.

اسمعیل (III.)—
بندهٔ شاهٔ ولایت اسمعیل 318—322

امام *see* جعفر, علی الرضا, محمد المهدی

ب

بابا—
السلطان بابا خان 456-7

بابر *see* محمد

بادشاه *see* محمد خدابنده

بهادر خان *see* اسمعیل (I.), حسین, طهماسب (I.)

بندهٔ شاه ولایت *see* اسمعیل (III.), حسین, سام, سلیمان (I.), عباس (I.) عباس (II.)

بندهٔ (؟) شاه کربلا (؟) *see* اسمعیل (I.)

ج

جعفر—
امام جعفر الصادق *see* Invocations

ح

حسن—
سالار حسن خان *see* محمد Mottoes

—حسین

السلطان العادل الهادی الکامل الوالی ابو المظفر السلطان ابن السلطان شاه سلطان حسین بهادر خان الصفوی 96

السلطان بن السلطان و الخاقان بن الخاقان 107

بندهٔ شاه ولایت حسین 88, &c.

کلب آستان علی حسین 115

کلب امیر المومنین سلطان حسین 89—95, 144. *See* Distichs

سام بن سلطان حسین *see* سام

—حسینعلی

(السلطان بن السلطان حسینعلی شاه قاجار), Introd., p. lxxiv.

الحسینی *see* اسمعیل (I.), طهماسب (I.), محمد خدابنده

خ

بهادر خان, بابا *see* خان

س

—سام

بندهٔ شاه ولایت سام بن سلطان حسین 275-6

— السلطان

السلطان *see* ابراهیم, اسمعیل (I.), بابا, حسین, شاه رخ, ناصر الدین, نادر, محمد خدابنده (I.), طهماسب

السلطان ابن (بن) السلطان *see* حسین, فتحعلی, ناصر الدین

سلطان *see* اسمعیل (I.), (بابر), فتحعلی

سلطان as part of name, *see* حسین, محمد خدابنده

سلطان خراسان *see* علی الرضا

سلیمان (صفی .II)—
بندهٔ شاه ولایت سلیمان 50, &c.
سلیمان 57, 71. *See* Distichs
سلیمان ثانی—
سلیمان ثانی 313
سلیمان شاه 314

ش

شاه رخ—
السلطان شاهرخ 293, 295, 296, 304, 305
کلب آستان رضا شاهرخ 294, 297—303, 306—308, 315. *See* Distichs.
شاهرخ 292. *See* Distichs
کلب سلطان خراسان شاهرخ [شاد] 316, 317. *See* Distichs
شاه, شه *passim*
شاه الدین *see* علی الرضا

ص

صاحب لزمان *see* محمد المهدی
صادق خان *see* Invocations
الصفوی *see* اسمعیل (I), اسمعیل (II.), حسین, طهماسب (I.)
صفی (I.)—
بندهٔ ساه ولایت صفی 35
صفی 34
شاه است از جان غلام صفی or شاه از جان غلام صفی است 34*a*
صفی *see* صفی (I.)
صفی (II.)—*see* سلیان
صفی Introd., p. lxxix. *See* Distichs

ط

طهماسب (I.)—

السلطان العادل الكامل الهادى الوالى ابو المظفر طهماسب شاه بهادر [خان] 24a

[السلطان العادل] الكامل الهادى الوالى شاه طهماسب [بهادر] خان الحسينى غلام 19, 22

السلطان العادل الكامل الهادى ابو المظفر شا[ه] طهماسب بهادر خان 25, 26

السلطان العادل الهادى ابو المظفر شاه طهماسب بهادر جان 20

السلطان الكامل الهادى ابو المظفر طهماسب شاه بهادر خان الصفوى الحسينى 27

السلطان العادل غلام على بن ابى طالب عليه السلام ابو المظفر الحسينى الصفوى 23, 24

طهماسب شاه 19 (Countermark)

شاه طهماسب 21

طهماسب (II.)—

طهماسب ثانى 145, &c. *See* Distichs

طهماسب بن اسمعيل *see* (II.)

ع

عادل—

عادل شاه *see* على الرضا ,على شاه Distichs

العادل *see* اسمعيل (I.), حسين, طهماسب (I.)

عباس (I.)—

ابو المظفر عباس شاه 28

بندهٔ شاه ولايت عباس 29—33

عباس (II.)—

عباس ثانی 36, &c. *See* Distichs

کلب علی عباس ثانی 47. *See* Distichs

بنده شاه ولایت عباس 48, 49

عباس (III.)—

ظل حق عباس ثالث ثانی صاحقرانی 205—212. *See* Distichs

علی شاه *see* عادل شاه and علی الرضا Distichs

علی شاه—

(السلطان بن السلطان بن السلطان علی شاه قاجار), Introd. p. lxxiv.

علی الرضا—

علی بن ابی طالب علیه السلام 23

علی ابی طالب علیه السلام 27*b*, 27*c*

علی بن (ابن) موسی الرضا *see* Distichs, Invocations

علی موسی رضا *see* Distichs

علی *see* Distichs, Invocations

امام رضا *see* Distichs *and* Mints, مشهد

رضا *see* Distichs

سلطان خراسان *see* Distichs.

شاه دین علی موسی رضا *see* Distichs

مقتدای انس و جان *see* Distichs

علی مراد خان *see* Invocations.

غ

غلام امام محمد مهدی الخ 27*a*, 27*a**, 27*a***, 27*a*.*** *See* محمد خدابنده

غلام صفی 34*a*. *See* صفی (I)

غلام علی بن ابی طالب الخ 23, 24. *See* طهماسب (I.)

غلام علی ابی طالب الخ 27*b*, 27*c*. *See* محمد خدابنده

ف

فتحعلی *see* بابا

السلطان ابن (بن) السلطان فتحعلی شاه قاجار 463—475, 501—524, 542—544

السلطان فتحعلی شاه قاجار 458—462, 488—490, 492—500, 541

السلطان فتحعلی شاه 477

سلطان فتحعلی شاه 476

فتحعلی شه خسرو صاحبقران 478—480, 525—539

فتحعلی شه خسرو کشورستان 481—483, 485—487, 540

فتحعلی شاه 484

ک

الکامل *see* اسمعیل (I.), حسین, طهماسب (I.)

کریم خان *see* Mottoes, Invocations

کلب آستان رضا *see* شاه رخ

کلب آستان علی *see* حسین

کلب امیر المومنین *see* حسین

کلب سلطان خراسان *see* شاه رخ

کلب علی *see* عباس (II.)

ل

لطفعلی خان—

لطفعلی بن جعفر 445

م

محمد خدابنده—

سلطان محمد خدابنده باد[شاه] غلام علی ابی طالب علیه السلام 27*b*, 27*c*

سلطان محمد غلام امام محمد مهدی السلام علیه و آبائه ابو المظفر بادشاه بن طهماسب شاه الحسینی 27*a**, 27*a***, cf. 27*a*

غلام امام محمد محدی .... باد[شاه الـ]ـلطان الحسینی 27*a****

محمد [آقا] *see* Distichs

محمد شاه *see* Mottoes

محمد حسن خان *see* Distichs

—محمود

شاه محمود جهانگیر 193—196, 197*a*. *See* Distichs

محمود شاه عالمگیر 197. *See* Distichs

—محمد المهدی

امام محمد مهدی 27*a*, 27*a**, 27*a***, 27*a****

امام بحق صاحب الزمان *see* Distichs

صاحب الزمان *see* Distichs, Invocations

ن

—نادر

السلطان نادر 215, 216*a*, 224—230, 236—244, 246—249, 251, 417—421.

شاه شاهان نادر صاحبقران 216, 217—220, 245, 250, 252—272. *See* Distichs

نادر ایران 221—223, 231—235. *See* Distichs

—ناصر الدین

السلطان ابن (بن) السلطان ناصر الدین شاه قاجار 578, &c.

السلطان ناصر الدین شاه قاجار 588 (in Tughrá), 593—595, 597—599, 606, 628—631, 640, 642—644, Med. 1.

السلطان ناصر الدین شاه 592, 607—609, 611—614, 621, 622

السلطان الاعظم والخاقان الافخم ناصر الدین شاه قاجار 596

ناصر الدین شاهنشاه Med. 2.

و

الوالی *see* اسمعیل (I.), حسین, طهماسب (I.)

ه

الهادی *see* اسمعیل (I.), حسین, طهماسب (I.)

III. A. INDEX OF DISTICHS.

از خراسان سکه بر زر شد بتوفیق خدا نصرت وامداد شاه دین علی موسی رضا	Ṭahmásp II., 'Alí Riẓa, 184-92 'Abbás III., 'Alí Riẓa, 213, 213*a*
باشرفی اثر نام آنجناب رسید شرف زسکهٔ اشرف بر آفتاب رسید	Ashraf, 198-9
بر زر و سیم تا نشان باشد سکهٔ صاحب الزمان باشد	Aḳa Muḥammad, 454-5
[بزر تا ؟] شاهرخ زد سکهٔ صاحبقرانی‌را [دو] باره (؟) دولت ایران گرفت از سرجوانی‌را	Sháh Rukh, 292
(بزر زد سکه از الطاف سرمد شه والا گهر سلطان محمد)	Sultán Muḥammad, Introd., p. lxxxi.
بزر سکه از میمنت زد قضا بنام علی بن (ابن) موسی الرضا	Muḥammad Ḥasan, 401—15 Aḳa Muḥammad, 446
بگیتی انکه اکنون سکه زد صاحبقرانی زتوفیق خدا کلب علی عباس ثانی	'Abbás II., 47
بگیتی سکهٔ صاحبقرانی زد از توفیق حق عباس ثانی	'Abbás II., 36—46
بگیتی سکهٔ صاحبقرانی زد از توفیق حق طهماسب ثانی	Ṭahmasp II., 145—183
بهر تحصیل رضای مقتدای انس و جان سکهٔ خیرات بر زر زد سلیمان جهان	Sulaimán I., 57, 71

تا زر و سیم در جهان باشد	Kerím Khán, 323, 326
سکهٔ صاحب الزمان باشد	Aḳa Muḥammad, 448-50
تا زر و سیم را نشان باشد	Aḳa Muḥammad, 447
سکهء صاحب الزمان باشد	
تا که آزاد در جهان باشد	
سکهء صاحبِ الزمان باشد	Ázád, 416
دست زد بر جلالهٔ اشرف شاه	
بود تعبیر سکه داد گناه	Ashraf, 200 – 202
زالطاف شاه اشرف حق شعار	
بزر نقش شد سکهء چار یار	Ashraf, 203, 204
(زبعد هستی عباس ثانی	
صفی زد سکهء صاحبقرانی)	Ṣafí II., (Sulaimán I.,) Introd., p. lxxix.
زد از لطف حق سکهء کامرانی	
شه عدل گشته سلیمان ثانی	Sulaimán II., 313
(زد زتوفیق حق بچهرهٔ زر	
سکه سلطان حسین دین پرور)	Ḥusain, Introd., p. lxxx.
زفیض حضرت باری و سرنوشت قضا	
رواج یافت بزر سکهٔ امام رضا	Ibráhím ('Alí Riẓa), 289—91
(زمشرق تا بمغرب گر امام است	
علی و آل او مارا تمام است)	Isma'íl II., Introd., p. lxxvii.
سکه بر زر زد بتوفیق الهی در جهان	
ظل حق عباس ثالث ثانی صاحبقران	'Abbás III., 205—212
سکه بر زر کرد نام سلطنت‌را در جهان	
نادر ایران زمین و خسرو گیتی ستان	Nádir, 214, 221-23, 231-33
سکه زد از سعیِ نادر ثانی صاحبقران	
کلب سلطان خراسان شاهرخ [شاه] جهان	Sháh Rukh, 316, 317

سکه زد از مشرق ایران چو قرص آفتاب
شاه محمود جهانگیر سیادت انتساب — Maḥmúd, 193-6, 197*a*

سکه زد بر هفت کشور چتر زد چون مهر و ماه
وارث ملك سلیمان گشت احمد پادشاه — Aḥmad, Introd., p. lxxxii.

سکه زد در جهان بحکم خدا
شاهرخ کلب آستان رضا — Sháh Rukh, 294, 297-303, [306-8, 315

سکه زد طهماسب ثانی بر زر کامل عیار
لا فتی الا علی لا سیف الا ذوالفقار — Tahmasp II., Introd., p. lxxx.

سکهٔ صاحبقرانی زد بتوفیق اله
همچو خورشید جهان افروز ابراهیم شاه — Ibráhím, 286, 288

سکهٔ مهر علی‌را تا زدم بر نقد جان
گشت از فضل خدا محکوم فرمانم جهان — Sulaimán I., 68

شد آفتاب و ماه زر و سیم در جهان
از سکهٔ امام بحق صاحب الزمان — Kerím Khán, 324-5, 328-30, 334-5, 338-52, 354-5, 356-65, 369-72, 374, 377, 380, 383-5, 387-8; Abu-l-Fet-ḥ, 422; Sádiḳ, 423-4, 426, 428-9; 'Alí Murád, 431, 433-37; Aḳa Muḥammad, 452-53.

گشت رایج بحکم لم یزلی
سکهٔ سلطنت بنام علی — 'ÁdilSháh ('Alí Riẓa?), 277-85

گشت زده سکه بر زر
لطفعلی بن جعفر — Luṭf-'Alí, 445

گشت صاحب سکه از توفیق رب المشرقین
در جهان کلب امیر المومنین سلطان حسین — Ḥusain, 89-95, 144

فرو رود بزمین ماه و آفتاب منیر
زرشك سکهٔ محمود شاه عالمگیر — Maḥmúd, 197

هر شیردل که دشمن شه‌را عن گرفت — Náṣir-ed-dín, Med. 1.
از آفتاب همت ما این نشان گرفت

هست سلطان بر سلاطین جهان شــاه شاهان نادر صاحبقران	[252-72 Nádir, 216-20, 245-8, 250,
برفروزد روی (?) زمی چون طلوع مهر و ماه وارث ملك شد سلیمان بن سادات شاه	Sulaimán II., 314

III. B. INVOCATIONS.

یا امام جعفر الصادق	Jaa'far Khán, *passim*
یا صاحب الزمان	Kerím Khán, 382, 386, 394—403
یا علی	'Alí Murád, *passim*. *See* Miscellaneous Inscriptions, ناد علیا الخ
یا علی بن موسی الرضا	Sháh Rukh (Alí Riẓa), 309—312
یا کریم	Kerím Khán, *passim*, Ṣádiḳ, *passim*. *See* Mottoes, هو کریم
یا محمد	Aḳa Muhammad Khán, *passim*

III. C. MOTTOES.

شاهنشه انبیا محمد	Muḥammad Sháh, *passim*
العزة لله	Fet-ḥ-'Alí, 458, &c.
الملك لله	Bábá Khán (Fet-ḥ-'Alí), 456
هو کریم	Kerím Khán, 328, 328*a* (from یا من هو یمن رجاه کریم). *See* Introd., p. lxxxix.
هو الناصر	Náṣir-ed-dín, Med. 3

IV. MISCELLANEOUS INDEX.

لا اله الا الله محمد رسول الله علی ولی الله *passim*

لا اله الا الله محمد نبی الله علی ولی الله 30, 32, 33, 326

لا اله الا الله محمد رسول الله (Afgháns) 193-9, 203-4, 416

علی حسن حسین علی محمد جعفر موسی علی محمد علی حسن محمد *passim* (order varied)

اللهم صل علی النبی و الولی والبتول والسبطین والسجاد والباقر والصادق والکاظم و الرضا و التقی و النقی والزکی والمهدی 47 cf. 18*b*, 651

ناد علیا مظهر العجائب
تجده عونا لك فی النوائب
کل هم وغم سینجلی
بولایتك یا علی یاعلی یا علی 15, 652

ابا بکر عمر عثمان علی (Afghán), 197*a*

خلد الله تعالی ملکه و سلطانه و.... †1

خلد الله تعلی ملکه و سلطانه 7, 26

خلد الله ملکه و سلطانه 2, 5, 8, 9, 12, 12*, 15,*a* 17, 17*a*, 21, 25, 96, 652

خلد الله ملکه 8, 12*a*, 18, 215, 216*a*, 224—230, 234—243, 246—249, 251-2, 272

خلد ملکه 10

† The phrases خلد ا ع often defective from condition of coins.

V. INDEX OF DENOMINATIONS, MARKS AND FORMULAS OF GENUINENESS, Etc.

دو دینار Kandahár 145-149
ده تومان 596
ربعی 631, 640, 644
یکهزار دینار 629—643
٥٠٠ دینار 630
٥٠ دینار 646, 648, 649
٢٥ دینار 647, 650

عدل ضرب طهماسب شاه 19
رائج Mesh-hed, 260. *See also* Distichs, Ádil Sháh.
فلوس رائج ممالك محمد شه و ایران 576.

VI. INDEX OF TYPES.

A.

Antelope, running.—Ḳandahár, 145—149.
Ape.—Eriván, 55, 56.

B.

Bird.—Urúmí, 24; Borujird, 60; Baghdád, 62; Khoï, 107
Boar (?) and lion.—Kermánsháhán, 160.
Bull, humped.—Tabríz, 88—91.
Bull, humped, on fish.—Tabríz, 92.

C.

Camel.—Eriván, 53; Ḳandahár, 140-3.
Cock.—Eriván, 58.

D.

Dragon.—Urúmí, 23.
Duck.—Ganja, 180.

E.

Eagle, devouring partridge?—Hamadán, 195.
Elephant.—Eriván, 49—52; Tabríz, 93; Túï, 100; Tíra? 102.
Elephant with Driver.—Kermánsháhán, 161; Mesh-hed, 190—192.

F.

Fet-ḥ-'Alí, *see* Sháh.
Fish.—Bandar-Abu-shahr, 20; Tíra? 101, 102.
Fish, Bull on, *see* Bull.
Fishes, Two.—Ḳandahár, 152, 153.
Flower.—Ḳandahár, 154.

G.

Goose.—Eriván 59; Ṭeherán, 124.
Geese, Two.—Sá-új Bulágh, 114.

H.

Hare.—Eriván, 57; Khoï, 106.
Horse.—Baghdád, 61; Shemákhi, 116; Ganja, 173—176.
Horse, galloping.—Ḳandahár, 138, 139; Herát, 194.
Horse, galloping, and sun.—Ḳazvín, 128.

I.

Ibex.—Shíráz, 119, 120; Ḳazvín, 130; Ganja, 177-9.
Ibex, recumbent, Eriván, 54.

L.

Lion.—Abu-shahr, 6, 7; Bandar-Abu-shahr, 15-19; Tiflís, 95, 96; Tíra? 101; Resht, 109, 110; Ḳazvín, 129; Ḳandahár, 134—136; Kermánsháhán, 159; Ganja, 170, 171.
Lion and Boar? see Boar?
Lion and cub.—Eriván, 47—48.
Lion and Sun.—Ṭeherán, Æ 593—595, Æ 628—631, 639, 640. 642—644. Med. Æ 1, Æ 2, 3.—Iṣfahán, 26—32; Eriván, 35—44; Bandar-'Abbás? 63, 64; Tabríz, 71—78; Khoï, 103—105; Demávend, 108; Ra'násh, 112, 113; Shemákhí, 115; Ṭeherán, 121; Ḳazvín, 125—127; Ḳandahár, 131—133; Káshán, 162—165; Ganja, 168, 169; Mazenderán, 182, 183; Mesh-hed, 188; Yazd, 196.
Lion, recumbent.—Tabríz, 82.

Lion, recumbent, and Sun.—No mint Bil, 542—544. Irán Æ (royal), 576. Irán, 1, 2; Urúmí, 22; Eriván, 45; Tabríz. 79—81.
Lion, rampant —Irán, 3.
Lions, rampant, Two.—Abu-shahr, 4, 5.
Lion, seizing bull.—Tiflís, 98, 99.
Lion, seizing stag.—Iṣfahán, 33, 34; Behbehán, 65—70; Ṭeherán, 122; Ḳandahar, 137; Mazenderán, 184—187.

N.

Naṣir-ed-dín, *see* Sháh.

O.

Ornamented Label.—Abu-shahr, 12, 13, 14.

P.

Parrot.—Resht 111.
Peacock.—Abu-shahr, 9; Ardebíl, 21; Tabríz, 94; Shemákhí, 117, 118; Ṭeherán, 123; Ḳandahár, 150, 151; Káshán, 167.
Peacocks, Two.—Abu-shahr, 10.

S.

Sabre.—Ḳandahár, 157, 158.
Sabre, Two-bladed.—(Zu-l-fiḳár) Ḳandahár, 155, 156; Ganja, 181.
Sháh (Fet-ḥ-'Alí) on horseback.—Zenján, *N* 476, 477.
Sháh (Fet-ḥ-'Alí) seated on throne.—Iṣfahán, *N* 484.
Sháh (Náṣir-ed-dín) seated.—*R* 611.
Sháh (Náṣir-ed-dín), Bust of.—Ṭeherán, *N* 592, 596—599, *R* 607–609, 612, 613; Ḳazvín, 614.
Shield, Arms of Persia, *see* Lion and Sun.
Ship.—Abu-shahr, 11.
Stag.—Ḳandahár, 144.

Sun, rayed.—Ṭeherán, Æ 646—650; Abu-shahr, 8; Eriván, 46; Tabríz, 83—87; Tiflís, 97; Káshán, 166; Mesh-hed, 189.

T.

Turtle.—Urúmí, 25.

Z.

Zu-l-fiḳár, *see* Sabre, Two-bladed.

COMPARATIVE TABLE OF THE YEARS OF THE HIJRAH AND OF THE CHRISTIAN ERA.

(This Table, after Wüstenfeld, gives the current Christian day, the Muḥammadan day beginning at sunset on the Christian day preceding. New style begins A.D. 1582. See Introd. p. xviii. for a caution.)

A.H.	A.D.		A.H.	A.D.	
900	1494 . .	Oct. 2	941	1534 . .	July 13
901	1495 . .	Sept. 21	942	1535 . .	„ 2
902	1496 . .	„ 9	943	1536 . .	June 20
903	1497 . .	Aug. 30	944	1537 . .	„ 10
904	1498 . .	„ 19	945	1538 . .	May 30
905	1499 . .	„ 8	946	1539 . .	„ 19
906	1500 . .	July 28	947	1540 . .	„ 8
907	1501 . .	„ 17	948	1541 . .	April 27
908	1502 . .	„ 7	949	1542 . .	„ 17
909	1503 . .	June 26	950	1543 . .	„ 6
910	1504 . .	„ 14	951	1544 . .	Mar. 25
911	1505 . .	„ 4	952	1545 . .	„ 15
912	1506 . .	May 24	953	1546 . .	„ 4
913	1507 . .	„ 13	954	1547 . .	Feb. 21
914	1508 . .	„ 2	955	1548 . .	„ 11
915	1509 . .	April 21	956	1549 . .	Jan. 30
916	1510 . .	„ 10	957	1550 . .	„ 20
917	1511 . .	Mar. 31	958	1551 . .	„ 9
918	1512 . .	„ 19	959	1551 . .	Dec. 29
919	1513 . .	„ 9	960	1552 . .	„ 18
920	1514 . .	Feb. 26	961	1553 . .	„ 7
921	1515 . .	„ 15	962	1554 . .	Nov. 26
922	1516 . .	„ 5	963	1555 . .	„ 16
923	1517 . .	Jan. 24	964	1556 . .	„ 4
924	1518 . .	„ 13	965	1557 . .	Oct. 24
925	1519 . .	„ 3	966	1558 . .	„ 14
926	1519 . .	Dec. 23	967	1559 . .	„ 3
927	1520 . .	„ 12	968	1560 . .	Sept. 22
928	1521 . .	„ 1	969	1561 . .	„ 11
929	1522 . .	Nov. 20	970	1562 . .	Aug. 31
930	1523 . .	„ 10	971	1563 . .	„ 21
931	1524 . .	Oct. 29	972	1564 . .	„ 9
932	1525 . .	„ 18	973	1565 . .	July 29
933	1526 . .	„ 8	974	1566 . .	„ 19
934	1527 . .	Sept. 27	975	1567 . .	„ 8
935	1528 . .	„ 15	976	1568 . .	June 26
936	1529 . .	„ 5	977	1569 . .	„ 16
937	1530 . .	Aug. 25	978	1570 . .	„ 5
938	1531 . .	„ 15	979	1571 . .	May 26
939	1532 . .	„ 3	980	1572 . .	„ 14
940	1533 . .	July 23	981	1573 . .	„ 3

A.H.	A.D.		A.H.	A.D.	
982	1574	April 23	1032	1622	Nov. 5
983	1575	„ 12	1033	1623	Oct. 25
984	1576	Mar. 31	1034	1624	„ 14
985	1577	„ 21	1035	1625	„ 3
986	1578	„ 10	1036	1626	Sept. 22
987	1579	Feb. 28	1037	1627	„ 12
988	1580	„ 17	1038	1628	Aug. 31
989	1581	„ 5	1039	1629	„ 21
990	1582	Jan. 26	1040	1630	„ 10
991	1583	„ 25*	1041	1631	July 30
992	1584	„ 14	1042	1632	„ 19
993	1585	„ 3	1043	1633	„ 8
994	1585	Dec. 23	1044	1634	June 27
995	1586	„ 12	1045	1635	„ 17
996	1587	„ 2	1046	1636	„ 5
997	1588	Nov. 20	1047	1637	May 26
998	1589	„ 10	1048	1638	„ 15
999	1590	Oct. 30	1049	1639	„ 4
1000	1591	„ 19	1050	1640	April 23
1001	1592	„ 8	1051	1641	„ 12
1002	1593	Sept. 27	1052	1642	„ 1
1003	1594	„ 16	1053	1643	Mar. 22
1004	1595	„ 6	1054	1644	„ 10
1005	1596	Aug. 25	1055	1645	Feb. 27
1006	1597	„ 14	1056	1646	„ 17
1007	1598	„ 4	1057	1647	„ 6
1008	1599	July 24	1058	1648	Jan. 27
1009	1600	„ 13	1059	1649	„ 15
1010	1601	„ 2	1060	1650	„ 4
1011	1602	June 21	1061	1650	Dec. 25
1012	1603	„ 11	1062	1651	„ 14
1013	1604	May 30	1063	1652	„ 2
1014	1605	„ 19	1064	1653	Nov. 22
1015	1606	„ 9	1065	1654	„ 11
1016	1607	April 28	1066	1655	Oct. 31
1017	1608	„ 17	1067	1656	„ 20
1018	1609	„ 6	1068	1657	„ 9
1019	1610	Mar. 26	1069	1658	Sept. 29
1020	1611	„ 16	1070	1659	„ 18
1021	1612	„ 4	1071	1660	„ 6
1022	1613	Feb. 21	1072	1661	Aug. 27
1023	1614	„ 11	1073	1662	„ 16
1024	1615	Jan. 31	1074	1663	„ 5
1025	1616	„ 20	1075	1664	July 25
1026	1617	„ 9	1076	1665	„ 14
1027	1617	Dec. 29	1077	1666	„ 4
1028	1618	„ 19	1078	1667	June 23
1029	1619	„ 8	1079	1668	„ 11
1030	1620	Nov. 26	1080	1669	„ 1
1031	1621	„ 16	1081	1670	May 21

* Here the change to the Gregorian New Style takes effect.

A.H.	A.D.		A.H.	A.D.	
1082	1671	May 10	1132	1719	Nov. 14
1083	1672	April 29	1133	1720	„ 2
1084	1673	„ 18	1134	1721	Oct. 22
1085	1674	„ 7	1135	1722	„ 12
1086	1675	Mar. 28	1136	1723	„ 1
1087	1676	„ 16	1137	1724	Sept. 20
1088	1677	„ 6	1138	1725	„ 9
1089	1678	Feb. 23	1139	1726	Aug. 29
1090	1679	„ 12	1140	1727	„ 19
1091	1680	„ 2	1141	1728	„ 7
1092	1681	Jan. 21	1142	1729	July 27
1093	1682	„ 10	1143	1730	„ 17
1094	1682	Dec. 31	1144	1731	„ 6
1095	1683	„ 20	1145	1732	June 24
1096	1684	„ 8	1146	1733	„ 14
1097	1685	Nov. 28	1147	1734	„ 3
1098	1686	„ 17	1148	1735	May 24
1099	1687	„ 7	1149	1736	„ 12
1100	1688	Oct. 26	1150	1737	„ 1
1101	1689	„ 15	1151	1738	April 21
1102	1690	„ 5	1152	1739	„ 10
1103	1691	Sept. 24	1153	1740	Mar. 29
1104	1692	„ 12	1154	1741	„ 19
1105	1693	„ 2	1155	1742	„ 8
1106	1694	Aug. 22	1156	1743	Feb. 25
1107	1695	„ 12	1157	1744	„ 15
1108	1696	July 31	1158	1745	„ 3
1109	1697	„ 20	1159	1746	Jan. 24
1110	1698	„ 10	1160	1747	„ 13
1111	1699	June 29	1161	1748	„ 2
1112	1700	„ 18	1162	1748	Dec. 22
1113	1701	„ 8	1163	1749	„ 11
1114	1702	May 28	1164	1750	Nov. 30
1115	1703	„ 17	1165	1751	„ 20
1116	1704	„ 6	1166	1752	„ 8
1117	1705	April 25	1167	1753	Oct. 29
1118	1706	„ 15	1168	1754	„ 18
1119	1707	„ 4	1169	1755	„ 7
1120	1708	Mar. 23	1170	1756	Sept. 26
1121	1709	„ 13	1171	1757	„ 15
1122	1710	„ 2	1172	1758	„ 4
1123	1711	Feb. 19	1173	1759	Aug. 25
1124	1712	„ 9	1174	1760	„ 13
1125	1713	Jan. 28	1175	1761	„ 2
1126	1714	„ 17	1176	1762	July 23
1127	1715	„ 7	1177	1763	„ 12
1128	1715	Dec. 27	1178	1764	„ 1
1129	1716	„ 16	1179	1765	June 20
1130	1717	„ 5	1180	1766	„ 9
1131	1718	Nov. 24	1181	1767	May 30

A.H.	A.D.	
1182	1768 . .	May 18
1183	1769 . .	„ 7
1184	1770 . .	April 27
1185	1771 . .	„ 16
1186	1772 . .	„ 4
1187	1773 . .	Mar. 25
1188	1774 . .	„ 14
1189	1775 . .	„ 4
1190	1776 . .	Feb. 21
1191	1777 . .	„ 9
1192	1778 . .	Jan. 30
1193	1779 . .	„ 19
1194	1780 . .	„ 8
1195	1780 . .	Dec. 28
1196	1781 . .	„ 17
1197	1782 . .	„ 7
1198	1783 . .	Nov. 26
1199	1784 . .	„ 14
1200	1785 . .	„ 4
1201	1786 . .	Oct. 24
1202	1787 . .	„ 13
1203	1788 . .	„ 2
1204	1789 . .	Sept. 21
1205	1790 . .	„ 10
1206	1791 . .	Aug. 31
1207	1792 . .	„ 19
1208	1793 . .	„ 9
1209	1794 . .	July 29
1210	1795 . .	„ 18
1211	1796 . .	„ 7
1212	1797 . .	June 26
1213	1798 . .	„ 15
1214	1799 . .	„ 5
1215	1800 . .	May 25
1216	1801 . .	„ 14
1217	1802 . .	„ 4
1218	1803 . .	April 23
1219	1804 . .	„ 12
1220	1805 . .	„ 1
1221	1806 . .	Mar. 21
1222	1807 . .	„ 11
1223	1808 . .	Feb. 28
1224	1809 . .	„ 16
1225	1810 . .	„ 6
1226	1811 . .	Jan. 26
1227	1812 . .	„ 16
1228	1813 . .	„ 4
1229	1813 . .	Dec. 24
1230	1814 . .	„ 14
1231	1815 . .	„ 3
1232	1816 . .	Nov. 21
1233	1817 . .	„ 11
1234	1818 . .	Oct. 31
1235	1819 . .	„ 20
1236	1820 . .	„ 9
1237	1821 . .	Sept. 28
1238	1822 . .	„ 18
1239	1823 . .	„ 7
1240	1824 . .	Aug. 26
1241	1825 . .	„ 16
1242	1826 . .	„ 5
1243	1827 . .	July 25
1244	1828 . .	„ 14
1245	1829 . .	„ 3
1246	1830 . .	June 22
1247	1831 . .	„ 12
1248	1832 . .	May 31
1249	1833 . .	„ 21
1250	1834 . .	„ 10
1251	1835 . .	April 29
1252	1836 . .	„ 18
1253	1837 . .	„ 7
1254	1838 . .	Mar. 27
1255	1839 . .	„ 17
1256	1840 . .	„ 5
1257	1841 . .	Feb. 23
1258	1842 . .	„ 12
1259	1843 . .	„ 1
1260	1844 . .	Jan. 22
1261	1845 . .	„ 10
1262	1845 . .	Dec. 30
1263	1846 . .	„ 20
1264	1847 . .	„ 9
1265	1848 . .	Nov. 27
1266	1849 . .	„ 17
1267	1850 . .	„ 6
1268	1851 . .	Oct. 27
1269	1852 . .	„ 15
1270	1853 . .	„ 4
1271	1854 . .	Sept. 24
1272	1855 . .	„ 13
1273	1856 . .	„ 1
1274	1857 . .	Aug. 22
1275	1858 . .	„ 11
1276	1859 . .	July 31
1277	1860 . .	„ 20
1278	1861 . .	„ 9
1279	1862 . .	June 29
1280	1863 . .	„ 18
1281	1864 . .	„ 6

A.H.	A.D.		A.H.	A.D.	
1282	1865 . .	May 27	1301	1883 . .	Nov. 2
1283	1866 . .	„ 16	1302	1884 . .	Oct. 21
1284	1867 . .	„ 5	1303	1885 . .	„ 10
1285	1868 . .	April 24	1304	1886 . .	Sept. 30
1286	1869 . .	„ 13	1305	1887 . .	„ 19
1287	1870 . .	„ 3	1306	1888 . .	„ 7
1288	1871 . .	Mar. 23	1307	1889 . .	Aug. 28
1289	1872 . .	„ 11	1308	1890 . .	„ 17
1290	1873 . .	„ 1	1309	1891 . .	„ 7
1291	1874 . .	Feb. 18	1310	1892 . .	July 26
1292	1875 . .	„ 7	1311	1893 . .	„ 15
1293	1876 . .	Jan. 28	1312	1894 . .	„ 5
1294	1877 . .	„ 16	1313	1895 . .	June 24
1295	1878 . .	„ 5	1314	1896 . .	„ 12
1296	1878 . .	Dec. 26	1315	1897 . .	„ 2
1297	1879 . .	„ 15	1316	1898 . .	May 22
1298	1880 . .	„ 4	1317	1899 . .	„ 12
1299	1881 . .	Nov. 23	1318	1900 . .	„ 1
1300	1882 . .	„ 12			

TABLE

OF THE

RELATIVE WEIGHTS OF

ENGLISH GRAINS and FRENCH GRAMMES.

Grains	Grammes.	Grains.	Grammes.	Grains.	Grammes.	Grains.	Grammes.
1	·064	41	2·656	81	5·248	121	7·840
2	·129	42	2·720	82	5·312	122	7·905
3	·194	43	2·785	83	5·378	123	7·970
4	·259	44	2·850	84	5·442	124	8·035
5	·324	45	2·915	85	5·508	125	8·100
6	·388	46	2·980	86	5·572	126	8·164
7	·453	47	3·045	87	5·637	127	8·229
8	·518	48	3·110	88	5·702	128	8·294
9	·583	49	3·175	89	5·767	129	8·359
10	·648	50	3·240	90	5·832	130	8·424
11	·712	51	3·304	91	5·896	131	8·488
12	·777	52	3·368	92	5·961	132	8·553
13	·842	53	3·434	93	6·026	133	8·618
14	·907	54	3·498	94	6·091	134	8·682
15	·972	55	3·564	95	6·156	135	8·747
16	1·036	56	3·628	96	6·220	136	8·812
17	1·101	57	3·693	97	6·285	137	8·877
18	1·166	58	3·758	98	6·350	138	8·942
19	1·231	59	3·823	99	6·415	139	9·007
20	1·296	60	3·888	100	6·480	140	9·072
21	1·360	61	3·952	101	6·544	141	9·136
22	1·425	62	4·017	102	6·609	142	9·200
23	1·490	63	4·082	103	6·674	143	9·265
24	1·555	64	4·146	104	6·739	144	9·330
25	1·620	65	4·211	105	6·804	145	9·395
26	1·684	66	4·276	106	6·868	146	9·460
27	1·749	67	4·341	107	6·933	147	9·525
28	1·814	68	4·406	108	6·998	148	9·590
29	1·879	69	4·471	109	7·063	149	9·655
30	1·944	70	4·536	110	7·128	150	9·720
31	2·008	71	4·600	111	7·192	151	9·784
32	2·073	72	4·665	112	7·257	152	9·848
33	2·138	73	4·729	113	7·322	153	9·914
34	2·202	74	4·794	114	7·387	154	9·978
35	2·267	75	4·859	115	7·452	155	10·044
36	2·332	76	4·924	116	7·516	156	10·108
37	2·397	77	4·989	117	7·581	157	10·173
38	2·462	78	5·054	118	7·646	158	10·238
39	2·527	79	5·119	119	7·711	159	10·303
40	2·592	80	5·184	120	7·776	160	10·368

TABLE

OF THE

RELATIVE WEIGHTS OF

ENGLISH GRAINS and FRENCH GRAMMES.

Grains.	Grammes.	Grains.	Grammes.	Grains.	Grammes.	Grains.	Grammes.
161	10·432	201	13·024	241	15·616	290	18·79
162	10·497	202	13·089	242	15·680	300	19·44
163	10·562	203	13·154	243	15·745	310	20·08
164	10·626	204	13·219	244	15·810	320	20·73
165	10·691	205	13·284	245	15·875	330	21·38
166	10·756	206	13·348	246	15·940	340	22·02
167	10·821	207	13·413	247	16·005	350	22·67
168	10·886	208	13·478	248	16·070	360	23·32
169	10·951	209	13·543	249	16·135	370	23·97
170	11·016	210	13·608	250	16·200	380	24·62
171	11·080	211	13·672	251	16·264	390	25·27
172	11·145	212	13·737	252	16·328	400	25·92
173	11·209	213	13·802	253	16·394	410	26·56
174	11·274	214	13·867	254	16·458	420	27·20
175	11·339	215	13·932	255	16·524	430	27·85
176	11·404	216	13·996	256	16·588	440	28·50
177	11·469	217	14·061	257	16·653	450	29·15
178	11·534	218	14·126	258	16·718	460	29·80
179	11·599	219	14·191	259	16·783	470	30·45
180	11·664	220	14·256	260	16·848	480	31·10
181	11·728	221	14·320	261	16·912	490	31·75
182	11·792	222	14·385	262	16·977	500	32·40
183	11·858	223	14·450	263	17·042	510	33·04
184	11·922	224	14·515	264	17·106	520	33·68
185	11·988	225	14·580	265	17·171	530	34·34
186	12·052	226	14·644	266	17·236	540	34·98
187	12·117	227	14·709	267	17·301	550	35·64
188	12·182	228	14·774	268	17·366	560	36·28
189	12·247	229	14·839	269	17·431	570	36·93
190	12·312	230	14·904	270	17·496	580	37·58
191	12·376	231	14·968	271	17·560	590	38·23
192	12·441	232	15·033	272	17·625	600	38·88
193	12·506	233	15·098	273	17·689	700	45·36
194	12·571	234	15·162	274	17·754	800	51·84
195	12·636	235	15·227	275	17·819	900	58·32
196	12·700	236	15·292	276	17·884	1000	64·80
197	12·765	237	15·357	277	17·949	2000	129·60
198	12·830	238	15·422	278	18·014	3000	194·40
199	12·895	239	15·487	279	18·079	4000	259·20
200	12·960	240	15·552	280	18·144	5000	324·00

TABLE

FOR

CONVERTING ENGLISH INCHES INTO MILLIMÈTRES AND THE MEASURES OF MIONNET'S SCALE.

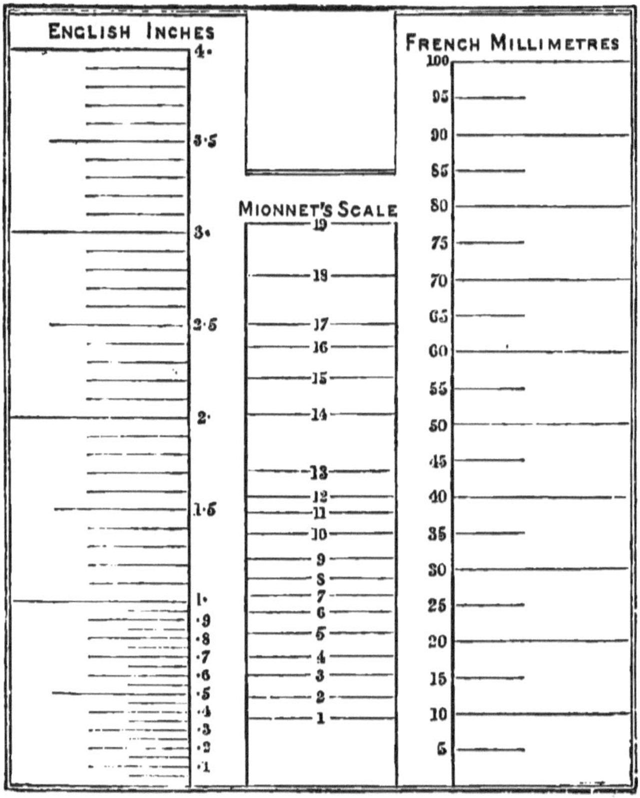

Gilbert & Rivington (Limited), 52, St. John's Square, Clerkenwell, E.C.

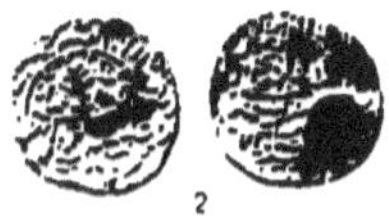

2

1

3

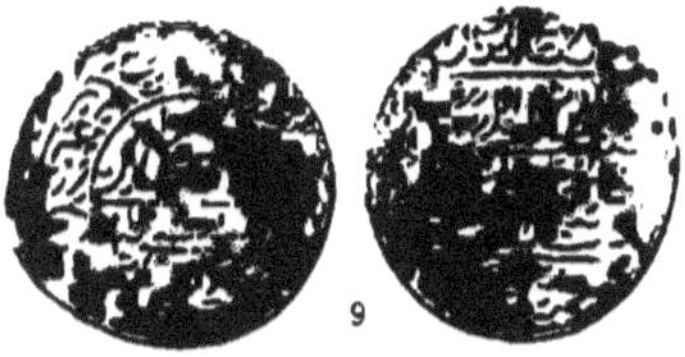

9

10

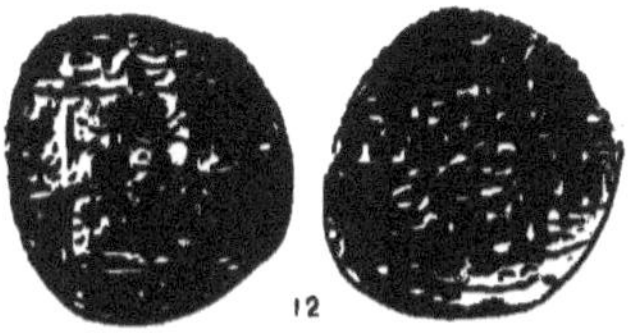

12

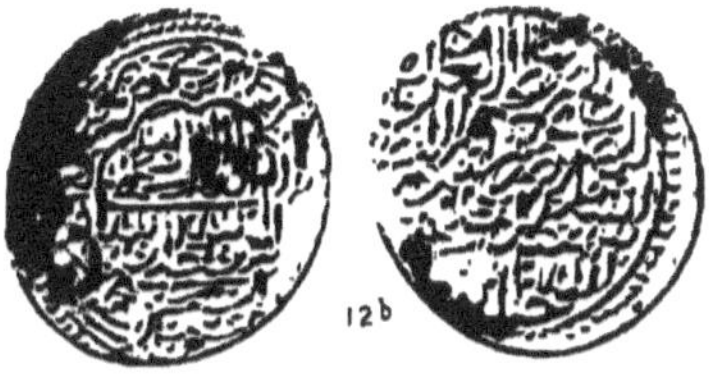

12b

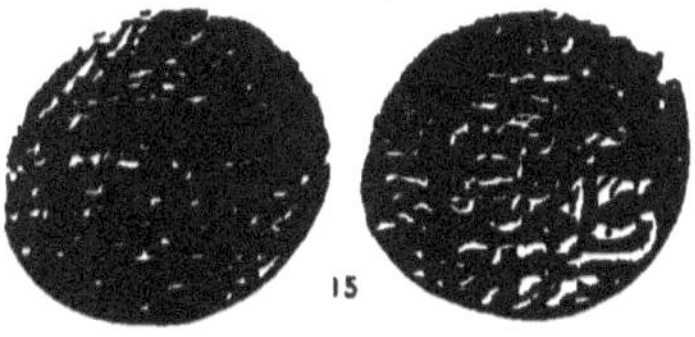

15

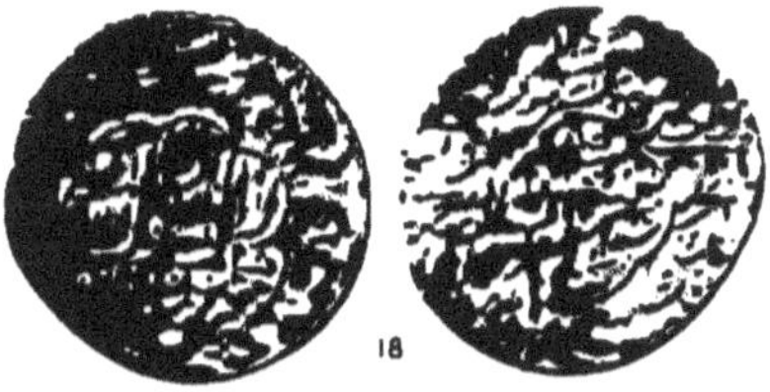

18

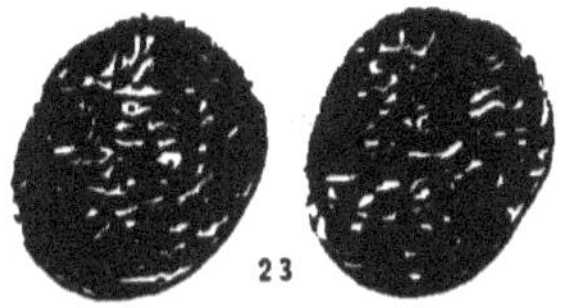

23

26

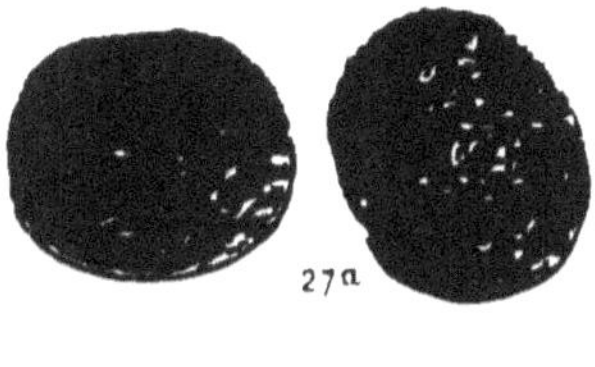

27a

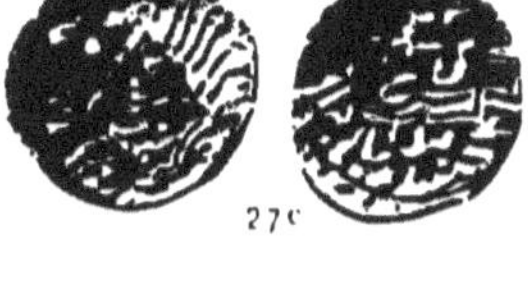

27c

28
29
30
34a
35
47
36
47
50
57

58

68 68

79 79

93 93

88

96

97

99

99

103
103
108
108
115
131
131
134
146
149
184
188

193

197

198

201

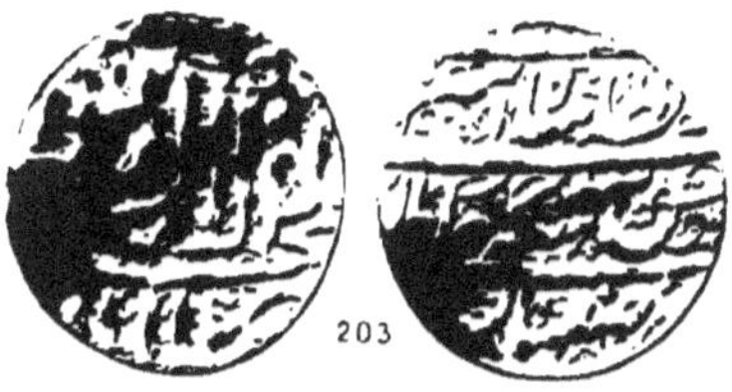
203

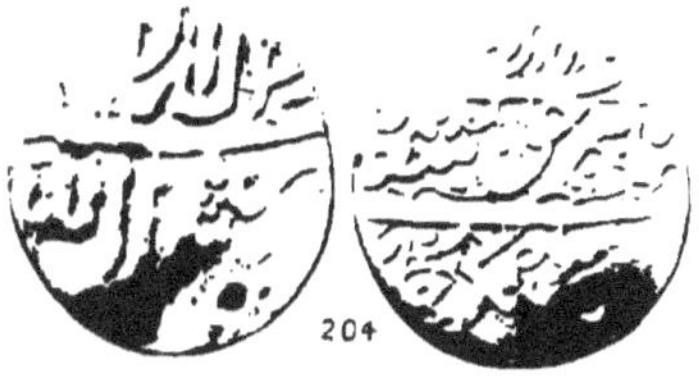
204

205

208

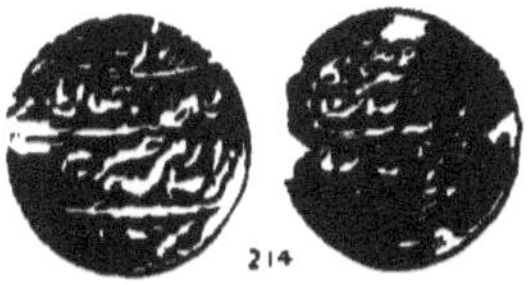
214

215

218

221

222

229

247

252

263

272

275
277
287
288
291
292
293
294
310
312
313
314

315

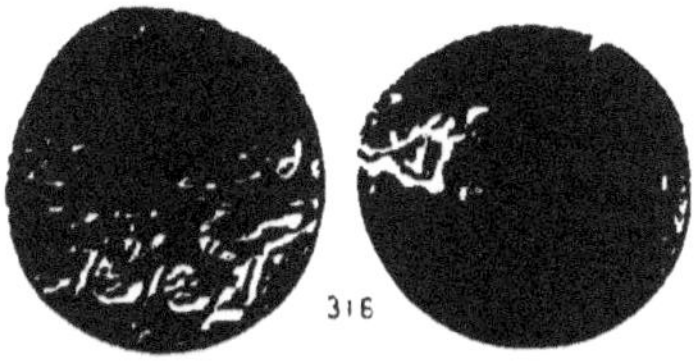
316

318

320

323

324

325

326

328

334

337

338

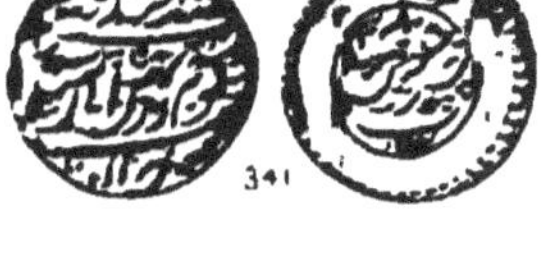
341

344

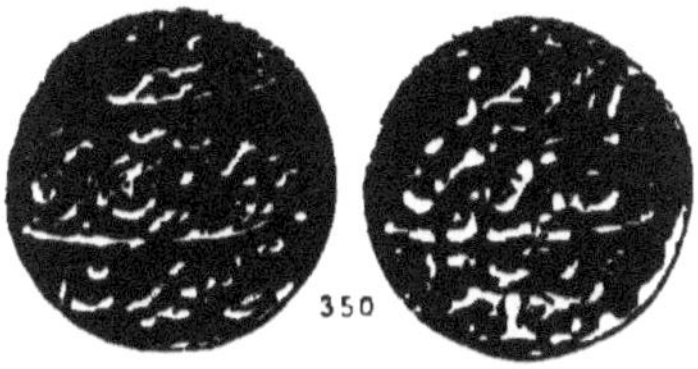
350

353

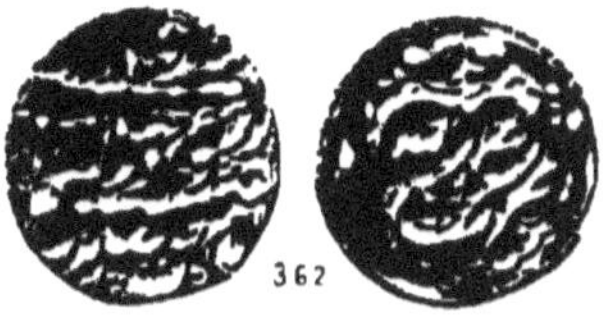
362

363

373

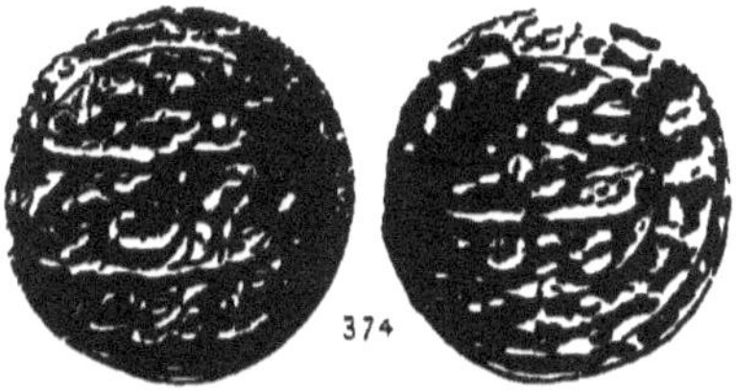
374

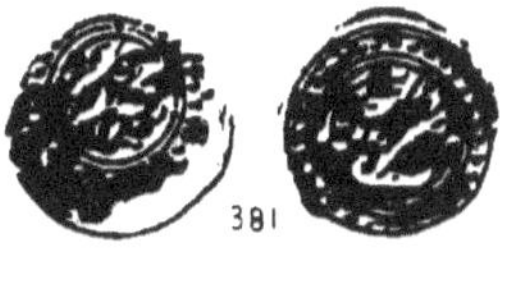
381

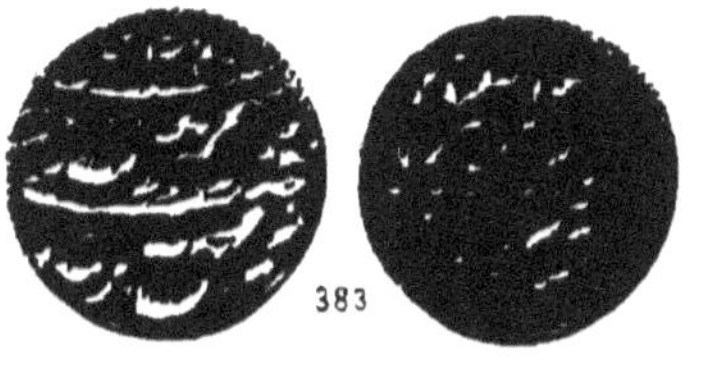
383

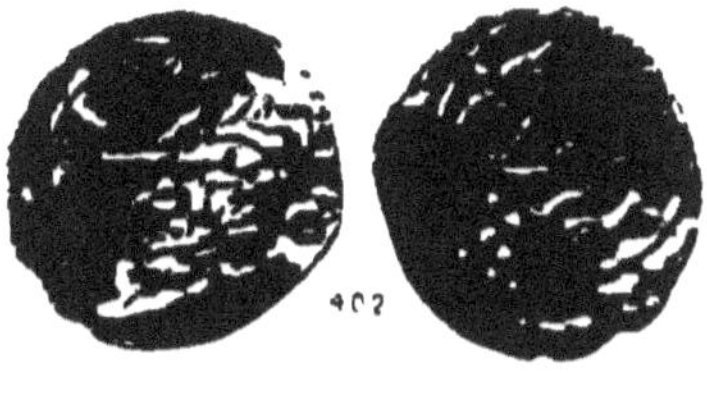
402

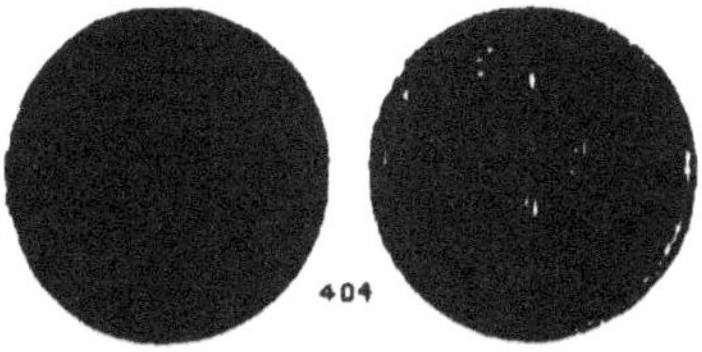

404

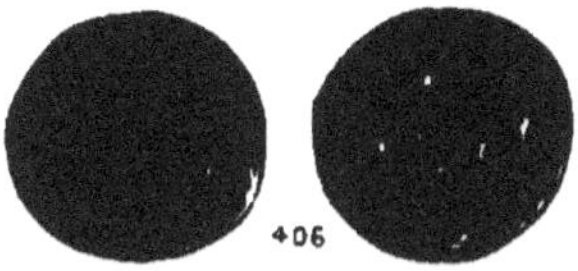

406

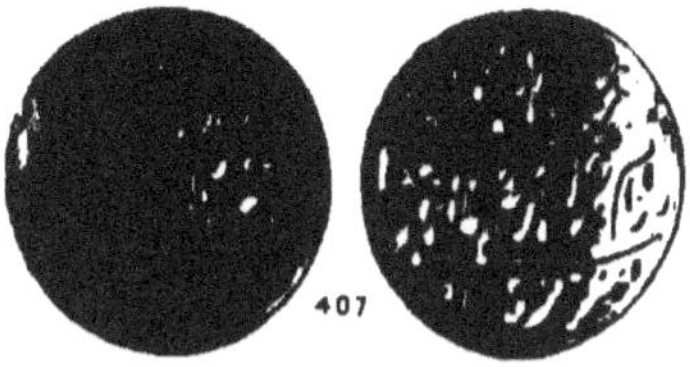

407

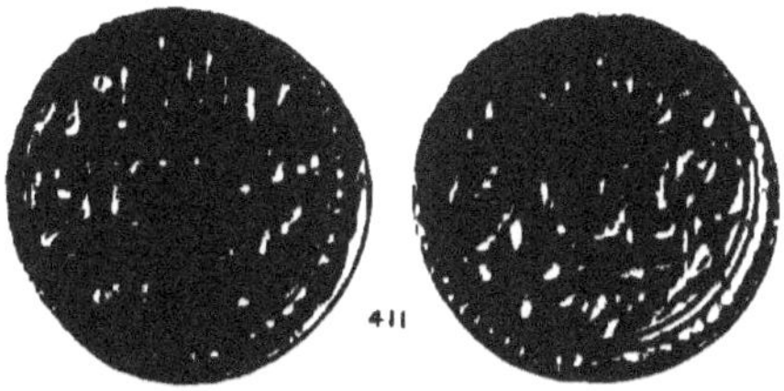

411

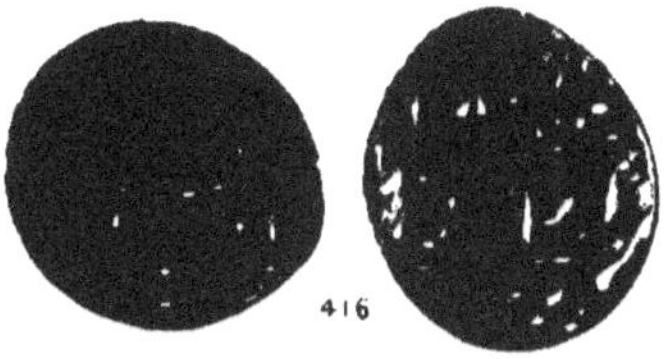

416

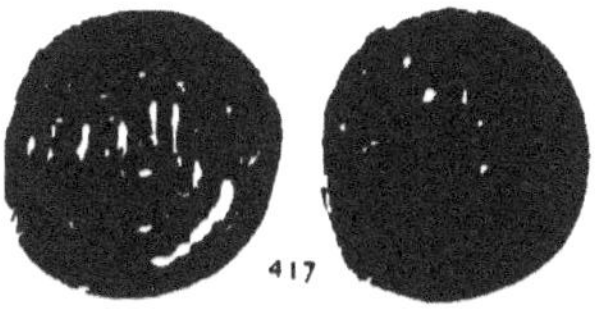

417

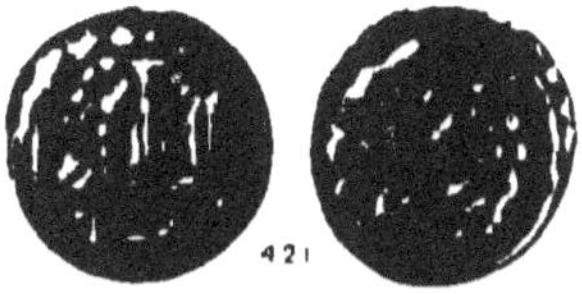

421

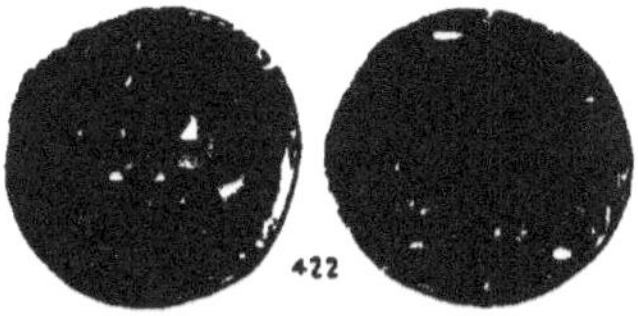
422

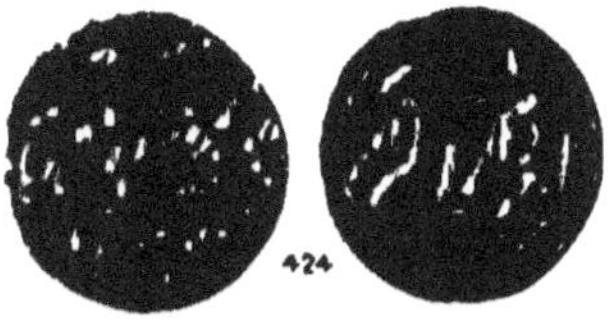
424

426

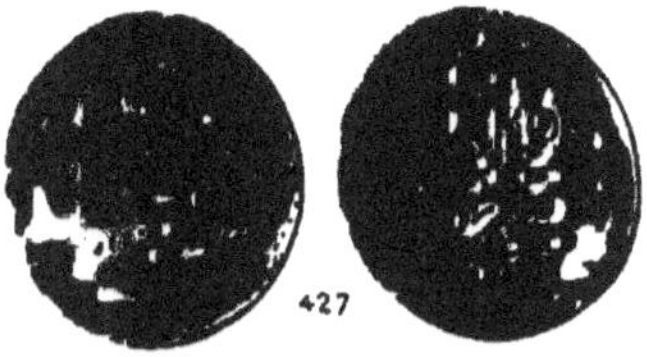
427

430

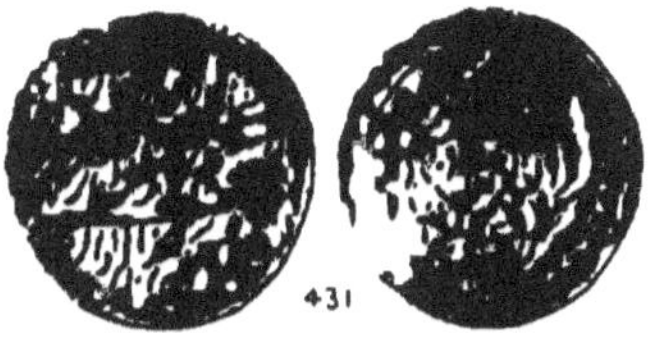
431

433

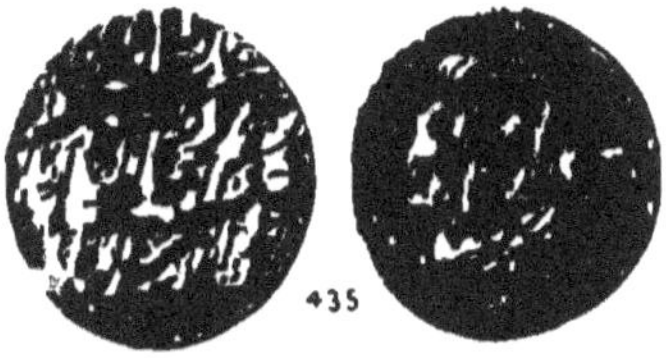
435

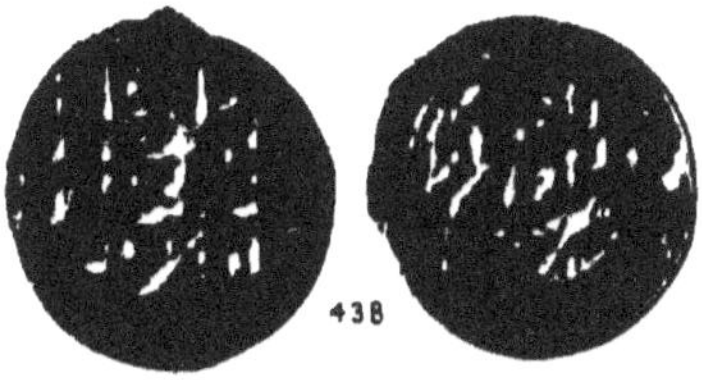
438

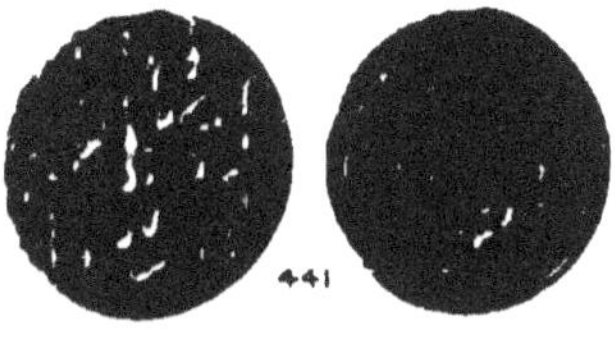
441

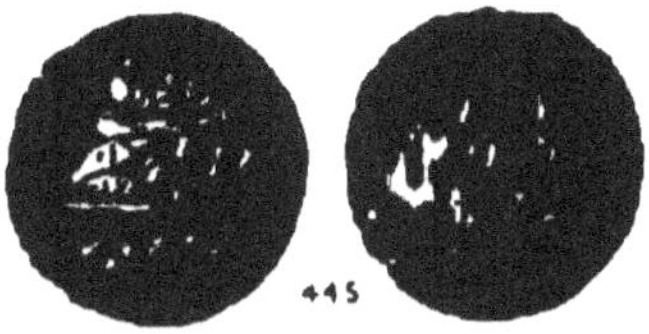
445

448

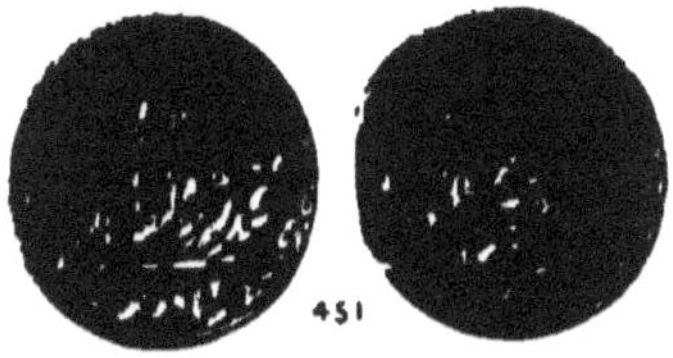

451

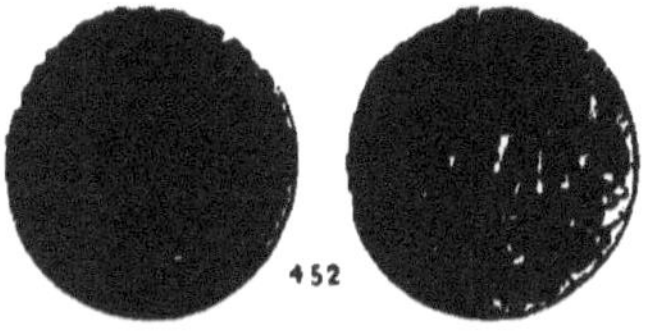

452

454

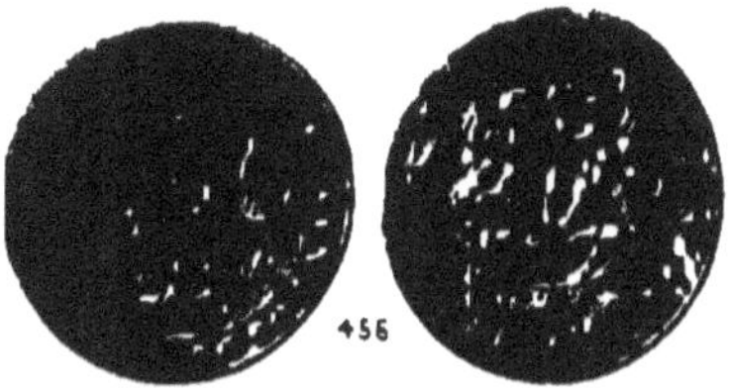

456

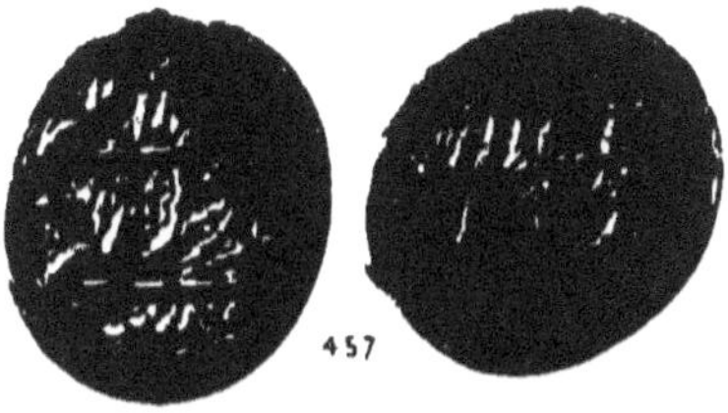

457

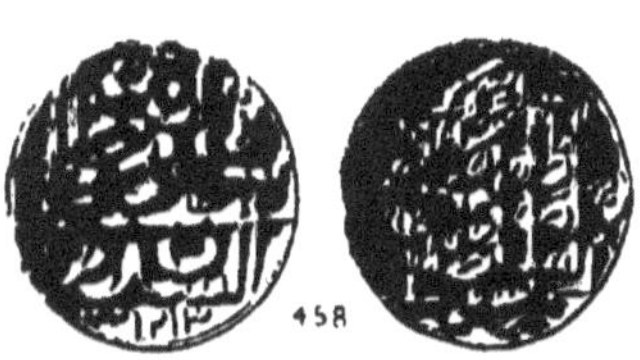

458

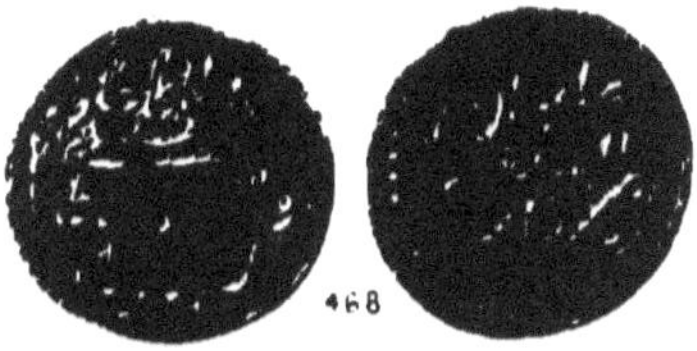

468

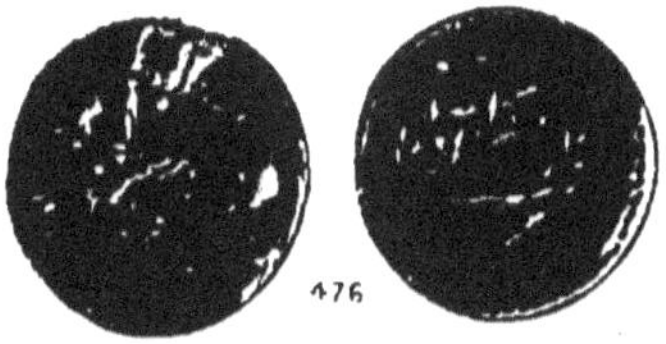

476

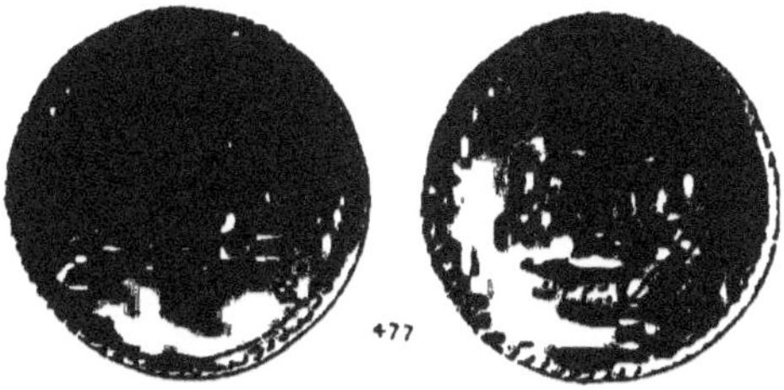

477

479

484

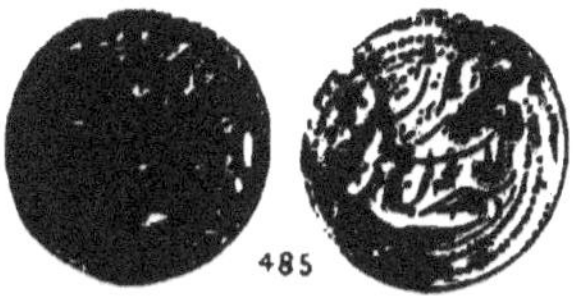

485

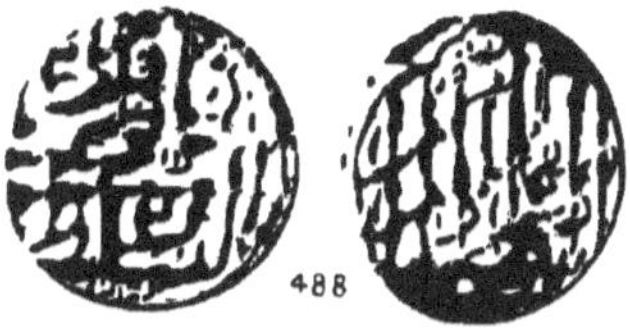

488

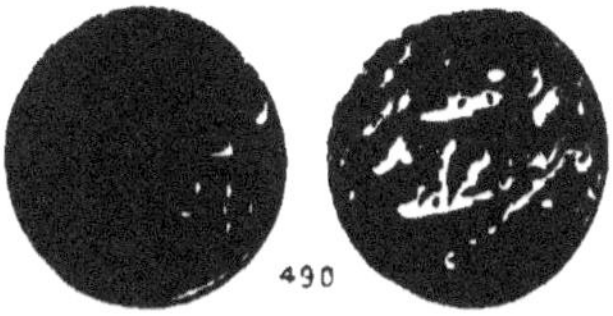

490

491

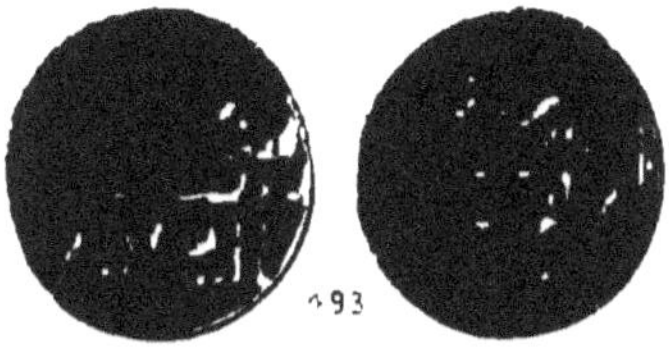

493

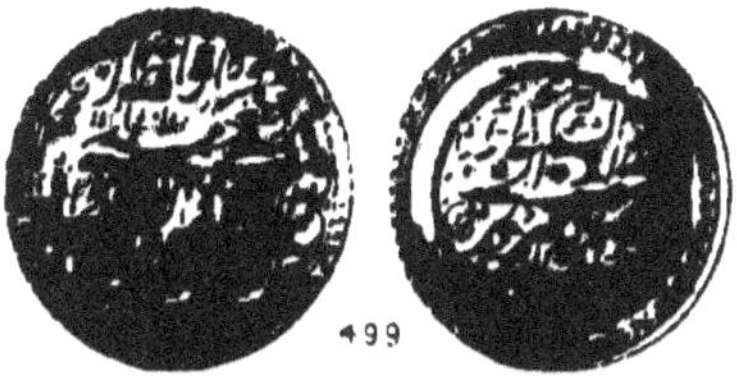

499

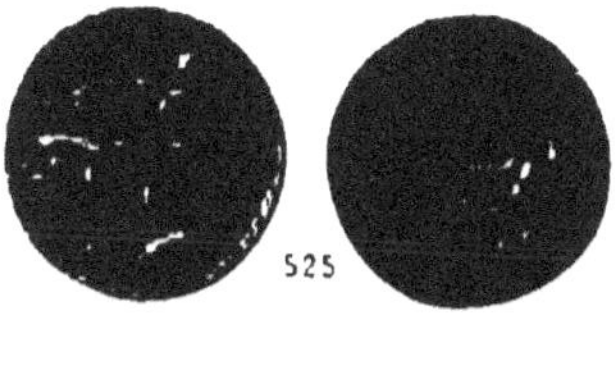

525

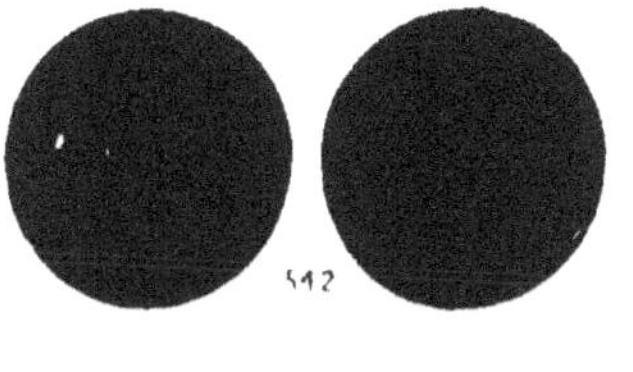

542

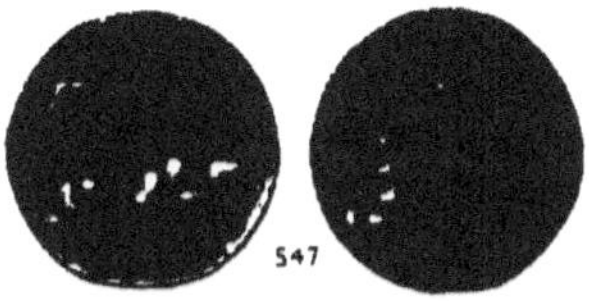
547

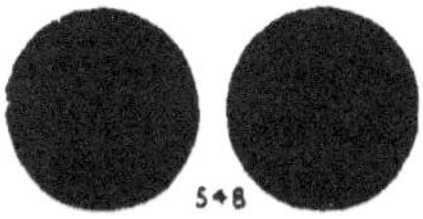
548

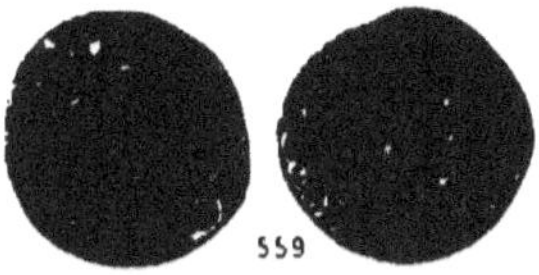
559

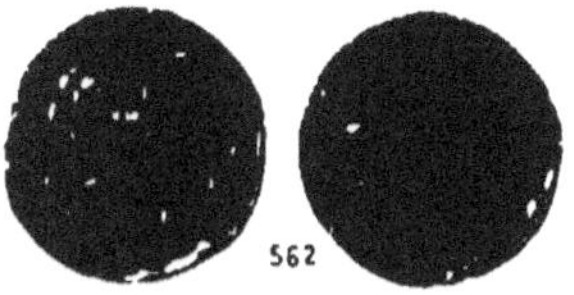
562

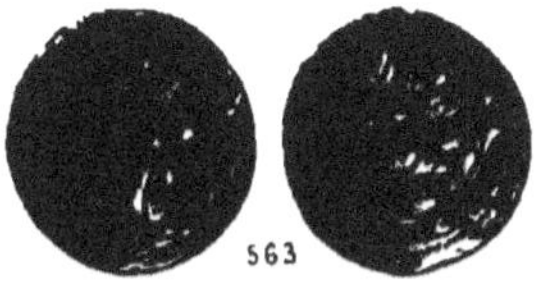
563

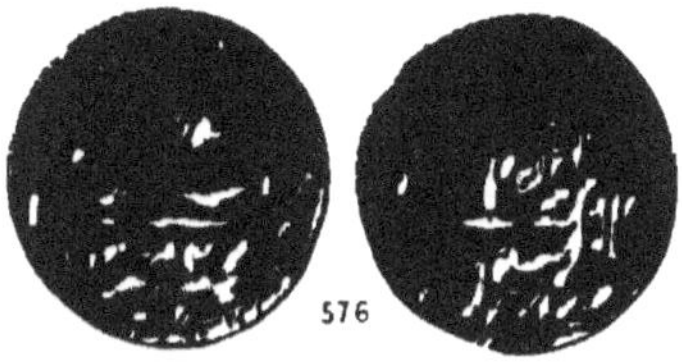
576

577

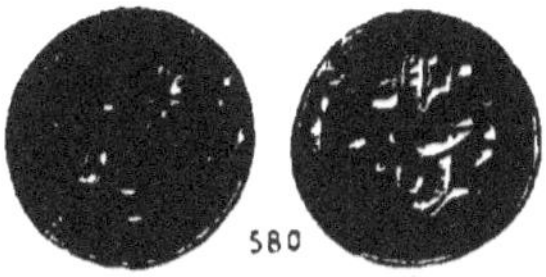
580

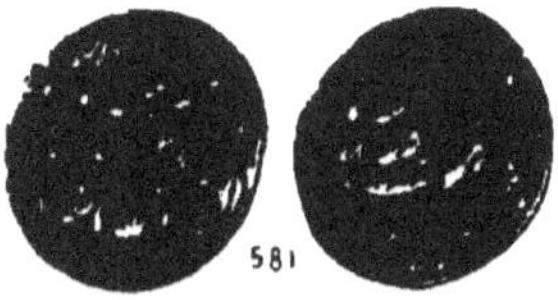
581

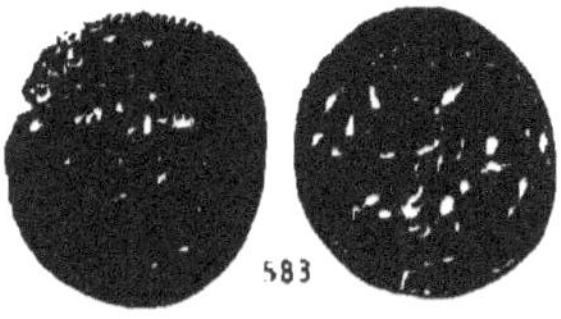
583

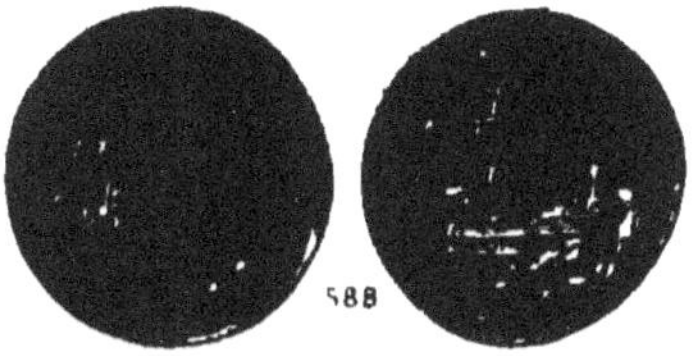
588

[illegible]45

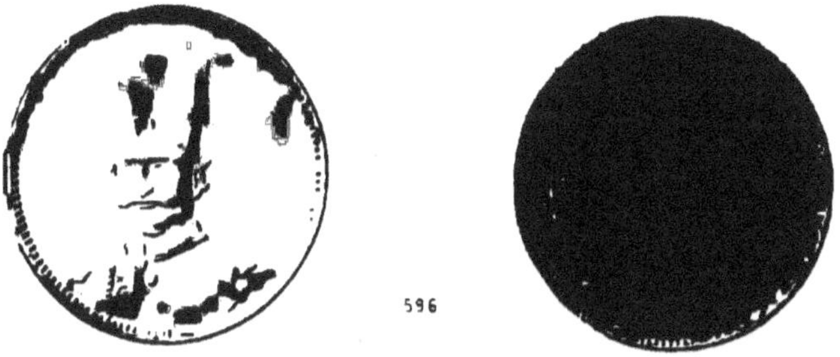

596

599

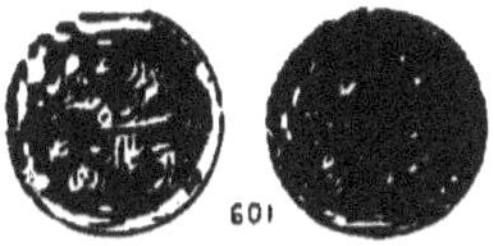

601

603

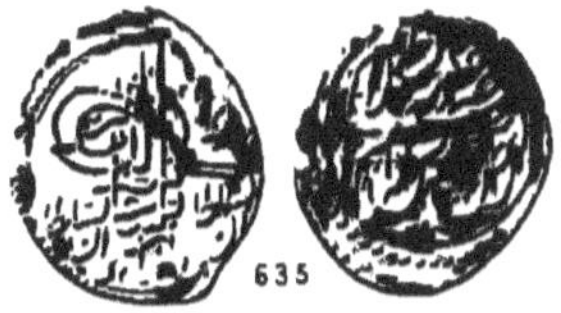

635

628

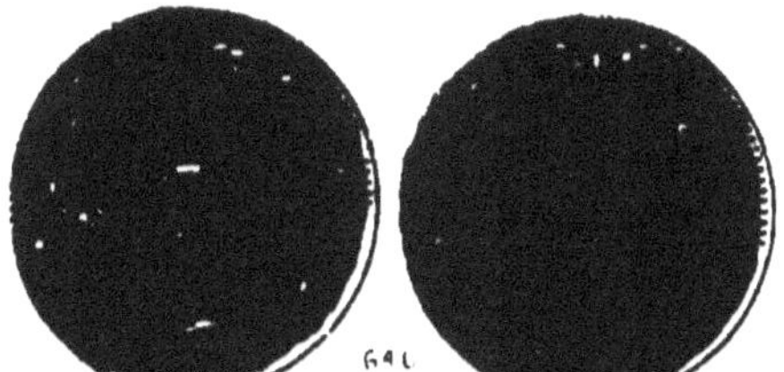

646

652

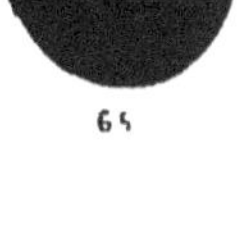

65

Pl XVII.

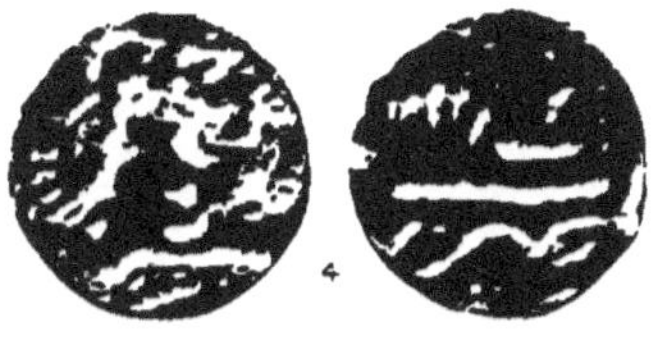

4

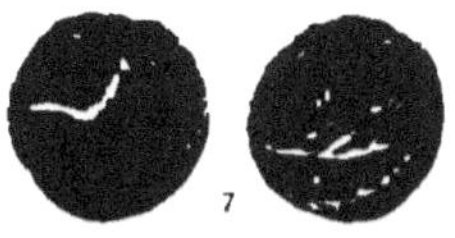

7

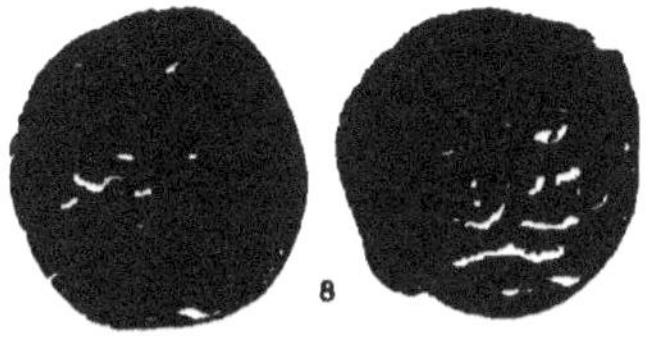

8

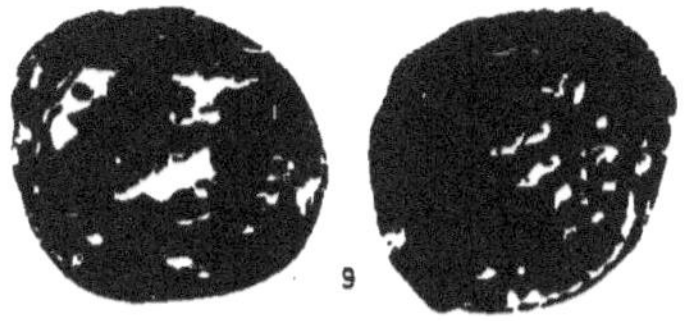

9

1

11

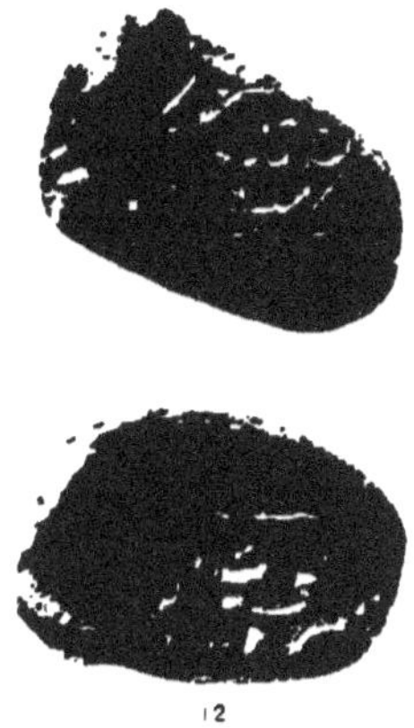

12

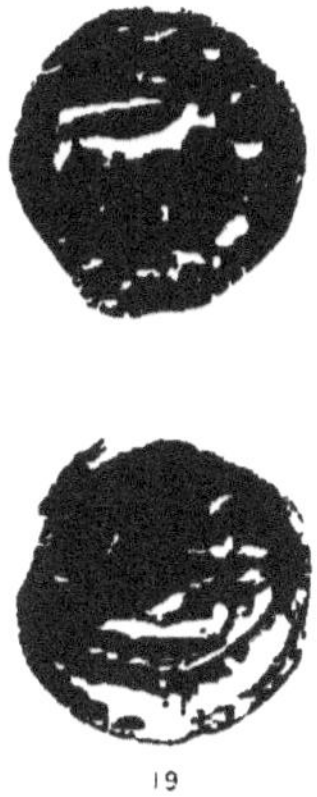

19

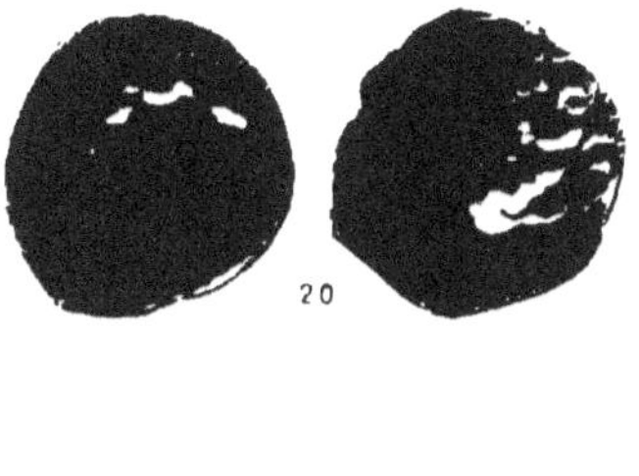

20

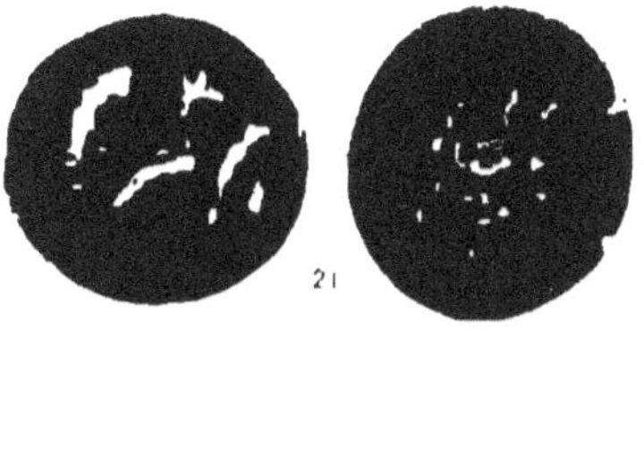

21

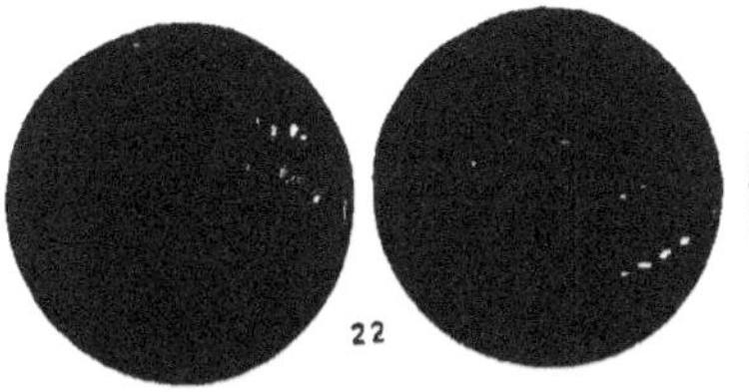

22

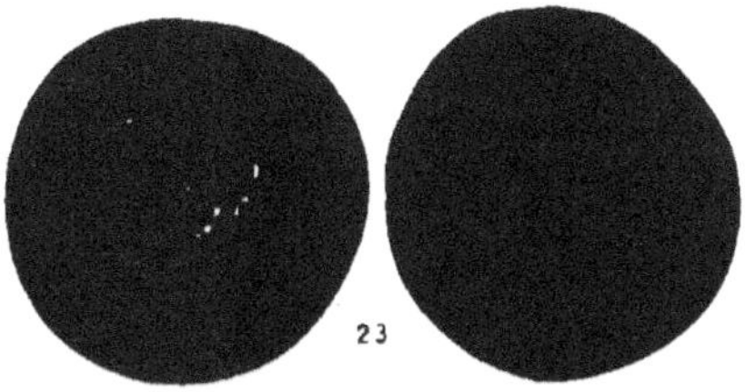

23

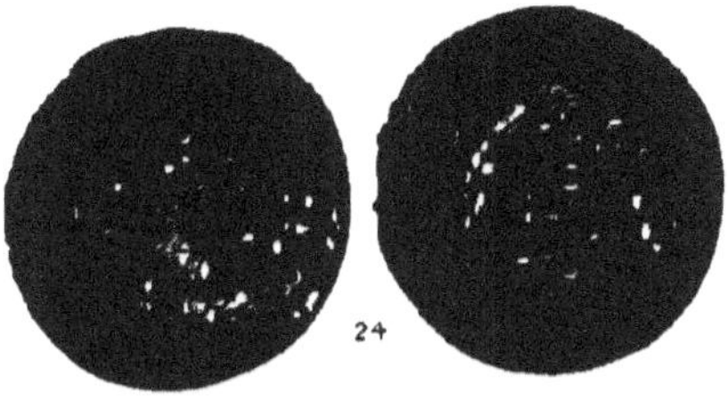

24

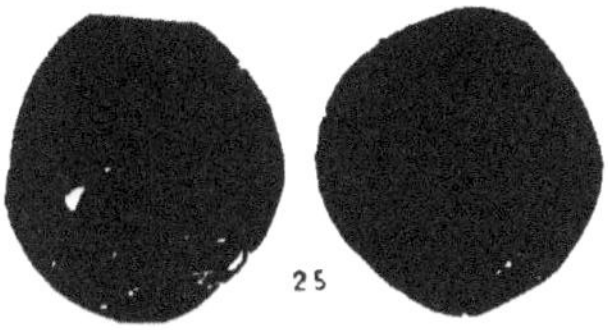

25

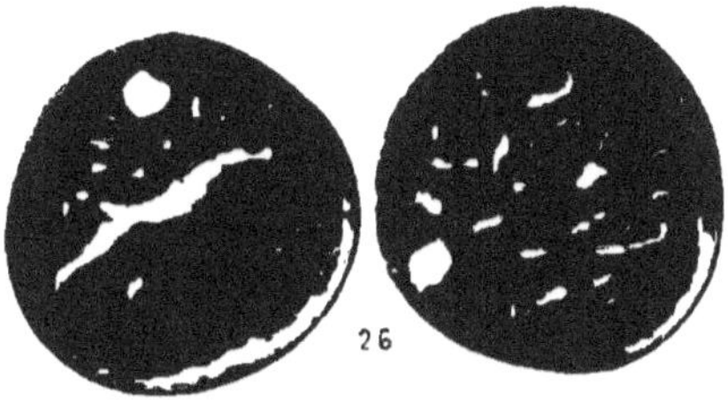

26

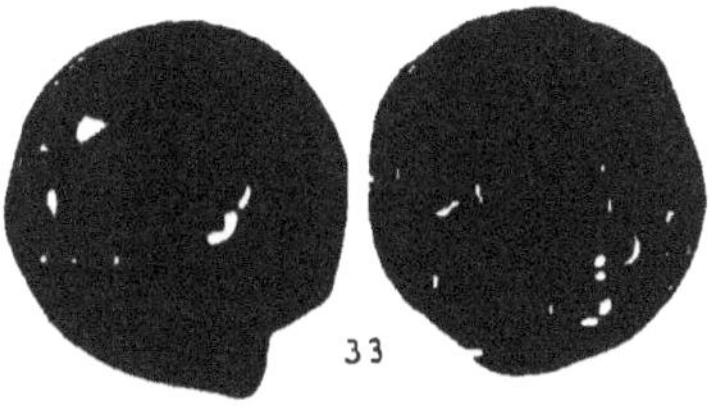

33

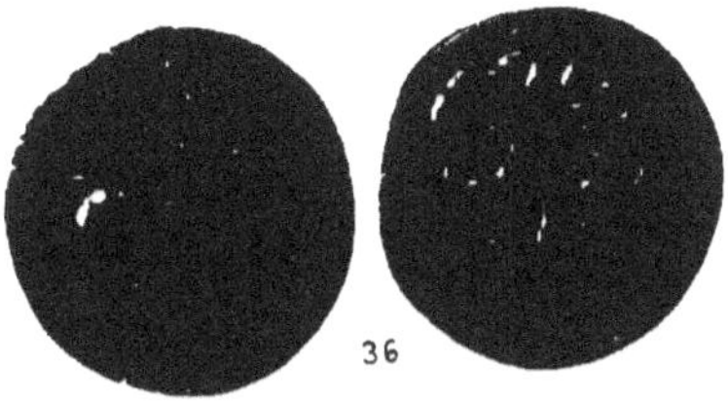

36

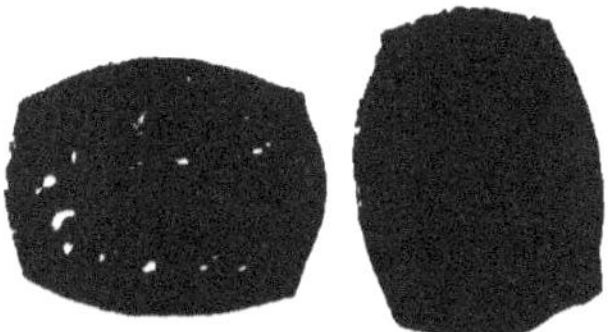

40

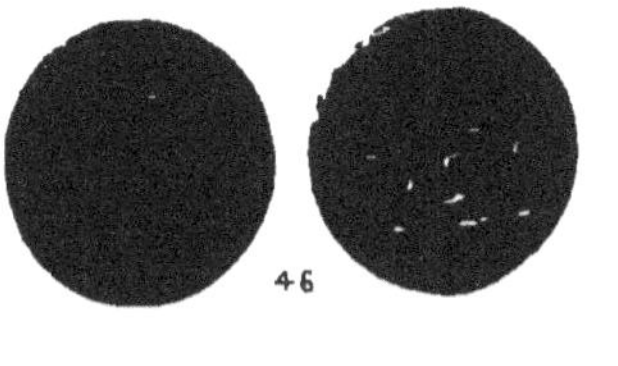

46

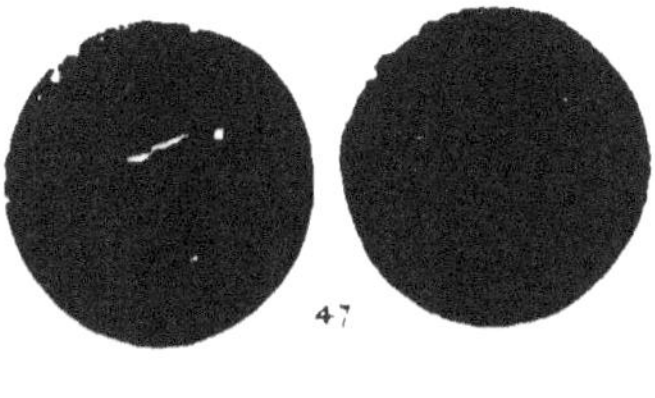

47

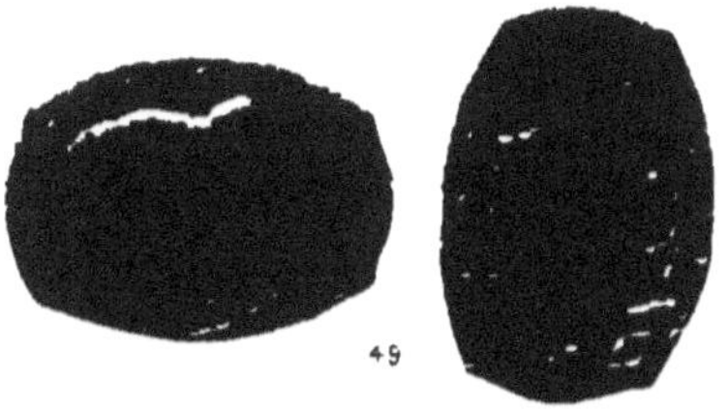

49

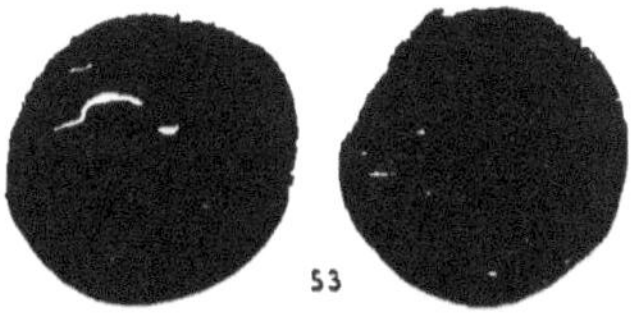

53

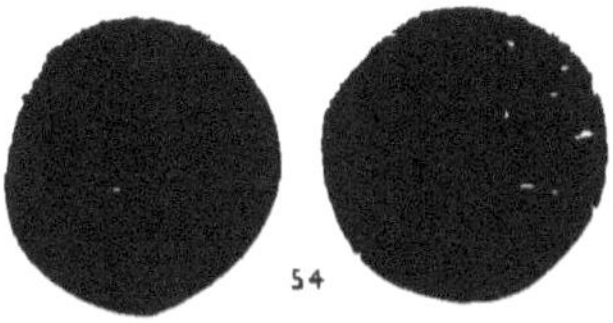

54

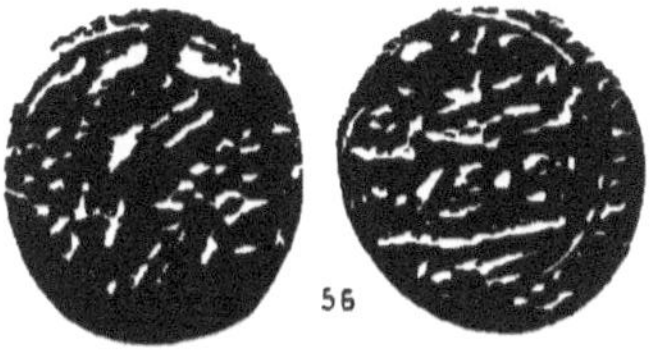

56

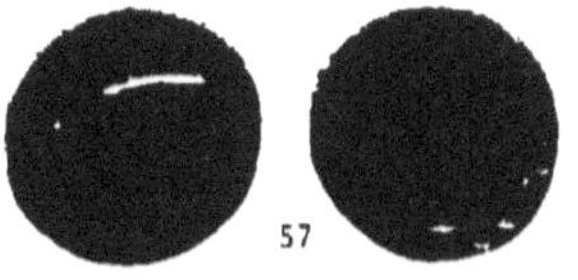

57

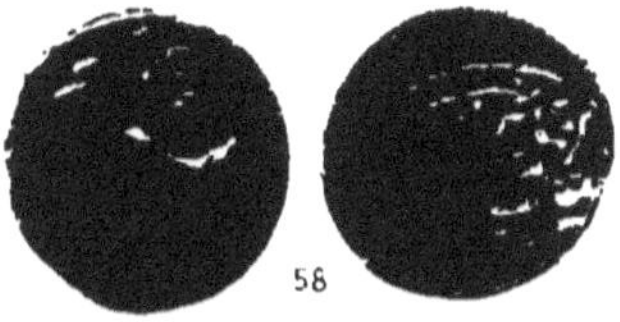

58

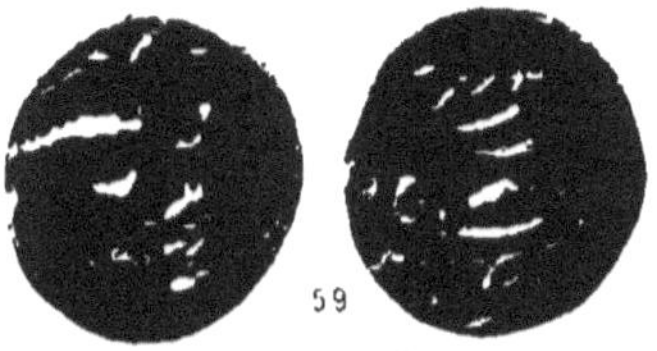

59

60

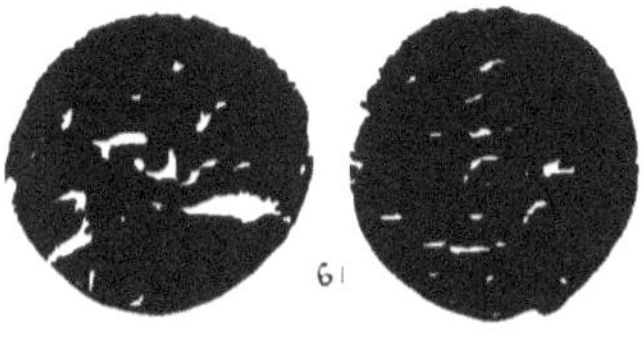

61

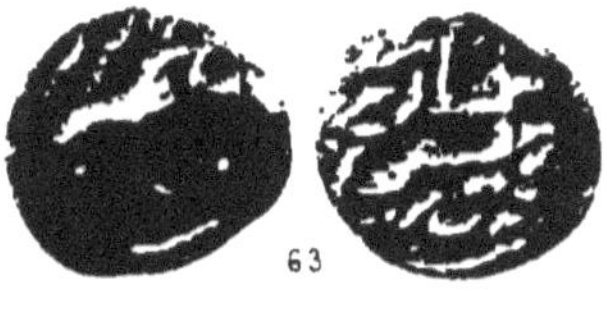

63

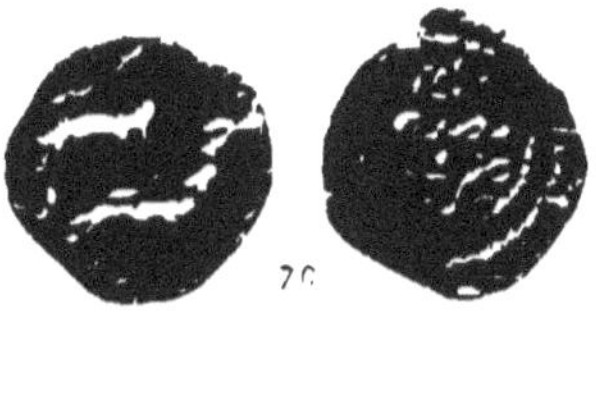

70

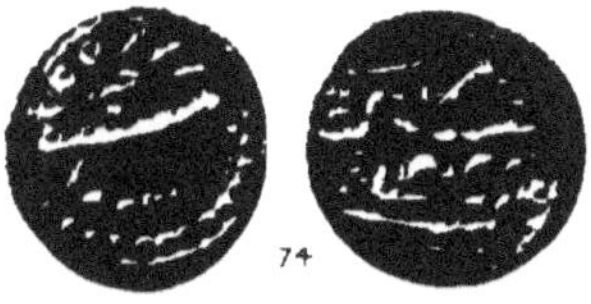

74

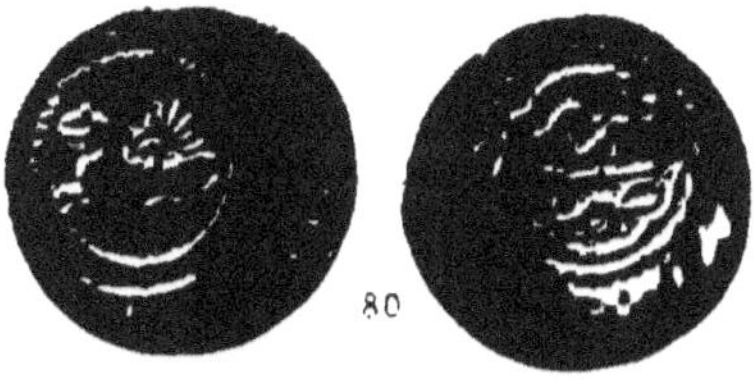

80

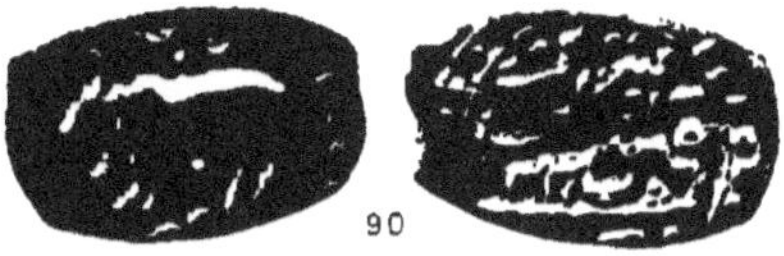

90

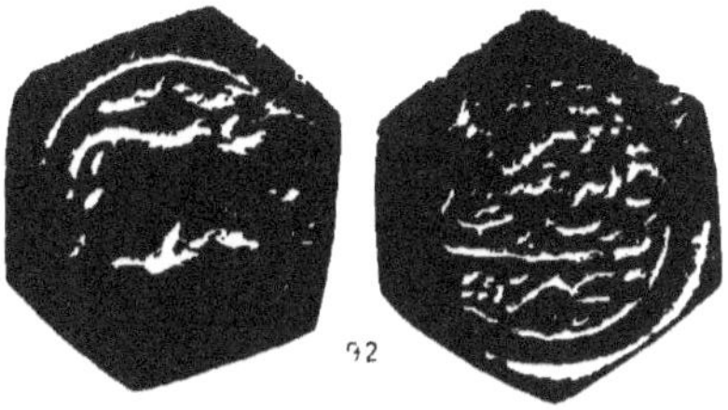

92

93

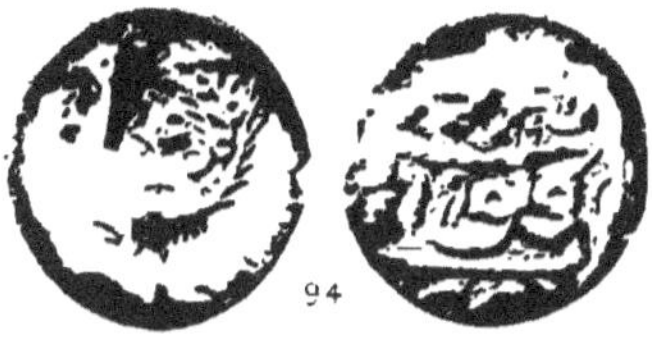

94

95

100

101

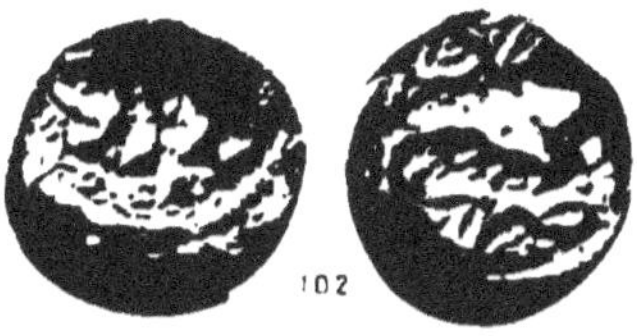

102

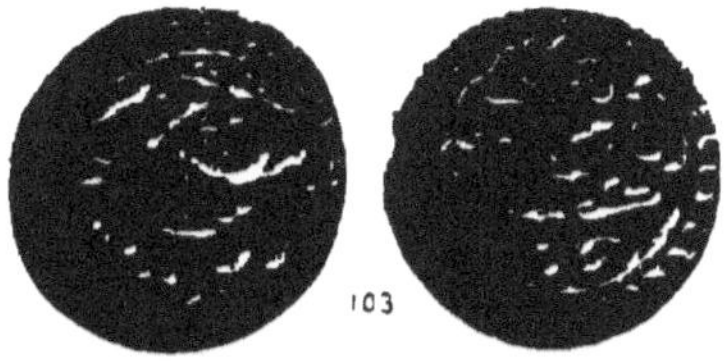

103

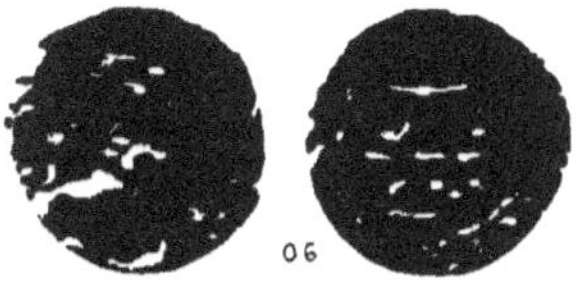

06

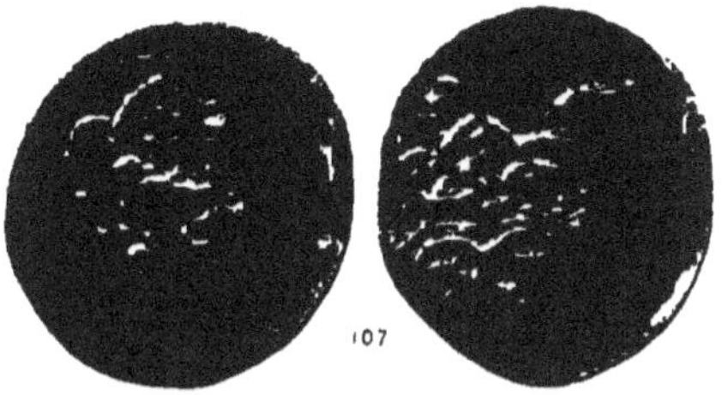

107

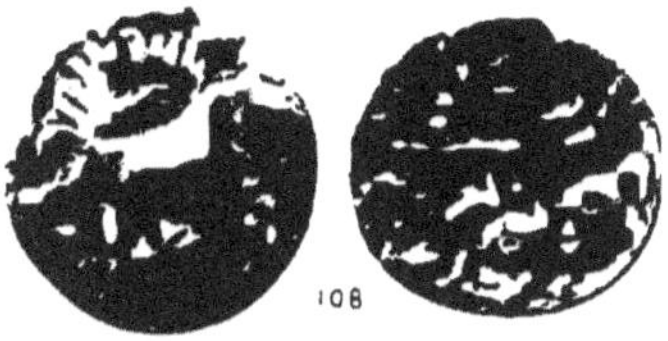

108

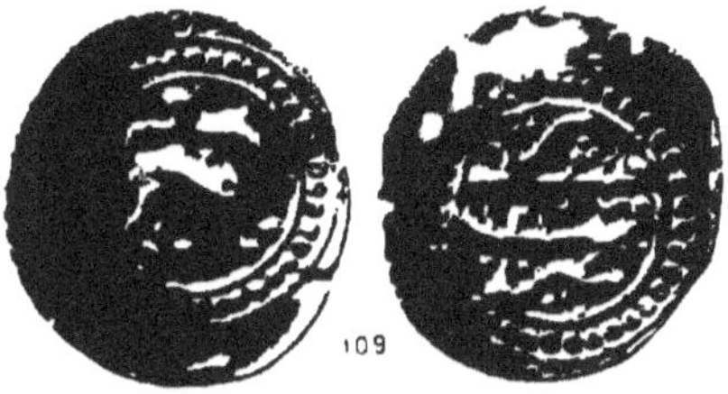

109

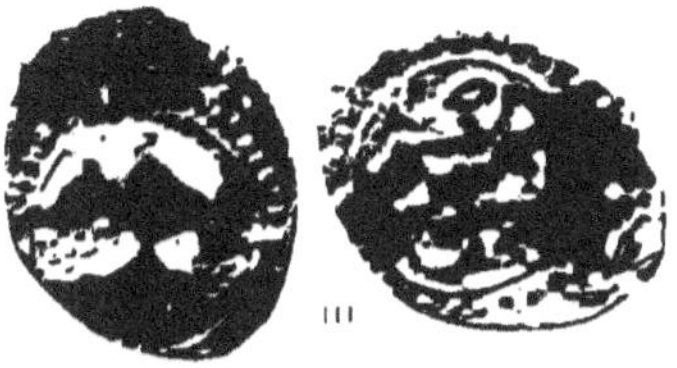

111

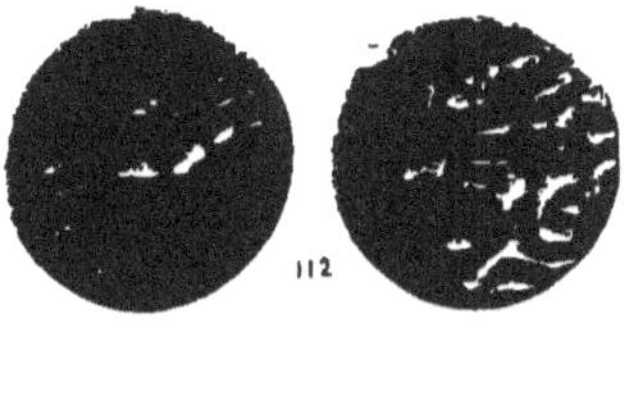

112

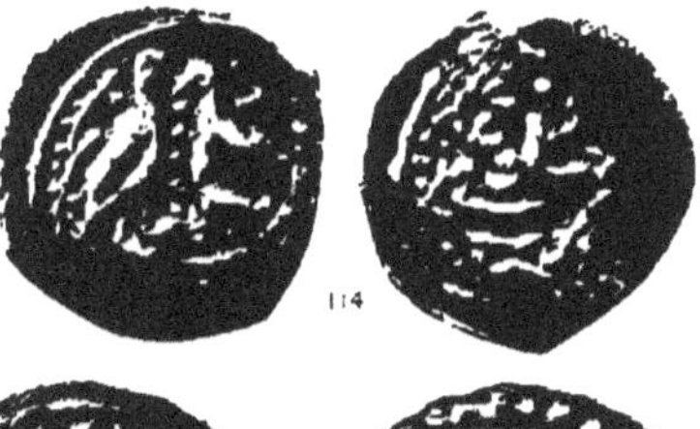

114

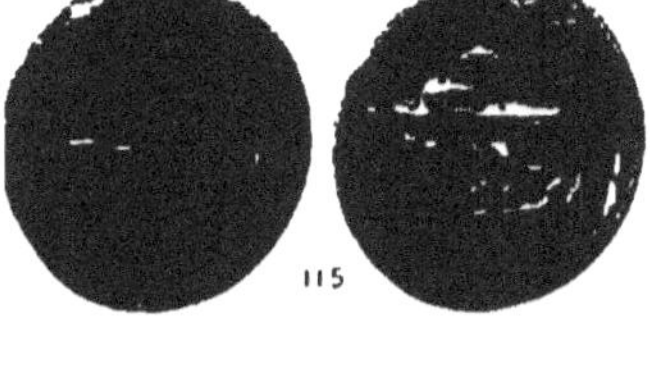

115

122

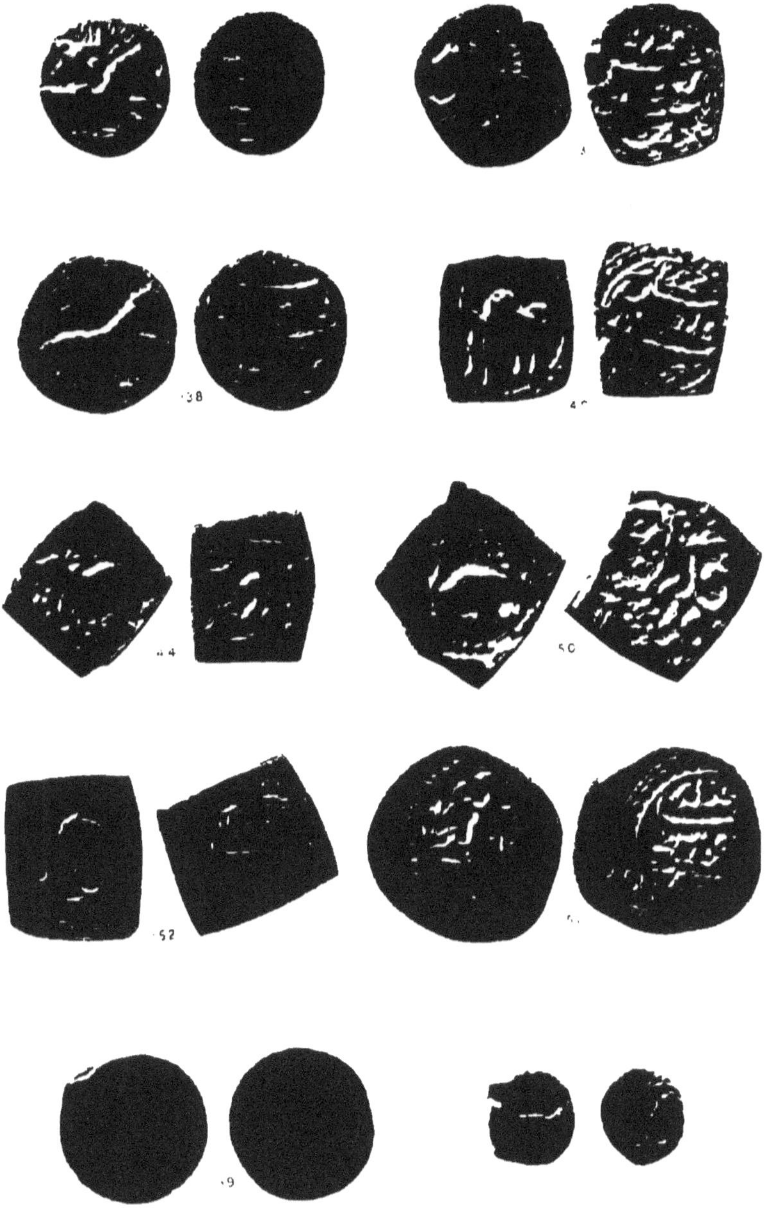
38
44
50
52

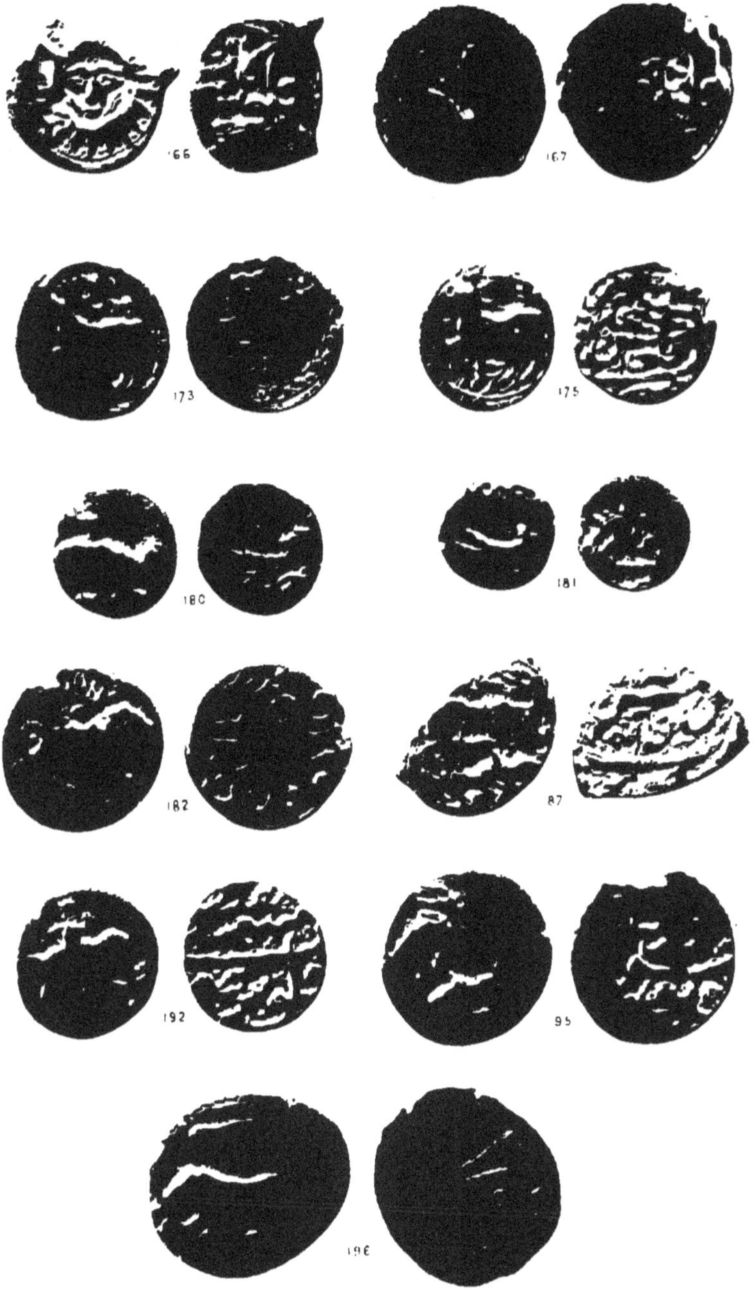
166
167
173
175
180
181
182
87
192
95
196

1

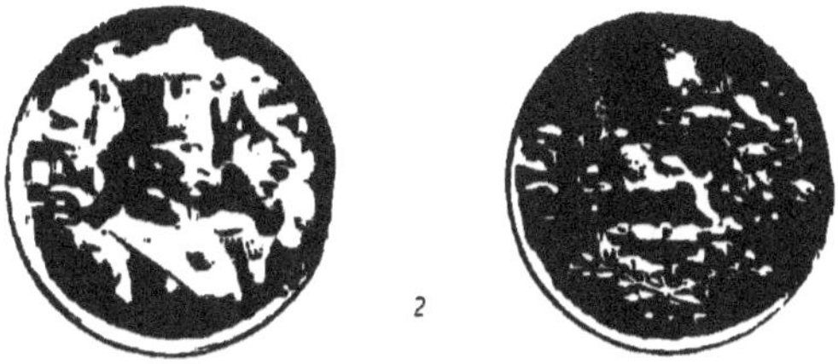

2

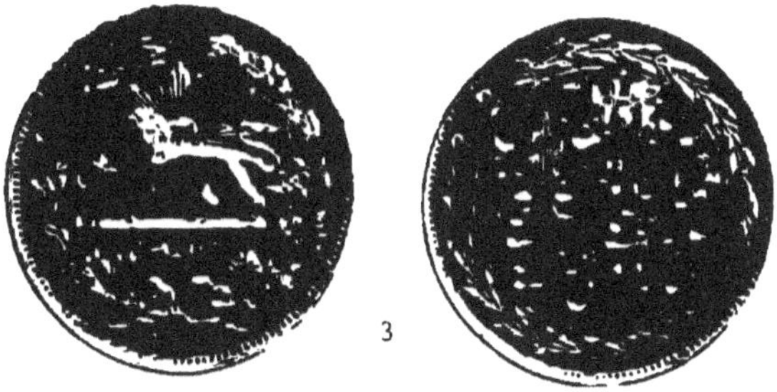

3

www.ingramcontent.com/pod-product-compliance
Lightning Source LLC
Chambersburg PA
CBHW020835020526
44114CB00040B/798
* 9 7 8 3 3 3 7 2 8 8 7 2 3 *